Common Pool Resources

Common pool resources (CPRs) include, for instance, fishing grounds, irrigation systems, forests, and the atmosphere. Now more than ever, how we responsibly share and use those goods is a vital issue. This textbook introduces students of economics, business, and policy studies to the key issues in the field. It uses a game-theory approach to help readers understand the mathematical representation of how to find equilibrium behavior in CPRs, how to identify the socially optimal appropriation, and how to measure the inefficiencies that arise. Algebra and calculus steps are clearly explained, so students can more easily reproduce the analysis and apply it in their own research. Finally, the book also summarizes experimental studies that tested theoretical results in controlled environments, introducing readers to a literature that has expanded over the last decades, and provides references for further reading.

ANA ESPINOLA-ARREDONDO is a professor in the School of Economic Sciences, Washington State University.

FELIX MUÑOZ-GARCIA is a professor in the School of Economic Sciences, Washington State University.

Common Pool Resources

Strategic Behavior, Inefficiencies, and Incomplete Information

ANA ESPINOLA-ARREDONDO
Washington State University

FELIX MUÑOZ-GARCIA
Washington State University

CAMBRIDGE
UNIVERSITY PRESS

University Printing House, Cambridge CB2 8BS, United Kingdom

One Liberty Plaza, 20th Floor, New York, NY 10006, USA

477 Williamstown Road, Port Melbourne, VIC 3207, Australia

314–321, 3rd Floor, Plot 3, Splendor Forum, Jasola District Centre, New Delhi – 110025, India

79 Anson Road, #06–04/06, Singapore 079906

Cambridge University Press is part of the University of Cambridge.

It furthers the University's mission by disseminating knowledge in the pursuit of education, learning, and research at the highest international levels of excellence.

www.cambridge.org
Information on this title: www.cambridge.org/9781108831031
DOI: 10.1017/9781108923095

© Ana Espinola-Arredondo and Felix Muñoz-Garcia 2022

First published 2022

A catalogue record for this publication is available from the British Library.

ISBN 978-1-108-83103-1 Hardback
ISBN 978-1-108-92627-0 Paperback

Additional resources for this publication at www.cambridge.org/9781108831031

Contents

Figures

Matrices

Preface

This textbook offers an introduction to the analysis of common pool resources, such as fishing grounds, aquifers, and forests, using game-theory tools familiar for most undergraduate students in economics, business, and social sciences.

Since Gordon (1954) and Hardin (1968), a large body of literature has emerged – theoretical, but especially experimental and field studies – seeking to understand the main incentives behind individuals and firms exploiting a common pool resource (CPR). These studies also focus on identifying which institutions and information contexts help ameliorate the so-called tragedy of the commons, where every individual ignores the effect that their appropriation causes on other individuals exploiting the resource, leading to its overexploitation. While several authors develop literature reviews, they mostly focus on the institutional arrangements that induce individuals to reduce their appropriation in the commons; see Ostrom (1990,1994, and 2000), Carpenter (2000), Faysee (2005), or Araral (2014).

These are important points, but literature reviews often overlook (or significantly summarize) the mathematical representation of how to find equilibrium behavior in CPRs, how to identify the socially optimal appropriation, how to measure the inefficiencies that arise, and how incomplete information affects equilibrium behavior. This textbook seeks to fill this gap by providing a relatively brief introduction to CPR models and results, specifically targeted to upper-level undergraduate and graduate students.

Our presentation emphasizes the intuition behind each modeling assumption, the steps we need to follow to solve similar CPR problems, and the economic interpretation of each result. In addition, it assumes only a basic background in intermediate microeconomics, and perhaps some game theory, but does not require readers to have a good command of dynamic programming techniques and differential game theory, as opposed to Dockner et al. (2000).[1] While CPR problems are often presented using these techniques, we believe that the main incentives behind players exploiting a resource can be discussed without the need to rely on advanced mathematical tools. As a result, we expect our text to be appropriate for undergraduate courses in environmental economics and in natural resource economics for students undergoing economics and business degrees, environmental policy for students undergoing public policy or political science degrees, or as a first introduction to the topic for graduate students.

ORGANIZATION OF THE BOOK

Introduction and Static Inefficiencies

Chapter 1 provides an introduction to CPRs and discusses their main features, how they differ from other goods, and why we can expect them to be more intensively exploited when firms (e.g., fishing or logging) do not coordinate their appropriation decisions. Chapter 2 presents the first model, where N firms exploit a CPR during a single period. While the setting is static, it helps us understand how to find equilibrium appropriation for each firm, and how to identify the socially optimal amount that maximizes welfare, where we present different definitions of social welfare. With these two ingredients, we can then evaluate whether equilibrium appropriation is more significant than socially optimal appropriation, and thus a socially excessive exploitation of the resource occurs in equilibrium. In other words, even when firms interact only once, a *static* inefficiency can arise in their equilibrium appropriation.

Dynamic Inefficiencies

Chapter 3 extends our analysis to settings where fishermen interact with each other dynamically. For simplicity, we consider a CPR where

[1] Other intermediate presentations of the topic include Dasgupta and Heal (1979), Conrad and Clark (1987), and Conrad (2010), which also focus on dynamic programming tools.

a single firm operates in the first period and a new firm joins the commons in the second period. In this context, we show that a new form of inefficiency arises: a *dynamic* inefficiency, since the firm exploiting the CPR in the first period ignores the effect of its first-period appropriation on its rival's profits during the second period. The static inefficiency still emerges, but only during the second period, as every firm ignores how its appropriation decisions affect its rival's current costs. We also identify the socially optimal amount of appropriation in each period, letting us precisely measure the size of the dynamic and static inefficiencies.

Greater Dynamic Inefficiencies: Entry Deterrence

In Chapter 4 we still consider the dynamic CPR from Chapter 3, but make an important observation: in the previous chapter, the incumbent exploiting the commons took future entry for granted, as if it could not do anything to prevent it during the first period.

This may, of course, not be the best strategy for the incumbent. In Chapter 4 we examine under which conditions the incumbent may have incentives to intensively deplete the resource during the first period to make entry unprofitable for the potential entrant in the second period. In short, we identify in which cases the incumbent practices "entry deterrence" by exploiting the CPR more intensively than in Chapter 3. Needless to say, this intense appropriation gives rise to a new form of inefficiency or, alternatively, expands the dynamic inefficiency found in Chapter 3; an inefficiency that is due to the incumbent facing an entry threat.

Repeated Interaction

Chapter 5 continues our exploration of dynamic settings, focusing now on CPRs where firms interact repeatedly, such as fishermen operating in the same fishing ground for several periods. For presentation purposes, we consider a context with two firms, each choosing between a high or low appropriation level. We start showing that, in the unrepeated version of the game (one-shot interaction) every firm finds high appropriation to be a strictly dominant strategy, that is, a strategy that provides the firm with an unambiguously higher payoff than low appropriation regardless of the strategy its opponent selects. In other words, every firm chooses a high appropriation in the equilibrium of the unrepeated game, while the social optimum would call for every firm to choose a low appropriation yielding a higher payoff.

We then consider the finitely repeated version of the game, showing that a similarly inefficient result emerges as when the game is unrepeated, namely, every firm selects a high appropriation in every period of the game. Finally, we consider the infinitely repeated version of the CPR game, demonstrating that cooperation (in the form of low appropriation levels) can now be sustained, as long as firms care enough about their future payoffs. We study different extensions and how the literature tested these theoretical results in controlled experiments.

Incomplete Information

Chapters 6 and 7 introduce elements of incomplete information into our previous CPR models. In Chapter 6, we consider settings where firms simultaneously choose their appropriation levels and one (or both) firms face uncertainty about the available stock. This can occur when firms' technology does not let them precisely know the available fish in a CPR, or how difficult the CPR is to access.

We first analyze a setting where all firms face uncertainty about the available stock, identifying the appropriation that emerges in equilibrium, the socially optimal appropriation, and the inefficiency that arises due to incomplete information. That is, we seek to measure if inefficiencies become greater than when all firms observe the stock (i.e., under complete information). We then consider a similar setting where only one firm is uninformed about the available stock while its rival accurately observes the stock, also finding equilibrium appropriation, socially optimal levels, and the inefficiencies that emerge.

Chapter 7 extends our analysis of incomplete information to settings where firms interact sequentially. Specifically, we consider a CPR where an incumbent firm operated for a long period, being able to accumulate precise information about the available stock, and a potential entrant, uninformed about the stock. The latter can, nonetheless, observe the incumbent's appropriation to infer the stock's abundance, e.g., if the incumbent appropriates large amounts (bringing tons of fish to port every day) the stock is likely abundant. The potential entrant uses this information to update its beliefs about the stock, and then choose whether to enter or stay out.

We find an equilibrium where the incumbent chooses to appropriate the resource less intensively than under complete information (underexploit) to "convey" the stock to the potential entrant, making the latter interpret that the stock is too low to merit entry. A similar equilibrium can be sustained where the incumbent facing a large stock chooses a low appropriation level to "conceal" the abundant stock from the potential entrant and deter entry. In both cases, underexploitation can help ameliorate the excessive exploitation of the resource that arises under complete information, thus mitigating the inefficiencies we encountered in previous chapters. We then discuss the role of information in the commons, and its welfare improving or reducing effects.

ANCILLARY MATERIALS

The following ancillary materials are available online at www.cambridge.org/9781108831031.

1. *Solutions Manual for "Common Pool Resources"* (only available to instructors). This includes step-by-step answer keys to all end-of-chapter exercises.
2. *PowerPoint slides* (only available to instructors). They cover the main topics in every chapter of the textbook. The slides include all definitions, equations, short explanations, and figures, thus facilitating class preparation. Slides can also be distributed to students as a first set of lectures notes they can complement with in-class explanations.

ACKNOWLEDGMENTS

Part of this manuscript is based on the Ph.D. Environmental Economics course that Ana teaches at Washington State University, while other sections are based on the lectures that Felix gave at the Department of Economics in the University of Wyoming as a visiting scholar. He is grateful to the Department's financial support and hospitality, particularly Klaas Van't Veld, Chuck Mason, and Jason Shogren. Several chapters in the book are based on papers presented at HEC-Montréal, where we received extremely useful feedback, which also helped us present the main results at a more intuitive level. Ana also thanks Gene Gruver for his encouragement and advising at the University of Pittsburgh.

We are particularly grateful to George Zaccour, Michéle Breton, Bernard Sinclair-Desgagné, Hassan Benchekroun, and Justin Leroux, for their insightful comments and suggestions. We also appreciate the continuous support of our institution, Washington State University, and our colleagues at the School of Economic Sciences, where many of the models presented in this book originated, while doing research, teaching, and advising Ph.D. students. We also thank students who helped us develop some of the answer keys, such as John Strandholm, Xueying Ma, Eric Dunaway, Dindu Lama, and Imisi Aiyetan; and the team at Cambridge University Press, especially Philip Good and Erika Walsh, for their constant support and suggestions. Last, but not least, we would like to thank our family and friends for encouraging us during the preparation of the manuscript.

I   **Introduction**

1.1   WHAT ARE COMMON POOL RESOURCES?

If we ask you to find examples of common pool resources (CPRs), you may consider fishing grounds, hunting grounds, or forests, along with oil fields, pastures, irrigation systems, and aquifers. Other, more recent, examples may include the use of a computer facility or Wi-Fi internet connections that require no password. But, what are the distinctive features that these examples, and CPRs in general, exhibit? For us to qualify a good or service as a CPR, it needs to satisfy two properties:

1. It must exhibit *rivalry* (rival goods), that is, its consumption by one individual reduces the amount of the good available to other individuals. This property holds in all the above examples, where a larger fishing catch by one fisherman reduces the available stock that other fisherman can catch; or the internet browsing by one more individual reduces the Wi-Fi speed other individuals can enjoy.
2. It must be *nonexcludable*, which means that preventing an individual from enjoying the good is costly or impossible. Again, the above examples satisfy this property, since preventing a new fisherman from accessing a fishing ground is relatively costly.

1.2   DIFFERENCES BETWEEN CPRS AND OTHER GOODS

How do CPRs differ from the other types of goods and services we encounter every day? Table 1.1 classifies different types of goods according to whether they satisfy the above two properties: the rows consider whether the good is rival, while the columns evaluate whether the good is excludable. As suggested above, CPRs are rival in

I

Table 1.1 *Different types of goods.*

	Excludable	*Nonexcludable*
Rival	private goods (e.g., apple)	common pool resources (e.g., fishing ground)
Nonrival	club goods (e.g., gym)	public goods (e.g., national defense)

consumption but nonexcludable, leaving us with three other types of goods to discuss:

a. **Private goods:** Starting from private goods, such as an apple, we see that its consumption is rival (if you eat it, I cannot enjoy the same apple) and excludable (if you don't pay for an apple, you cannot eat it).

b. **Club goods:** We can then move on to club goods, such as a gym membership. Club goods are nonrival since the good can be enjoyed by several members without affecting each other's utility, unless the gym becomes congested. In addition, they are excludable since gym owners can easily prevent nonmembers from accessing the center by requiring users to show a membership card.[1]

c. **Public goods:** Finally, public goods are rival (consumption by one individual does not reduce the amount of the good available to other individuals) and nonexcludable (preventing an individual from enjoying the good is extremely expensive, or impossible). A common example is national defense, since my consumption does not reduce your consumption, and if you were to not pay your taxes tomorrow it would be essentially impossible for the government to prevent you from enjoying national defense even if you didn't help in its funding.[2] Another common example is clean air, since it also satisfies the two features of nonrivalry

---

[1] A more recent example of club goods is satellite TV, or pay-TV channels, since their consumption is indeed nonrival (if you watch my favorite TV series, my consumption is not reduced), but excludable since you cannot watch a specific TV channel if you did not pay for it. Generally, most types of copyrighted works, such as books, movies, and software, are club goods since they all satisfy nonrivalry and excludability.

[2] Well, the government could deport you so you don't get to enjoy national defense, but this is not a penalty for tax evasion. At least not yet!

(your consumption of clean air does not reduce my own) and nonexcludability (how can we prevent you from not enjoying clean air?). Other examples include public fireworks, official statistics, and publicly available inventions through unpatented R&D.

1.3 OVEREXPLOITING THE COMMONS

CPRs share a key feature with public goods, namely that both are nonexcludable, thus making it difficult to prevent individuals or firms from enjoying the good. This can lead to an excessive number of agents seeking to enter into the CPR, as they know that their exclusion is rather costly or, in some cases, infeasible. Unlike public goods, however, CPRs are rival in consumption, which, informally, "makes things worse." To see this, consider a fishing ground. As a rival good, each fisherman's appropriation (e.g., 10 tons of fish) cannot be appropriated by other fishermen; a feature that does not apply to public goods where all agents can benefit without affecting each other's utility (think again about national defense).

The rivalry feature of CPRs can, alternatively, be understood as a negative externality: When a fisherman appropriates one more ton of fish, this ton is not available to other fishermen, which increases their appropriation costs if they seek to maintain their appropriation level unaltered. Intuitively, the commons is more scarce after fisherman i increased his appropriation, forcing all other fishermen $j \neq i$ to spend more time or resources to catch the same amount of fish than before. From this perspective, we can then anticipate that, when fisherman i chooses her appropriation level, she considers her private benefits and costs from appropriation, but ignores the external effects that this imposes on other fishermen (less stock available to catch). If, instead, all fishermen coordinated their appropriation decisions – or if a regulator set appropriation decisions to each fisherman using policy instruments like fishing quotas – they would consider the joint profits of all, internalizing the external effects that each of their appropriations would impose on other fishermen's costs.

I.4 THE "TRAGEDY OF THE COMMONS" – STATIC AND DYNAMIC COMPONENTS

From our discussion above, the appropriation decisions that each fisherman chooses when left unregulated (which we refer to as the "equilibrium appropriation") exceed the appropriation level that they would choose if they coordinated their decisions (which is often known as "socially optimal appropriation" as it maximizes welfare for all agents in the society). This means that equilibrium appropriation is *socially excessive* or, more compactly, that the resource is overexploited. This problem is often referred to as the "tragedy of the commons," as we highlight directly below, and is recurrent in many CPRs such as fishing grounds, forests, and aquifers simultaneously being exploited by several firms, and extends nowadays to policies mitigating climate change.[3]

Tragedy of the Commons: Equilibrium appropriation exceeds the socially optimal appropriation.

Importantly, the "tragedy of the commons" arises even in static settings where fishermen exploit the commons during only one period, as we discuss in Chapter 2; is emphasized when firms interact during several periods in a dynamic setting, as we show in Chapter 3; and further augmented when firms face entry threats in future periods and use their current appropriation to deter entry of potential competitors, as demonstrated in Chapter 4. This can inform regulators about the relative size of inefficiencies in different CPRs, namely, being:

- nil in those resources where a single firm operates during all periods, as this firm fully considers the effect of its appropriation decisions (i.e., it internalizes these effects), both in its current and future profits;
- larger in commons where more than one firm operates (even if they only interact once) since they ignore the external effects that their individual appropriation imposes on the other firm or firms costs or profits;

---

[3] In the Middle Ages the commons was a meadow that belonged to all farmers in a region (often known as the "commoners").

- larger in CPRs where a single firm expects (with certainty) that another firm or firms will enter in future periods; and
- even larger in those commons facing entry threats where the incumbent can use her current appropriation to deter the potential entrant from joining the CPR.

1.5 THE "TRAGEDY OF THE COMMONS" UNDER INCOMPLETE INFORMATION

In Chapters 5–7, we insert the standard CPR problem in a different setting. First, Chapter 5 considers contexts in which firms interact repeatedly, either for a finite or infinite rounds, and identifies under which conditions firms have incentives to cooperate, decreasing their appropriation, and thus protecting the commons. Chapters 6 and 7, instead, insert the CPR problem into a setting where firms interact under incomplete information. Chapter 6 considers environments in which all firms face a common source of uncertainty, such as what the available stock is or how they will be affected by each other's appropriation decisions. In that context, we seek to evaluate whether firms' appropriation is lower when they operate under certainty than under uncertainty, as that could help policy makers predict which CPRs will experience a more intense overexploitation.

Chapter 7 considers, instead, a context in which the incumbent is better informed than the potential entrant about the initial stock, which could occur when the incumbent has operated in the CPR for a long time thus accumulating detailed information about the stock. In this setting, the potential entrant observes the incumbent's appropriation, using it as a signal of the (unobserved) initial stock. This signal helps the entrant decide whether the stock is sufficiently abundant to merit entry, or scarce enough to remain outside the CPR. We investigate under which conditions the incumbent has incentives to decrease its appropriation of the resource enough to signal that the stock is low, thus deterring entry. This type of behavior will actually protect the commons, and arises because of the incomplete information setting in which firms interact. In other words, incomplete information can serve to reduce the above inefficiencies – so prevalent in the commons – if they induce the incumbent to reduce its appropriation to deter future entry. However, we also identify conditions for which the incumbent chooses to increase its appropriation to deter entry.

We then evaluate under which conditions this appropriation reduction is welfare improving – implying that incomplete information generates a larger welfare than complete information settings – and in which contexts incomplete information becomes welfare reducing. These results suggest a role for information management (i.e., regulators choosing to disseminate or conceal information about the stock, or other properties of the commons) that is often ignored in policy discussions.

2   Common Pool Resources
in a Static Setting

2.1 INTRODUCTION

In this chapter, we start our analysis of CPRs from a stylized setting, namely, a one-shot interaction between the agents exploiting the resource, such as the fishermen operating in a fishing ground. This is, of course, a simplifying assumption, since a key feature of CPRs is that an initial stock can be depleted over time. Such depletion affects the intensity with which agents exploit the resource in each period, which we will examine in future chapters. By abstracting from the dynamic aspects of the CPR, however, we gain a clearer understanding of the incentives that agents face within a period, and which are not driven by the stock depletion.

We first investigate appropriation in a CPR such as a fishing ground, a forest, or an aquifer, e.g., how many tons of fish each fishing boat catches. We analyze how this appropriation is affected by the available stock and the number of agents exploiting the resource. Section 2.3 then identifies the socially optimal appropriation of the resource and how it differs from the equilibrium appropriation that agents choose when left unregulated. Section 2.4 elaborates on policies commonly used to induce these agents to exploit the CPR at a socially optimal level.

2.2   MODELING THE CPR

Assume that N firms (or individuals) have free access to the resource. Every unit of appropriation (e.g., a ton of fish) is sold in the international market that, for simplicity, is assumed to be perfectly competitive. Intuitively, every fisherman's appropriation (e.g., 20 tons of cod) represents a small share of industry catches, thus not affecting market prices for this variety of fish. As a result, every firm takes the market price p as given, which we normalize to $p = \$1$ to facilitate our analysis. (We examine how our results are affected by this assumption in Subsection 2.3.2.)

Cost Function: In addition, every firm faces the following cost function

$$C(q_i, Q_{-i}) = \frac{q_i(q_i + Q_{-i})}{S},$$

where $S > 0$ denotes the stock of the resource, which reduces fisherman i's cost when the resource becomes more abundant (intuitively, fish are easier to catch). In addition, q_i represents fisherman i's appropriation, and $Q_{-i} = \sum_{j \neq i} q_j$ reflects aggregate appropriations by individuals other than i. For instance, when only two fishermen exploit the resource (fisherman 1 and 2), the above total cost function simplifies to

$$C(q_1, q_2) = \frac{q_1(q_1 + q_2)}{S}$$

for fisherman 1 (so that $Q_{-1} = q_2$), and similarly $C(q_2, q_1) = \frac{q_2(q_2 + q_1)}{S}$ for fisherman 2 (so that $Q_{-2} = q_1$).[1]

Importantly, this cost function is increasing in fisherman i's own appropriation, q_i, and in his rival's appropriations, Q_{-i}.[2] In words, the fishing ground becomes more depleted as other firms appropriate fish, making it more difficult to catch fish for fisherman i.

Agent i's Profit-Maximization Problem: Therefore, every fisherman chooses their appropriation level q_i to maximize their profits as follows:

$$\max_{q_i \geq 0} \pi_i = q_i - \frac{q_i(q_i + Q_{-i})}{S}, \tag{2.1}$$

---

[1] In the case of three fishermen, Q_{-i} becomes $Q_{-1} = q_2 + q_3$ for fisherman 1, $Q_{-2} = q_1 + q_3$ for fisherman 2, and $Q_{-3} = q_1 + q_2$ for fisherman 3. In addition, the market can still be perfectly competitive if several other fishermen, located in other fishing grounds but appropriating the same type of fish, sell their catches in the international market.

[2] To confirm this result mathematically, note that the cost function $C(q_i, Q_{-i})$ satisfies $\frac{\partial C(q_i, Q_{-i})}{\partial q_i} = \frac{2q_i + Q_{-i}}{S}$, which is positive for all appropriation levels, and $\frac{\partial C(q_i, Q_{-i})}{\partial Q_{-i}} = \frac{q_i}{S}$, which is also positive for all appropriation levels.

where the first term represents the fisherman's revenue from additional units of appropriation (recall that the price of every unit was normalized to $p = \$1$ for simplicity), while the second term indicates the total cost that the fisherman incurs when appropriating q_i units of fish while his rivals appropriate Q_{-i} units.

2.3 FINDING EQUILIBRIUM APPROPRIATION

We next find the appropriation that each fisherman chooses in equilibrium. Technically, this is a setting where every agent chooses their appropriation level simultaneously, and where information about the stock and agents' cost functions is common knowledge. In short, this means that this is a setting that can be analyzed as a simultaneous-move game of complete information, like the Cournot game of simultaneous quantity competition.

To solve this type of game, as you may remember, we need to first solve each player's profit-maximization problem (2.1), which provides us with the player's best response function. Second, we use the best response function of all players to identify the Nash equilibrium of the game. In our context, a Nash equilibrium is a list of appropriation levels (one for each fisherman) that are mutual best responses, that is, every fisherman uses a best response to their opponents' appropriation levels. We discuss each of these steps below.[3]

Step 1: *Find fisherman i's best response function.* Differentiating with respect to q_i in the above maximization problem for fisherman i we obtain

$$\underbrace{1}_{MR} - \underbrace{\frac{2q_i + Q_{-i}}{S}}_{MC} = 0.$$

---

[3] For an introduction to game theory tools, see Tadelis (2013) and Muñoz-Garcia and Toro-Gonzalez (2019). For game theory applications to industrial organizations, see Belleflamme and Peitz (2015), and for applications to environmental economics, see Lambertini (2015).

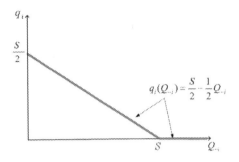

FIGURE 2.1 Fisherman i's best response function.

In words, the first term captures the marginal revenue from catching additional units of fish, MR, whereas the second term indicates the marginal cost that the firm experiences from these additional catches, MC. That is, the fisherman increases appropriation until the marginal revenue and cost exactly offset each other. Rearranging the above expression yields $S = 2q_i + Q_{-i}$, and solving for q_i, we find

$$q_i(Q_{-i}) = \frac{S}{2} - \frac{1}{2}Q_{-i}. \qquad \text{(BRF}_i)$$

Intuitively, $q_i(Q_{-i})$ represents fisherman i's best response function, since it describes how many units to appropriate, q_i, as a response to how many units his rivals appropriate, Q_{-i}. In particular, he appropriates half of the available stock, $\frac{S}{2}$, when his rivals do not appropriate any units, $Q_{-i} = 0$, but his appropriation decreases as his rivals appropriate positive amounts, $Q_{-i} > 0$, as depicted in Figure 2.1.[4]

Firms are symmetric in our setting since they face the same price for each unit of fish ($\$1$), and the same cost function. Therefore, the best response function of any other firm j (where $j \neq i$) is symmetric to the best response function we wrote above, that is, $q_j(Q_{-j}) = \frac{S}{2} - \frac{1}{2}Q_{-j}$, so we only change the subscript.

---

[4] Recall that, to find the horizontal intercept of the best response function in Figure 2.1, we only need to set it equal to zero, $\frac{S}{2} - \frac{1}{2}Q_{-i} = 0$, rearrange, $\frac{S}{2} = \frac{1}{2}Q_{-i}$, and solve for Q_{-i} to obtain $Q_{-i} = S$. In words, this point represents that, if fisherman i's rivals appropriate all the available stock, $Q_{-i} = S$, then fisherman i responds by not appropriating anything, $q_i = 0$.

Step 2: *Using best response functions to find the Nash equilibrium.*
In a symmetric equilibrium, each fisherman appropriates the same
amount of fish, implying that $q_1^* = q_2^* = \cdots = q_N^* = q^*$, which helps
us ignore the subscripts since all firms' catches coincide.[5] Therefore,
Q_{-i}^* becomes

$$Q_{-i}^* = \sum_{j \neq i} q^* = (N-1)q^*$$

given that we sum over all $N-1$ fishermen different from i. Inserting
this result in the above best response function yields

$$q^* = \frac{S}{2} - \frac{1}{2}(N-1)q^*,$$

which is now a function of q^* alone (recall that the stock S and
the number of fishermen N are both parameters, as opposed to q
that is the only variable we seek to solve for). Rearranging the above
expression yields

$$\frac{2q^* + (N-1)q^*}{2} = \frac{S}{2},$$

or $(N+1)q^* = S$, which solving for q^* entails an equilibrium
appropriation of

$$q^* = \frac{S}{N+1}.$$

For instance, if the stock is $S = 100$ tons of fish and $N = 9$ fishermen,
equilibrium appropriation becomes $q^* = \frac{100}{9+1} = 10$ tons. Therefore,
aggregate equilibrium appropriation becomes

$$Q^* = Nq^* = N\frac{S}{N+1}.$$

Only Two Firms: In the case of two firms, i and j, aggregate appropriation by i's rivals simplifies to $Q_{-i} = q_j$, implying that the best
response function of firm i is

$$q_i(q_j) = \frac{S}{2} - \frac{1}{2}q_j,$$

[5] Firms are symmetric since they all face the same problem (2.1). Intuitively, every firm
receives the same price per ton of fish and has the same cost function (e.g., access to the
same technology).

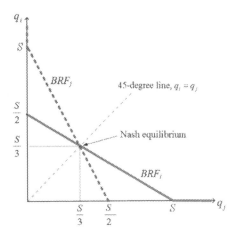

FIGURE 2.2 Equilibrium appropriation in the case of $N = 2$ firms.

and similarly for firm j's best response function. In this context, the Nash equilibrium can be depicted as the point where both firms' best response functions cross each other, as illustrated in Figure 2.2. We can evaluate our above results at $N = 2$ firms, obtaining an equilibrium appropriation of

$$q^* = \frac{S}{N+1} = \frac{S}{2+1} = \frac{S}{3},$$

lying on the 45-degree line of Figure 2.2, while aggregate appropriation is $Q^* = 2\frac{S}{3}$.

2.3.1 Comparative Statics

After finding an equilibrium result, like the above equilibrium appropriation level q^*, we often discuss how this result is affected by changes in one of the parameters, which we refer to as "comparative statics."

Equilibrium appropriation q^* only depends on the stock of the resource, S, and the number of firms competing for it, N. We can observe that equilibrium appropriation q^* increases in S, but decreases in N. This is intuitive as fishermen increase their catches as the resource becomes more abundant (higher S) but decrease them as their competition becomes fiercer (higher N).

For illustration purposes, Figure 2.3a depicts equilibrium appropriation q^* as a function of the number of firms exploiting the commons, N. (We fixed the stock at $S = 100$, so $q^* = \frac{100}{N+1}$.) Figure 2.3b

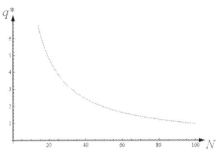

FIGURE 2.3A Equilibrium appropriation q^* as a function of N.

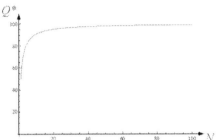

FIGURE 2.3B Aggregate equilibrium appropriation Q^* as a function of N.

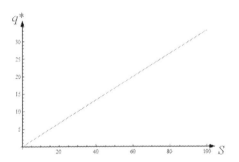

FIGURE 2.4 Equilibrium appropriation q^* as a function of S.

illustrates aggregate equilibrium appropriation $Q^* = N\frac{S}{N+1}$, where Q^* increases as the number of firms, N, increases. Together with Figure 2.3a, this says that, while the entry of more firms in the CPR leads each individual firm to decrease its own appropriation, the additional appropriation from the newcomer offsets such reduction in individual appropriations, ultimately yielding an overall increase in aggregate appropriation.

Figure 2.4 depicts q^* now as a function of the available stock, S, where the number of firms was fixed at $N = 2$, so appropriation simplifies to $q^* = \frac{S}{2+1} = \frac{S}{3}$.

To run comparative statics, we generally differentiate the equilibrium variable we just found (as the equilibrium appropriation q^* above) with respect to the parameter of interest (e.g., stock S). If this derivative is positive (negative) we can claim that our equilibrium result increases (decreases, respectively) in the parameter, and by how much.

2.3.2   Extension – What if Fishermen Have Some Market Power?

Our previous discussion considered that fishermen sell their appropriation at an international perfectly competitive market, where they take the price p as given. While this may be the case in some CPRs with a large amount of firms selling a relatively homogeneous product, other CPRs can be characterized by a few firms, each selling a relatively large share of total appropriations.[6] In that setting, we can no longer assume that fishermen take prices as given. Instead, they consider market demand $p(Q) = a - bQ$ where Q denotes aggregate appropriation, and $a, b > 0$ are both positive parameters. Recall that $b > 0$ indicates that a larger appropriation decreases the market price at which all fishermen sell their product. Since aggregate appropriation Q is the sum of fisherman i's appropriation and that of all his rivals, $Q = q_i + Q_{-i}$, we can express price $p(Q) = a - bQ$ as

$$p(Q) = a - b\left(q_i + Q_{-i}\right) = a - bq_i - bQ_{-i}.$$

As a practice, we repeat our previous analysis, starting by writing fisherman i's profit-maximization problem

$$\max_{q_i \geq 0} \ \pi_i = \underbrace{(a - bq_i - bQ_{-i})q_i}_{\text{Total revenue}} - \underbrace{\frac{q_i(q_i + Q_{-i})}{S}}_{\text{Total costs}}, \tag{2.2}$$

where the first term represents the total revenue from selling q_i units of appropriation (e.g., tons of fish) at price $p(Q)$, while the second term is the total cost of appropriating q_i units. We next apply Steps 1 and 2 to this setting.

[6] This is, for instance, the case with the highly concentrated fisheries in the North Sea, the Bering Sea, and the Western Pacific.

Step 1: *Finding fisherman i's best response function.* Differentiating the profit function in (2.2) with respect to q_i yields

$$a - 2bq_i - bQ_{-i} = \frac{2q_i + Q_{-i}}{S}$$

and solving for q_i, we find fisherman i's best response function

$$q_i(Q_{-i}) = \frac{aS}{2(1 + bS)} - \frac{1}{2}Q_{-i}.$$

When $a = 1$ and $b = 0$, market price collapses to $p(Q) = \$1$, and the best response function simplifies to $q_i(Q_{-i}) = \frac{S}{2} - \frac{1}{2}Q_{-i}$; as in our above discussion that assumed that market prices are insensitive to sales. However, when b increases, the vertical intercept of the best response function, $\frac{aS}{2(1+bS)}$, decreases, producing a downward shift without affecting its slope, $-\frac{1}{2}$. In words, this indicates that, for a given appropriation by fisherman i's rivals (treating Q_{-i} as given), the appropriation by fisherman i decreases when the market price becomes more sensitive to aggregate appropriation (when parameter b increases). The opposite effect arises when demand increases (as captured by an increase in a), as the vertical intercept of the best response function, $\frac{aS}{2(1+bS)}$, now increases, shifting the function upward.

Step 2: *Using best response functions to find the Nash equilibrium.* In a symmetric equilibrium, each fisherman appropriates the same amount of fish, $q_1^* = q_2^* = \cdots = q_N^* = q^*$, implying that Q_{-i}^* becomes

$$Q_{-i}^* = \sum_{j \neq i} q^* = (N - 1)q^*.$$

Inserting this result in the above best response function yields

$$q^* = \frac{aS}{2(1 + bS)} - \frac{1}{2}(N - 1)q^*,$$

which is now a function of q^* alone. Rearranging the above expression, and solving for q^*, yields an equilibrium appropriation of

$$q^* = \frac{aS}{(N + 1)(1 + bS)}.$$

When $a = 1$ and $b = 0$, equilibrium appropriation simplifies to $q^* = \frac{S}{N+1}$, as in our above discussion assuming that firms are price takers. In contrast, when b increases, each firm decreases its equilibrium appropriation q^*, since its sales now create a negative effect on market price that did not exist when such a price was given. Intuitively, the firm anticipates that selling more units will reduce market prices, so it does not appropriate as much fish as when prices are insensitive to its catches.

In this setting, aggregate equilibrium appropriation is

$$Q^* = Nq^* = N\frac{aS}{(N+1)\,(1+bS)}$$

thus exhibiting the same comparative statics as individual appropriation q^* discussed above.

2.4 COMMON POOL RESOURCES – SOCIALLY OPTIMAL APPROPRIATION

A natural question at this point is:

Is equilibrium appropriation excessive from a social point of view?

To answer that question we must, of course, start by defining the socially optimal appropriation. For simplicity, many authors in the CPR literature assume that the socially optimal appropriation is the one maximizing the fishermen's joint profits. That is, they consider that the social planner's welfare function is

$$W = PS, \tag{2.3}$$

where $PS = \sum_{i=1}^{N} \pi_i$ denotes the sum of all firms' profits. In the case of only two fishermen, W collapses to $W = \pi_1 + \pi_2$. This is a reasonable welfare function when catches are sold in an international market, thus making consumer surplus irrelevant. Importantly, the appropriation levels in this case coincide with those in a CPR cartel with firms seeking to maximize joint profits.

We could alternatively consider a more general welfare function that includes both consumer and producer surplus, as follows:

$$W = CS + PS, \tag{2.4}$$

where $CS = \int_0^Q p(Q)dQ$ denotes consumer surplus (i.e., the area below the demand curve $p(Q)$ between the origin and Q), and PS represents the producer surplus (i.e., sum of profits from all firms). This welfare function is more common in CPRs where catches are sold in the domestic market, thus affecting domestic consumers.

Welfare function $W = CS + PS$ can be further generalized to

$$W = (1 - \lambda)CS + \lambda PS, \tag{2.5}$$

where $\lambda \in [0,1]$ denotes the weight that the social planner (e.g., regulator) assigns to producer surplus, while $(1 - \lambda)$ captures the weight that she assigns to consumer surplus. This representation allows for several welfare functions as special cases:

1. When $\lambda = 1$, the welfare function in (2.5) collapses to $W = PS$, as in expression (2.3), thus indicating that the social planner does not care about consumer surplus. This can be the case when all appropriation is sold overseas so domestic consumers are not affected by the price of the good as, in short, they do not buy the product.
2. When $\lambda = \frac{1}{2}$, the social planner assigns the same importance to consumers and producers. Therefore, the welfare function in (2.5) simplifies to $W = \frac{1}{2}(CS + PS)$. Since $\frac{1}{2}$ enters as a constant, it can be graphically understood as a vertical shifter of $CS + PS$. As a result, the appropriation levels maximizing $W = \frac{1}{2}(CS + PS)$ coincide with those maximizing $W = CS + PS$, as in expression (2.4).
3. When $\lambda = 0$, the welfare function in (2.5) reduces to $W = CS$, so the social planner does not assign any weight to fishermen's profits, which could be the case if they are all foreign firms operating at a CPR overseas that does not have effects on domestic welfare, other than those channeled through the demand function and CS.

The following subsections find the socially optimal appropriation that maximizes welfare. For presentation purposes, we first consider the welfare function in (2.3), $W = PS$, and then the most general expression in (2.5). (As discussed in point 1 in the above list, (2.5) embodies (2.3) and (2.4) as special cases, when $\lambda = 1$ and $\lambda = 1/2$, respectively.) For simplicity, we focus on the case in which fishermen take prices as given, $p = \$1$, and consider two fishermen, $N = 2$, but a similar argument applies to CPRs where more than two fishermen consider a downward-sloping demand curve.

2.4.1   Socially Optimal Appropriation When only Profits Matter

When the social planner considers welfare function $W = PS$, she finds catches q_1 and q_2 to solve

$$\max_{q_1, q_2 \geq 0} \quad W = PS = \pi_1 + \pi_2, \tag{2.6}$$

which can be written as

$$\max_{q_1, q_2 \geq 0} \quad \pi_1 + \pi_2 = \underbrace{\left(q_1 - \frac{q_1(q_1 + q_2)}{S} \right)}_{\pi_1} + \underbrace{\left(q_2 - \frac{q_2(q_2 + q_1)}{S} \right)}_{\pi_2}.$$

This problem is, then, equivalent to that of a fishermen's cartel where fishermen 1 and 2 coordinate their catches, q_1 and q_2, to maximize their joint profits, $\pi_1 + \pi_2$. Differentiating with respect to q_1, we find

$$1 - \frac{2(q_1 + q_2)}{S} = 0,$$

and the same result emerges after differentiating with respect to q_2. Intuitively, the first term represents the marginal revenue from additional catches while the second term captures fisherman i's marginal cost, $\frac{2(q_1 + q_2)}{S}$. Relative to the individual decision problem analyzed in Section 2.3, increasing catches now produces twice as many marginal costs since each fisherman takes into account not only the increase in their own costs but also the increase in their rival's costs. In short, each fisherman internalizes now the cost externality that their appropriation imposes on other fishermen, as a larger q_i increases the cost of fisherman j.

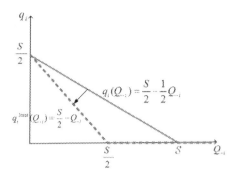

FIGURE 2.5 Equilibrium vs. joint profit maximization in the commons.

Rearranging the above expression, we obtain $S = 2(q_1 + q_2)$, and solving for q_1 we find

$$q_1(q_2) = \frac{S}{2} - q_2.$$

As depicted in Figure 2.5, this line originates at the same height as fisherman i's best response function in Figure 2.1, $\frac{S}{2}$, but decreases in their rival's appropriation faster than that in Figure 2.1, thus lying below. In words, this indicates that, for a given amount of appropriation from firm 2, q_2, firm 1 chooses to appropriate fewer units when firms coordinate their exploitation of the resource (jointly maximizing profits) than when each firm independently selects its own appropriation.[7]

To confirm this finding, let us simultaneously solve for appropriation levels q_1 and q_2 in the above equations, $q_1(q_2) = \frac{S}{2} - q_2$ for fisherman 1 and $q_2(q_1) = \frac{S}{2} - q_1$ for fisherman 2. These equations perfectly overlap on top of each other, indicating that a continuum of optimal pairs (q_1, q_2) solves the above joint-profit maximization problem, graphically illustrated by all points along the line $q_1(q_2) = \frac{S}{2} - q_2$. Since firms are symmetric, the literature often

---

[7] To find the horizontal intercept of expression $q_1(q_2) = \frac{S}{2} - q_2$, we only need to set it equal to zero, $0 = \frac{S}{2} - q_2$, rearrange, $\frac{S}{2} = q_2$, and solve for q_2 to obtain $q_2 = \frac{S}{2}$, as illustrated in the horizontal intercept of Figure 2.4. Intuitively, this point represents that, if fisherman 2 appropriates half of the available stock, $q_2 = \frac{S}{2}$, fisherman 1 responds by not appropriating anything, $q_1 = 0$.

considers that, among all optimal pairs, a natural equilibrium is that in which both firms appropriate the same amount, $q_1^{SO} = q_2^{SO} = q^{SO}$, where the superscript SO indicates "socially optimal" appropriation.

Inserting $q_1^{SO} = q_2^{SO} = q^{SO}$ in equation $q_1(q_2) = \frac{S}{2} - q_2$ and solving for q^{SO} entails a socially optimal appropriation

$$q^{SO} = \frac{S}{4}.$$

Comparing this result against the equilibrium appropriation when agents independently choose their appropriation levels (evaluated at the case of $N = 2$ fishermen), $q^* = \frac{S}{2+1} = \frac{S}{3}$, yields that

$$q^* > q^{SO} \text{ since } \frac{S}{3} > \frac{S}{4}.$$

In words, this result says that agents exploit the resource less intensively when they coordinate their appropriation decisions (and thus internalize the cost externalities their appropriation imposes on others) than when they do not coordinate their exploitation. This is often referred to as the "tragedy of the commons" as the CPR is exploited more intensively in equilibrium than if agents could coordinate their appropriation decisions, as in a CPR cartel.

2.4.2 Socially Optimal Appropriation with Consumers and Profits Matter

When the social planner considers welfare function $W = (1 - \lambda) CS + \lambda PS$, she chooses the level of catches q_1 and q_2 to solve

$$\max_{q_1, q_2 \geq 0} W = (1 - \lambda) CS + \lambda PS \tag{2.7}$$

where $CS = \int_0^Q (1 - Q) dQ$. Since inverse demand function $p(Q) = 1 - Q$ is linear in aggregate appropriation Q, consumer surplus can be expressed as the area of the triangle below the demand function, that is,

$$CS = \frac{1}{2} \underbrace{[1 - (1 - Q)]}_{\text{height}} \underbrace{(Q - 0)}_{\text{base}} = \frac{1}{2} Q^2.$$

Since aggregate appropriation can be expanded as $Q = q_1 + q_2$, we can rewrite problem (2.7) as follows:

$$\max_{q_1, q_2 \geq 0} W = (1 - \lambda) \frac{1}{2} (q_1 + q_2)^2 + \lambda (\pi_1 + \pi_2).$$

Differentiating with respect to q_1 and q_2 yields

$$\frac{\partial W}{\partial q_1} = (1 - \lambda)(q_1 + q_2) + \lambda \left(1 - \frac{2(q_1 + q_2)}{S} \right) = 0$$

$$\frac{\partial W}{\partial q_2} = (1 - \lambda)(q_1 + q_2) + \lambda \left(1 - \frac{2(q_1 + q_2)}{S} \right) = 0$$

where both expressions are symmetric since firms face the same demand and cost functions. In a symmetric social optimum, firms exploit the CPR at the same rate, $q_1^{SO} = q_2^{SO} = q^{SO}$. Inserting this property into either of our first-order conditions above, we obtain

$$2(1 - \lambda)q + \lambda \left(1 - \frac{4q}{S} \right) = 0.$$

Solving for q, we find the socially optimal appropriation

$$q^{SO}(\lambda) = \frac{S\lambda}{2 [2\lambda - S(1 - \lambda)]}.$$

As a confirmation, note that when $\lambda = 1$, this expression simplifies to $q^{SO}(1) = \frac{S}{4}$, as in our discussion at the beginning of this section where the social planner only considered producer surplus. More generally, differentiating $q^{SO}(\lambda)$ with respect to λ, we find

$$\frac{\partial q^{SO}(\lambda)}{\partial \lambda} = -\frac{S^2}{2 [2\lambda - S(1 - \lambda)]^2},$$

which is negative. In words, the regulator decreases the socially optimal appropriation when she assigns a larger weight to producer surplus.

2.5 FACING OUR FIRST INEFFICIENCY

Our above results help identify the first inefficiency in the exploitation of the commons by individual firms. Despite operating in a static

context, firms' equilibrium appropriation is larger than a social planner would select. This happens regardless of the welfare function that
she considers, that is, both when she only seeks to maximize firms'
joint profits, $W = \pi_1 + \pi_2$, and when her objective is to maximize a
weighted sum of consumer and producer surplus, $W = (1 - \lambda)CS +
\lambda PS$. Intuitively, every individual fisherman ignores the negative cost
externality that their appropriation produces on other fishermen, and
thus exploits the resource above the socially optimal level.[8]

This result is analogous to that in the standard Cournot model
of quantity competition, where firms tend to produce too much,
relative to the output that would maximize their joint profits in a
cartel, since they ignore the negative effect that their sales impose
on their rivals' revenues (as these sales decrease the market price,
which in turn reduces the total revenue of all firms in the industry).
This negative effect is, however, internalized when firms coordinate
their production decisions to maximize their joint profits or, more
generally, when a social planner determines individual output levels.

In the next chapters, we analyze CPRs in dynamic settings,
where today's stock is affected by aggregate exploitation decisions
in previous periods. In those settings, the above (purely static) inefficiency still arises, but other forms of inefficiencies (dynamic in
nature) will emerge.

2.6   INEFFICIENT EXPLOITATION WITH MORE
GENERAL FUNCTIONS

For presentation purposes, our previous analysis considered a specific
cost function for every firm i, $C_i(q_i, Q_{-i}) = \frac{q_i(q_i + Q_{-i})}{S}$, to show that
appropriation is excessive relative to the social optimum, $q^* > q^{SO}$,

---

[8] Examples of commons being overexploited abound. For instance, the Food and Agriculture
Organization (2005) identifies such overexploitation for the blue whiting in the Northeast
Atlantic, the Chilean jack mackerel in the Southeast Pacific, and the Peruvian anchovy in
the Southeast Pacific.

or, more compactly, that equilibrium appropriation is "socially excessive." In this section, we show this result without assuming a specific cost function. Instead, we only assume that firm i's marginal cost, $MC_i = \frac{\partial C_i(q_i, Q_{-i})}{\partial q_i}$, satisfies the following assumptions:

1. positive, $MC_i > 0$, and increasing in firm i's own appropriation, $\frac{\partial MC_i}{\partial q_i} > 0$;
2. decreasing in the available stock, $\frac{\partial MC_i}{\partial S} < 0$;
3. increasing in the appropriation of any rival firm j, $\frac{\partial MC_i}{\partial q_j} > 0$ where $j \neq i$.

Both assumptions hold in the cost function we considered in all previous sections, $C(q_i, Q_{-i}) = \frac{q_i(q_i + Q_{-i})}{S}$, since marginal cost in that setting was $MC_i = \frac{2q_i + Q_{-i}}{S}$, which is positive and increasing in q_i (as required by Assumption 1), decreasing in the stock S (as required by Assumption 2), and increasing in the appropriation by firm i's rivals, Q_{-i} (as required by Assumption 3). Intuitively, Assumption 1 says that each fisherman i faces a positive and increasing cost for every additional unit the firm appropriates; Assumption 2 suggests that fisherman i can capture q_i tons of fish more easily when the stock is abundant than otherwise; while Assumption 3 indicates that, when other fishermen increase their appropriation Q_{-i}, the resource becomes more scarce, increasing the time and effort that fisherman i needs to spend to appropriate a given amount q_i.

Equilibrium Appropriation: In this context, every firm i solves a problem like (2.1) but with a more general cost function, as follows:

$$\max_{q_i \geq 0} \ \pi_i = q_i - C_i(q_i, Q_{-i}).$$

Differentiating with respect to q_i, we obtain

$$1 - \frac{\partial C_i(q_i, Q_{-i})}{\partial q_i} = 0$$

and since marginal cost was defined as $MC_i = \frac{\partial C_i(q_i, Q_{-i})}{\partial q_i}$, we can express the above result more compactly as

$$MC_i = 1.$$

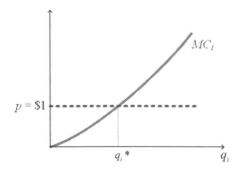

FIGURE 2.6 Equilibrium appropriation q_i^*.

In words, every fisherman i increases their individual appropriation until the point where their marginal revenue from additional sales (i.e., the price of this additional appropriation, which is normalized at $p = \$1$) coincides with the marginal cost of this additional appropriation. Figure 2.6 depicts condition $MC_i = 1$, by separately plotting the price $p = \$1$, and the marginal cost MC_i. This marginal cost is increasing in firm i's appropriation q_i since, by Assumption 1, $\frac{\partial MC_i}{\partial q_i} > 0.$[9]

While condition $MC_i = 1$ is an implicit equation, rather than the typical best response function found in previous sections, it helps us understand firm i's strategic incentives. When firm j increases its individual appropriation q_j, firm i's marginal cost MC_i decreases, since $\frac{\partial MC_i}{\partial q_j} > 0$ by Assumption 3, whereas the marginal revenue in the right-hand side of $MC_i = 1$ is unaffected. In Figure 2.6, curve MC_i shifts upward, entailing that the crossing point between MC_i and $\$1$ moves to the left, reducing firm i's equilibrium appropriation q_i. Graphically, this is exactly the negative slope of firm i's best response function $q_i(q_j)$ with respect to q_j, as depicted in Figure 2.1.

We next investigate the socially optimal appropriation, and subsequently compare it with that arising in equilibrium.

---

[9] Figure 2.6 depicted MC_i as increasing in q_i at an increasing rate (that is, convex in q_i). Assumptions 1-3, however, did not impose any structure on the concavity or convexity of MC_i. Therefore, our results still apply if MC_i is linear (a straight, increasing, line in Figure 2.6) or concave (increasing in q_i but at a decreasing rate).

Social Optimum: Assuming, for simplicity, that the welfare function considers only joint profits, the social planner solves a problem analogous to (2.6), that is

$$\max_{q_1,.....q_N \geq 0} W = PS = \sum_{i=1}^{N} \pi_i = \sum_{i=1}^{N} \left[q_i - C_i(q_i, Q_{-i}) \right],$$

which, for clarity, can be expanded as the sum of firm i's profits plus the profits of all its rivals, $\pi_i + \sum_{j \neq i} \pi_j$, as follows:

$$\max_{q_1,.....q_N \geq 0} W = \left[q_i - C_i(q_i, Q_{-i}) \right] + \sum_{j \neq i} \left[q_j - C_j(q_j, Q_{-j}) \right].$$

Differentiating with respect to every q_i, we find

$$1 - \frac{\partial C_i(q_i, Q_{-i})}{\partial q_i} - \sum_{j \neq i} \frac{\partial C_j(q_j, Q_{-j})}{\partial q_i} = 0$$

since Q_{-j} includes q_i as one of its components. As we did in our discussion of equilibrium appropriation, we can rearrange this expression as

$$MC_i + \underbrace{\sum_{j \neq i} \frac{\partial C_j(q_j, Q_{-j})}{\partial q_i}}_{\text{New term (Cost externality)}} = 1.$$

Our result then coincides with equilibrium condition $MC_i = 1$, except for the new term $\sum_{j \neq i} \frac{\partial C_j(q_j, Q_{-j})}{\partial q_i}$. Intuitively, every firm i increases its individual appropriation until the point where its marginal revenue from appropriating one more unit ($p = \$1$) coincides with the sum of its own additional cost, MC_i, and the additional cost that its appropriation imposes on all other firms, $\sum_{j \neq i} \frac{\partial C_j(q_j, Q_{-j})}{\partial q_i}$. Relative to the equilibrium condition $MC_i = 1$, every firm now internalizes the negative cost externality that its individual appropriation q_i produces on its rivals. As a result of this additional cost, firm i chooses a lower exploitation in the social optimum than in equilibrium, $q_i^{SO} < q_i^*$. Figure 2.7 illustrates this result and compares it against that emerging from equilibrium condition $MC_i = 1$.

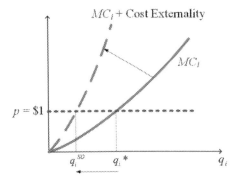

FIGURE 2.7 Equilibrium and socially optimal appropriation.

2.7   POLICY INSTRUMENTS

In this section, we briefly discuss some policy instruments to correct the socially excessive exploitation that we identified in our previous results.

2.7.1   Quotas

The regulator can set a quota that lets fisherman i catch as much fish as the socially optimal level, q_i^{SO}, facing stringent penalties if they exceed this allowance. Quotas are fairly common in several CPRs such as the "Common Fisheries Policy" in the European Union, which sets quotas on fish catches for each member state, and the "individual transferable quotas" assigned to each fisherman in the USA or New Zealand.

In these quotas, also known as "catch share," the regulator starts by setting a total allowable catch for each species of fish and for a given time period, and then a dedicated portion is assigned to individual fishermen in the form of quotas, which are transferable, and thus can be bought, sold, and leased to other fishermen. In 2008, for instance, 148 major fisheries and 100 smaller fisheries around the world had adopted some form of individual transferable quota; see Costello et al. (2008) for more details.

Quotas are often initially assigned according to each fisherman's recent catch history, implying that those who more intensively appropriate the resource receive larger quotas. This assignment rule can, then, induce fishermen to increase their relative appropriation of the resource to receive a larger transferable quota, which they can keep or sell in future periods.[10] Quota auctions have been proposed as an alternative allocation mechanism, which may prevent the above perverse incentives to increase appropriation before the quota is allocated and, in addition, raise public funds for access to fisheries. For a theoretical analysis of these auctions in the commons, see Montero (2008) and for an institutional and empirical discussion, see Libecap (2009) and Chu (2009).

Quotas regarding aquifers are less common, but countries such as Mexico and Spain set limits on private use; otherwise, the farmer can lose their water permit. For current empirical analysis, see Esteban and Albiac (2011) and Pereau et al. (2018), and references therein.

Finally, other command-and-control regulations include restrictions on the boat size, fishing gear (such as mesh or net size), limits on the days certain boats can fish, or prohibiting the catch of juvenile fish, among others.

2.7.2 Appropriation Fees

Alternatively, the regulator can set an emission fee for fisherman i, t_i, that induces them to appropriate the socially optimal level q_i^{SO}. In this setting, every fisherman i solves a problem analogous to that in (2.1) but with marginal costs increased by t_i, which yields a first-order condition

$$\underbrace{1}_{MR} - \underbrace{\left(\frac{2q_i + Q_{-i}}{S} + t_i\right)}_{MC} = 0.$$

---

[10] Another drawback from assiging quotas based on catch history is that small fishermen may be excluded from receiving any quota if they do not own a boat.

Solving for appropriation q_i, we find best response function

$$q_i(Q_{-i}) = \frac{S(1 - t_i)}{2} - \frac{1}{2}Q_{-i},$$

which coincides with that in Section 2.3 when the appropriation fee is absent, $t_i = 0$. Otherwise, a more stringent fee decreases the vertical intercept of the best response function, $\frac{S(1-t_i)}{2}$, without affecting its slope, graphically implying a parallel downward shift of fisherman i's best response function. Intuitively, for a given aggregate appropriation from their rivals Q_{-i}, fisherman i decreases their individual appropriation when facing a more stringent fee. This comes at no surprise since this fee increases the fisherman's marginal cost of additional appropriation, reducing their incentives to exploit the resource.

In a symmetric equilibrium, $q_i^* = q_j^* = q^*$, which entails that $Q_{-i}^* = (N - 1)q_i^*$. Inserting this property in the above best response function, we obtain

$$q^* = \frac{S(1 - t_i)}{2} - \frac{1}{2}(N - 1)q^*,$$

which only depends on q^*. Rearranging yields $q^*(N + 1) = S(1 - t)$. Solving for q^*, we find that equilibrium appropriation is

$$q^*(t_i) = \frac{S(1 - t_i)}{N + 1}.$$

As a confirmation, note that when the appropriation fee is absent, $t_i = 0$, we obtain the same equilibrium appropriation as in Section 2.3. When this fee is positive, nonetheless, equilibrium appropriation is lower. As in Section 2.3, this appropriation is increasing in the stock, S, but decreasing in the number of firms exploiting the CPR, N.

Our main question still remains: How can the regulator find the appropriation fee t_i that induces fisherman i to exploit the resource at the socially optimal level, q_i^{SO}? This question can be alternatively formulated as: What is the emission fee t_i, inserted in fisherman i's equilibrium appropriation $q^*(t_i)$, that induces this fisherman to appropriate q_i^{SO} tons of fish? Intuitively, this question says that the regulator seeks to achieve $q^*(t_i) = q_i^{SO}$, which we can expand as

$$\frac{S(1-t_i)}{N+1} = \frac{S}{4}.$$

Rearranging, we find $4 - 4t_i = N+1$ and, solving for t_i, we obtain that the optimal fee is

$$t_i^* = \frac{3-N}{4},$$

which is decreasing in the number of firms, N, and positive for $N \le 3$. Intuitively, the regulator seeks to induce the same socially optimal output per firm, $q_i^{SO} = \frac{S}{4}$, regardless of the number of firms. When few firms operate in the commons, the equilibrium exploitation of each firm, $q^*(t_i)$, is substantially larger than q_i^{SO}, requiring a stringent fee to reduce exploitation. When several firms compete, however, the equilibrium appropriation of each firm, $q^*(t_i)$, is relatively lower, while $q_i^{SO} = \frac{S}{4}$ is unaffected, leading the regulator to set a lax appropriation fee, which may become a subsidy when $N > 3$. While appropriation fees are less common in fisheries, they are relatively frequent in groundwater agricultural use (e.g., aquifer exploitation) such as in Israel.[11]

2.8   EXERCISES

2.1   Allowing for different cost externalities. Consider the setting in Section 2.3 and, for simplicity, assume $N = 2$ firms. In addition, consider that every firm's cost function is

$$C_i(q_i, q_j) = \frac{q_i(q_i + \theta q_j)}{S},$$

where $\theta \ge 0$ denotes the severity of the cost externality. When $\theta = 0$, firm i's costs are unaffected by its rival's appropriation q_j, whereas when $\theta > 0$, firm i's costs are affected by q_j. As a remark, note that our

[11] For an interesting application of emission fees in the commons, and how they can help firms increase their profits under certain conditions, see Kotchen and Salant (2011).

setting in Section 2.3 can be interpreted as a special case of this more general model, where $\theta = 1$.

(a) Find every firm i's best response function, $q_i(q_j)$.
(b) How is $q_i(q_j)$ affected by an increase in parameter θ? Interpret.
(c) Find the equilibrium appropriation q_i^*.
(d) How is q_i^* affected by an increase in parameter θ? Interpret.

2.2 Asymmetric firms. Consider the setting in Section 2.3 and, for simplicity, assume $N = 2$ firms. In this case, consider that firms face a different cost function

$$C_1(q_1, q_2) = \frac{q_1(q_1 + q_2)}{S} \quad \text{and} \quad C_2(q_2, q_1) = \frac{\alpha q_2(q_1 + q_2)}{S}$$

where $\alpha \in [0, 1]$ denotes firm 2's cost advantage. When $\alpha = 1$, both firms face the same cost function, as in Section 2.3. However, when $\alpha < 1$, firm 2 benefits from a cost advantage relative to firm 1.

(a) Find firm 1's best response function, $q_1(q_2)$. How is it affected by an increase in parameter α? Interpret.
(b) Find firm 2's best response function, $q_2(q_1)$. How is it affected by an increase in parameter α? Interpret.
(c) Compare firm 1 and firm 2's best response functions.
(d) Find the equilibrium appropriation pair (q_1^*, q_2^*). [*Hint*: Since firms are asymmetric, you cannot invoke symmetric appropriation as we did in Section 2.3. Instead, you will need to insert the best response function of one of the firms into that of its rival, as when you solve a system of two equations with two unknowns.]
(e) Which firm appropriates more in equilibrium?
(f) Show that the equilibrium appropriation you found in part (d) coincides with that in Section 2.3 when firms are symmetric, $\alpha = 1$.
(g) How is equilibrium appropriation affected by an increase in parameter α? Interpret.

2.3 Finding socially optimal appropriation in a CPR with N firms. Consider the setting in Section 2.4.1, which assumed a CPR with $N = 2$ firms. Repeat the analysis allowing for $N \geq 2$ firms.

(a) Find the socially optimal appropriation q_i^{SO}.
(b) How is q_i^{SO} affected by the number of firms, N?

2.4 Firms facing a downward-sloping demand. Consider the setting in Section 2.4.1 where fishermen face a linear inverse demand function $p(Q) = a - bQ$, where $a, b > 0$, and Q denotes aggregate appropriation.

(a) Assume that the social planner only considers producer surplus in the welfare function, $W = PS$. Show that equilibrium appropriation is socially excessive.

(b) Assume that the social planner considers consumer and producer surplus in the welfare function, $W = CS + PS$. Show that equilibrium appropriation is socially excessive.

(c) Let the difference $q_i^* - q_i^{SO}$ measure the inefficiency that arises when firms choose their appropriation level in equilibrium. Find this difference in parts (a) and (b).

(d) Is difference $q_i^* - q_i^{SO}$ larger when the social planner's welfare function considers only $W = PS$, as in part (a), or when it considers $W = CS + PS$, as in part (b)? Interpret.

(e) How is the difference $q_i^* - q_i^{SO}$ affected by the number of firms operating in the CPR, N? Interpret.

2.5 Profit-enhancing appropriation fees – I. Consider the setting in Section 2.3. Assume that a regulator sets a fee t on all firms (this is a generic fee t, rather than the socially optimal fee t^* found in Section 2.7.2).

(a) Find individual equilibrium appropriation $q^*(t)$, as a function of fee t.

(b) Show that $q^*(t)$ is decreasing in fee t. How is your result affected by the number of firms, N?

(c) Show that aggregate equilibrium appropriation, $Q^*(t)$, is also decreasing in fee t. How is your result affected by the number of firms, N?

(d) Evaluate equilibrium profits $\pi^*(t)$, and find if they are increasing/decreasing in fee t. Interpret your results.

2.6 Profit-enhancing appropriation fees – II. Repeat the analysis of Exercise 2.5, but allowing now for firms to sustain market power. That is, firms face a linear inverse demand curve $p(Q) = 1 - Q$, where Q denotes aggregate appropriation. How are your results from Exercise 2.5 affected? Interpret.

2.7 Finding appropriation fees. Consider the setting in Exercise 2.2. Let us use the approach to appropriation fees we discussed in Section 2.7, as follows:

(a) Find the equilibrium appropriation $q_1(t_1)$ and $q_2(t_2)$ for each firm. (Note that each appropriation is a function of a firm-specific appropriation fee.)

(b) Find the emission fee t_i that induces every firm i to appropriate q_i^{SO} units.

(c) What happens if the regulator cannot set a firm-specific appropriation fee, (t_1, t_2), but must rather set a uniform fee t to both firms? Discuss your results.

2.8 Appropriation fees under a different welfare function. Consider the discussion on appropriation fees in Section 2.7. Assume now that the social planner considers a welfare function $W = CS + PS$.

(a) Find the socially optimal appropriation, q_i^{SO}.

(b) Find the emission fee t_i that induces every firm i to appropriate q_i^{SO} units.

2.9 Equity shares, based on Ellis (2001) and Heintzelman et al. (2009). Consider our discussion of equilibrium appropriation levels in Section 2.3. Assume now that, before choosing its appropriation level q_i, every firm i selects an equity share $\alpha_i \in [0, 1/2]$ into firm j's profit to solve

$$\max_{\alpha_i \geq 0} \ (1 - \alpha_j)\pi_i + \alpha_i \pi_j.$$

In words, when $\alpha_j = \alpha_i = 0$, firm i's objective function reduces to its own profits, $(1 - 0)\pi_i + 0\pi_j = \pi_i$; if $\alpha_j = 0$ but $\alpha_i > 0$, firm i's objective function is $(1 - 0)\pi_i + \alpha_i \pi_j = \pi_i + \alpha_i \pi_j$, that is, its own profits plus a share on firm j's; and if both equity shares are positive, $\alpha_j, \alpha_i > 0$, firm i maximizes a weighted average of its own and firm j's profits.

For simplicity, we next consider equity shares α_i and α_j as given (exogenous) and study how appropriation levels are affected by these shares.

(a) For a given pair of equity shares α_i and α_j, find firm i's best response function $q_i(q_j)$. This function should depend on equity shares α_i and α_j. How is it affected by a marginal increase in α_i? And how is it affected by a marginal increase in α_j? Interpret.

(b) Find the equilibrium appropriation levels, q_i^* and q_j^*, and evaluate second-period profits, π_i^*. How are they affected by a marginal increase in each firm's equity shares?

(c) Is the "tragedy of the commons" ameliorated by the presence of equity shares? Interpret.

3   Common Pool Resources
in a Dynamic Setting

3.1   INTRODUCTION

In this chapter we examine another form of inefficiency in CPRs. While Chapter 2 analyzed a *static* inefficiency – that emerged when firms ignore the negative externality that their current appropriation imposes on other firms' current costs – this chapter explores a *dynamic* inefficiency, arising from firms ignoring the negative externality that their current appropriation imposes on other firms' *future* costs.

For presentation purposes, we consider a sequential-move game where, in the first period, only one firm operates in the CPR (e.g., the incumbent), but in the second period two firms compete for the resource (the incumbent and an entrant). This stylized setting helps us isolate the dynamic inefficiency that the incumbent's first-period appropriation imposes on the entrant's second-period costs, separating it from the static inefficiency that arises from the two firms' simultaneous appropriation of the CPR in the second period. Our analysis can be extended to settings with two or more firms operating in both the first and second period, which gives rise to static inefficiencies in each period (where equilibrium appropriation is socially excessive) and a dynamic inefficiency across periods (as every firm ignores the negative externality that its first-period appropriation has on its rivals' future costs), and to contexts where two or more firms interact during more than two periods.

This chapter considers, for simplicity, the entrant's decision as exogenous, that is, the entrant has either joined or not joined the CPR. In subsequent chapters, however, we make this entry decision endogenous, that is, we allow for the potential entrant to evaluate whether entry is profitable. Interestingly, we will also examine which actions the incumbent can take during the first period to prevent entry of potential competitors, and how these actions can, paradoxically, protect the resource from overexploitation or, at least, ameliorate aggregate appropriation.

3.2 MODELING CPRS IN A DYNAMIC SETTING

How can we alter the basic setting presented in Chapter 2 to account for dynamic effects in the CPR? In a two-period sequential-move model, every firm i chooses its individual appropriation x_i, facing a cost function similar to that in Chapter 2:

$$C(x_i, X_{-i}) = \frac{x_i(x_i + X_{-i})}{S},$$ (first-period cost)

where X_{-i} denotes aggregate appropriation by firm i's rivals, $X_{-i} = \sum_{j \neq i} x_j$. As in Chapter 2, $S \geq 0$ represents the available stock. If only one firm operates in the first period, then $X_{-i} = 0$, and the above cost function collapses to $C(x_i, X_{-i}) = \frac{x_i^2}{S}$.

In the second period, however, every firm faces a slightly different cost function, which accounts for the resource exploitation, as follows:

$$C(q_i, Q_{-i}) = \frac{q_i(q_i + Q_{-i})}{S - (1 - r)X},$$ (second-period cost)

where q_i denotes firm i's second-period appropriation and $Q_{-i} = \sum_{j \neq i} q_j$ is the aggregate appropriation by its rivals. Parameter $r \in [0, 1]$ represents the regeneration rate of the resource. To understand its role in second-period costs, consider the following cases:

- When $r = 1$, the resource fully regenerates, implying that the second-period cost function simplifies to $C(q_i, Q_{-i}) = \frac{q_i(q_i + Q_{-i})}{S}$, thus becoming symmetric to that in the first period. In this case, first-period aggregate appropriation, X, does not affect the firm's second-period costs since the stock fully regenerates across periods.[1]

---

[1] Resources that fully regenerate across periods are also known as renewable, such as solar energy or hydropower. In contrast, resources whose stock does not regenerate at all (or with an extremely slow regeneration process) are known as nonrenewable, and include oil extraction, natural gas, or coal.

- In contrast, when the regeneration rate is nil, $r = 0$, the second-period cost function becomes $C(q_i, Q_{-i}) = \frac{q_i(q_i + Q_{-i})}{S - X}$, suggesting that the stock available at the beginning of the second period is $S - X$, namely, the initial stock S diminished exactly by every unit of first-period appropriation, X.

Like the cost function presented in Chapter 2, this cost function exhibits a marginal cost of $MC_i = \frac{2q_i + Q_{-i}}{S - (1-r)X}$, which satisfies Assumptions 1–3. (You may check this as a practice.) Furthermore, marginal cost is decreasing in the regeneration rate r, indicating that exploiting the resource becomes easier for the fisherman as a larger proportion of first-period appropriation is replenished with new fish before the beginning of the second period.

Since this is a sequential-move game of complete information, we operate by backward induction to find the Subgame Perfect Equilibrium (SPE), also known as "rollback equilibrium." Intuitively, we start by analyzing firms' behavior in the second period of the game, taking first-period appropriation as given, and then move on to examine first-period appropriation where firms perfectly anticipate their profits in the second period of the game.

3.3 FINDING EQUILIBRIUM APPROPRIATION

As described in Section 3.1, we first study the following sequential-move game:

1. *First period:* Only one firm operates, which, for compactness, we refer to as the "incumbent." In this period, the incumbent chooses its first-period appropriation x.
2. *Second period:* The incumbent and an entrant simultaneously and independently select their second-period appropriation, q_1 and q_2, respectively.

3.3.1 *Equilibrium Appropriation in the Second Period*

Operating by backward induction, we start analyzing appropriation decisions in the second period. Taking first-period aggregate appropriation X as given, in the second period every firm i solves[2]

---

[2] The second-period cost function is evaluated at the first-period aggregate appropriation X, which coincides with x since only one firm (the incumbent) operates in that period. We

$$\max_{q_i \geq 0} \pi_i^{2nd} = q_i - \frac{q_i(q_i + q_j)}{S - (1 - r)x}. \tag{3.1}$$

Differentiating with respect to q_i yields

$$\underbrace{1}_{MR_i} - \underbrace{\frac{2q_i + q_j}{S - (1 - r)x}}_{MC_i} = 0. \tag{3.2}$$

Solving for q_i, we obtain firm i's best response function

$$q_i(q_j) = \frac{S - (1 - r)x}{2} - \frac{1}{2}q_j.$$

When the stock fully regenerates across periods, $r = 1$, this best response function collapses to $q_i(q_j) = \frac{S}{2} - \frac{1}{2}q_j$, thus becoming analogous to that in the static model of Chapter 2 and first-period aggregate appropriation X plays no role in firm i's second-period decisions. However, when $r < 1$, first-period aggregate appropriation X decreases the vertical intercept of the best response function, $\frac{S-(1-r)x}{2}$, graphically entailing a downward parallel shift of the best response function. Intuitively, the resource did not fully regenerate across periods, and then firms find a more depleted CPR at the beginning of the second period, making their appropriation more difficult. A similar argument applies when, for a given regeneration rate $r < 1$, first-period appropriation increases, as that decreases the stock available in the second period.

Firms are then symmetric in their production costs. In a symmetric equilibrium, they all extract the same second-period appropriation, $q_i^* = q_j^* = q^*$, which simplifies the above best response function to

$$q^* = \frac{S - (1 - r)x}{2} - \frac{1}{2}q^*.$$

Rearranging, we find $\frac{3}{2}q^* = \frac{S-(1-r)x}{2}$ and, solving for q^*, we obtain the second-period appropriation as a function of first-period appropriation

$$q^*(X) = \frac{S - (1 - r)x}{3}.$$

Second-period appropriation is, as expected, increasing in the initial stock, S, and in the regeneration rate, r, but decreasing in

present a model based on X to allow for more general settings in which more than one firm operates in the first period, as we discuss in exercise 3.7.

first-period aggregate appropriation, X. Overall, this comparative statics can be understood as second-period appropriation increasing in the "net stock" available at the beginning of the second period, $S - (1-r)X$.[3]

Therefore, inserting $q^*(x)$ into second-period profits, π_i^{2nd}, we find

$$\Pi_i^{2nd} = q^*(x) - \frac{q^*(x)(q^*(x) + q^*(x))}{S - (1-r)x}$$
$$= \frac{S - (1-r)X}{9}$$

that are also increasing in the net stock available at the beginning of the second period, $S - (1-r)x$. (We use Π_i^{2nd} to denote profit evaluated in second-period equilibrium appropriation $q^*(X)$, distinguishing it from π_i^{2nd} that is evaluated in any second-period appropriation.) This second-period equilibrium profit, Π_i^{2nd}, is an important element we will need in our analysis of first-period appropriation, since at that point of the game firms anticipate the profits they will obtain in the second period.

3.3.2 Equilibrium Appropriation in the First Period

In this period, the incumbent is the only firm operating, and chooses its appropriation x to maximize the sum of first- and second-period profits. Since $X = x$ in this context, we can express the incumbent's first-period problem as follows:

$$\max_{x \geq 0} \ \underbrace{\pi^{1st}}_{\pi^{1st}} + \delta \underbrace{\Pi_i^{2nd}}_{\Pi_i^{2nd}} = \underbrace{\left[x - \frac{x^2}{S} \right]}_{\pi^{1st}} + \delta \underbrace{\left[\frac{S - (1-r)x}{9} \right]}_{\Pi_i^{2nd}} \qquad (3.3)$$

where $\delta \in [0,1]$ denotes the firm's discount factor. When $\delta = 0$, second-period profits are irrelevant for the firm, while when $\delta = 1$

---

[3] As a confirmation, note that when $X = 0$ and/or $r = 1$, this expression collapses to $q^*(X) = \frac{S}{3}$, coinciding with the equilibrium appropriation in the static model of Chapter 2.

second-period profits receive the same weight as first-period profits.[4] In words, in problem (3.3) the incumbent chooses its first-period appropriation, x, seeking to maximize the sum of first-period profits and the discounted value of second-period profits.

Importantly, profits in both periods are affected by the firm's catches today, x: (1) first-period profits are a direct function of first-period appropriation and (2) second-period profits depend on the net stock available at the beginning of the second period, $S - (1 - r)x$, which decreases in first-period appropriation x.

Differentiating with respect to x, we find

$$1 - \frac{2x}{S} - \delta\frac{(1-r)}{9} = 0, \qquad \text{(FOC of (3.3))}$$

which, solving for x, yields a first-period equilibrium appropriation of

$$x^* = \frac{S\left[9 - \delta(1-r)\right]}{18}.$$

When the incumbent does not assign any value to future payoffs, $\delta = 0$, this first-period equilibrium appropriation collapses to $x^* = \frac{S}{2}$, as in the static model of Chapter 2. Intuitively, first- and second-period appropriation decisions become independent in this case. A similar argument applies if $r = 1$, where first-period equilibrium appropriation also simplifies to $x^* = \frac{S}{2}$. In this case, the available stock completely regenerates across periods, as if the stock hit a "reset button," letting the incumbent treat each period appropriation as independent decisions, since in both periods the initial stock, S, is fully available.

However, when the incumbent assigns a positive value to future payoffs, $\delta > 0$, and/or the stock does not fully regenerate across periods, $r < 1$, first-period equilibrium appropriation x^* is lower than $\frac{S}{2}$. In words, the incumbent anticipates that its first-period appropriation depletes part of the resource, which will not be fully regenerated, and the firm cares about its future profits. As a consequence, the

---

[4] The case where $\delta = 0$ can represent settings in which the firm does not operate in the second period, or it is planning to move its operations to a different CPR.

incumbent reduces its appropriation x^* to balance its profits across periods. When this firm assigns the same weight to both periods, $\delta = 1$, and the stock does not regenerate at all across periods, $r = 0$, first-period equilibrium appropriation becomes $x^* = \frac{8}{18}S \simeq 0.44S$.

Subgame Perfect Equilibrium (SPE): As a summary, we report below the SPE of this two-period appropriation game between the incumbent and the entrant:

- The incumbent chooses first-period appropriation $x^* = \frac{S[9-\delta(1-r)]}{18}$, and second-period appropriation $q^*(x) = \frac{S-(1-r)x}{3}$.
- The entrant responds to any first-period appropriation x from the incumbent choosing second-period appropriation $q^*(x) = \frac{S-(1-r)x}{3}$.

Note that we do not report second-period appropriation evaluated at the equilibrium first-period appropriation x^*, that is, we do not report $q^*(x^*) = \frac{S-(1-r)x^*}{3} = \frac{S[9+\delta+r[9-\delta(2-r)]]}{54}$. Instead, we report each firm's second-period appropriation as a function of *any* first-period appropriation x, $q^*(x)$, which lets firms respond to both equilibrium first-period appropriation x^* and to off-the-equilibrium appropriation levels $x \neq x^*$.[5]

3.4   SOCIALLY OPTIMAL APPROPRIATION

In this section, we evaluate the socially optimal appropriation. To do that in a dynamic setting, we operate by backward induction too, but only considering one player (the social planner) who first chooses second-period appropriation levels q_i and q_j, taking first-period appropriation as given, and then selects first-period appropriation x. For simplicity, we assume that the social planner seeks to maximize welfare function $W = PS$, that is, she only considers producer surplus. (The case in which she considers consumer and producer surplus, $W = CS + PS$, is left for the reader as Exercise 3.8.)

---

[5] This is a common property of SPE, since it provides equilibrium strategies for each player at any point of the game when this player is called on to move, both after observing equilibrium behaviors by players acting before her and after observing deviations from such equilibrium strategies. For more details, see Tadelis (Tadelis (2013), chapter 8).

Second Period: Taking first-period appropriation x as given, the social planner solves

$$\max_{q_i, q_j \geq 0} W^{2nd} = \pi_i^{2nd} + \pi_j^{2nd}$$

$$= \underbrace{\left[q_i - \frac{q_i(q_i + q_j)}{S - (1 - r)x} \right]}_{\pi_i^{2nd}} + \underbrace{\left[q_j - \frac{q_j(q_i + q_j)}{S - (1 - r)x} \right]}_{\pi_j^{2nd}}.$$

$$(3.4)$$

Differentiating with respect to q_i yields

$$1 - \frac{2q_i + q_j}{S - (1 - r)x} - \underbrace{\frac{q_j}{S - (1 - r)x}}_{\text{New term}} = 0 \qquad (3.5)$$

that coincides with the first-order condition in (3.2) except for the last term, capturing the cost externality that a greater second-period appropriation by firm i imposes on firm j.

A symmetric expression applies after differentiating the objective function in (3.4) with respect to q_j. Solving for q_i in (3.5), we obtain

$$q_i(q_j) = \frac{S - (1 - r)x}{2} - \frac{1}{2} q_j.$$

In a symmetric appropriation profile $q_i^{SO} = q_j^{SO} = q^{SO}$, which simplifies the above expression to

$$\frac{3}{2} q^{SO} = \frac{S - (1 - r)x}{2}.$$

Solving for q^{SO} yields the socially optimal second-period appropriation, as a function of first-period appropriation,

$$q^{SO}(X) = \frac{S - (1 - r)x}{4}$$

that is increasing in the net stock available at the beginning of the second period, $S - (1 - r)x$. In this context, second-period welfare becomes

$$W^{2nd}(q^{SO}, q^{SO})$$

$$= \left[q^{SO} - \frac{q^{SO}(q^{SO} + q^{SO})}{S - (1-r)x} \right] + \left[q^{SO} - \frac{q^{SO}(q^{SO} + q^{SO})}{S - (1-r)x} \right]$$

$$= \frac{S - (1-r)x}{4}.$$

First Period: The social planner anticipates the second-period welfare, and how it depends on first-period appropriation, solving

$$\max_{x \geq 0} \ \underbrace{\pi^{1st} + \delta W^{2nd}(q^{SO}, q^{SO})}_{} = \underbrace{\left[x - \frac{x^2}{S} \right]}_{\pi^{1st}} + \delta \underbrace{\left[\frac{S - (1-r)x}{4} \right]}_{W^{2nd}(q^{SO}, q^{SO})},$$

$$(3.6)$$

where, for simplicity, we assume that the social planner's discount factor δ coincides with that of the incumbent. (You are asked to consider a setting in which discount factors differ in exercise 3.9.) Differentiating with respect to x, we obtain

$$1 - \frac{2x}{S} - \delta \frac{(1-r)}{4} = 0$$

that we can rearrange to compare it against the first-order condition in expression (3.3), $1 - \frac{2x}{S} - \delta \frac{(1-r)}{9} = 0$, as follows:

$$1 - \frac{2x}{S} - \delta \frac{(1-r)}{9} - \underbrace{\delta \frac{5(1-r)}{36}}_{\text{New term}} = 0. \qquad \text{(FOC of (3.6))}$$

Comparing this result against that chosen by the incumbent firm in equilibrium – see first-order condition of equation (3.3) – we see that the result coincides, except for the last term. Intuitively, this term captures the negative effect that an increase in first-period appropriation has *on the entrant's* second-period profits. The incumbent considered the effect of first-period appropriation on its own second-period profits but overlooked the effect on the entrant's. The social planner, however, internalizes that dynamic external effect.

Solving for x, we find the first-period equilibrium appropriation

$$x^{SO} = \frac{S[4 - \delta(1-r)]}{8}$$

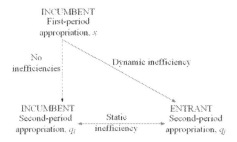

FIGURE 3.1 Static and dynamic inefficiencies.

that is lower than that in equilibrium, $x^* = \frac{S[9-\delta(1-r)]}{18}$, since the difference

$$x^* - x^{SO} = \frac{S\left[9 - \delta(1 - r)\right]}{18} - \frac{S\left[4 - \delta(1 - r)\right]}{8}$$

$$= \frac{5\left[S\delta(1 - r)\right]}{72}$$

is clearly positive.

3.5 STATIC AND DYNAMIC INEFFICIENCIES

We can now evaluate the inefficiencies that arise in this setting by comparing equilibrium behavior against the socially optimal appropriation. We separately identify each inefficiency below:

- *Static inefficiency (SI).* The social planner chooses a lower second-period appropriation to correct the static inefficiency (i.e., firms exploit the resource at socially excessive levels). In particular, this inefficiency can be measured by the difference

$$SI = q^*(x) - q^{SO}(x) = \frac{S - (1 - r)x}{3} - \frac{S - (1 - r)x}{4}$$

$$= \frac{S - (1 - r)x}{12}$$

for a given first-period appropriation X. The static inefficiency SI is, then, increasing in the net stock available at the beginning of the second period, $S - (1 - r)x$, entailing that SI expands as the initial stock and regeneration rate increase, but shrinks as first-period appropriation increases.[6]
Figure 3.1 illustrates the static inefficiency as occurring because two firms simultaneously choose their second-period appropriation without considering the cost externalities that their actions impose on their rivals.

---

[6] Note that when the resource fully regenerates, $r = 1$, the static inefficiency is still positive.

- *Dynamic inefficiency (DI)*. The social planner also selects a lower first-period appropriation to correct the dynamic inefficiency, namely, that the incumbent ignores how a more depleted resource impacts the entrant's profits. Specifically, this inefficiency is captured by the difference

$$DI = x^* - x^{SO} = \frac{S\left[9 - \delta(1 - r)\right]}{18} - \frac{S\left[4 - \delta(1 - r)\right]}{8}$$

$$= \frac{5\left[S\delta(1 - r)\right]}{57}.$$

When $\delta = 0$, the dynamic inefficiency DI collapses to zero. Intuitively, regulator and incumbent do not assign any value to future payoffs, making appropriation decisions in each period independent, thus eliminating the potential for dynamic inefficiencies. The static inefficiency, however, still arises in this context, since SI is not a function of discount factor δ. A similar argument applies if the resource fully regenerates across periods, $r = 1$, since in this setting appropriation decisions in each period become independent. Finally, for a given $\delta \neq 0$ and $r \neq 1$, the dynamic inefficiency becomes more severe as the initial stock S expands.

3.6   EQUILIBRIUM VS. SOCIALLY OPTIMAL NUMBER OF FIRMS

We now study the equilibrium number of firms that enter a CPR. We then find the socially optimal number of firms, that is, the number of firms that maximizes social welfare, and ultimately compare whether equilibrium entry is socially excessive.[7]

3.6.1   Equilibrium Entry

Consider a firm evaluating whether or not to operate in a CPR where $N - 1$ firms already operate. If it enters, the resource is exploited by N firms, yielding the same profits we identified in Chapter 2. That is, every firm i's equilibrium appropriation is $q^* = \frac{S}{N+1}$, entailing entry profits of

$$\pi_i^{Entry} = q^* - \frac{q^*(q^* + (N - 1)q^*)}{S}$$

$$= \frac{S}{(N + 1)^2}$$

---

[7] For a more detailed analysis of the optimal number of firms in the commons, see Cornes et al. (1986), Mason et al. (1988), and Mason and Polasky (1997).

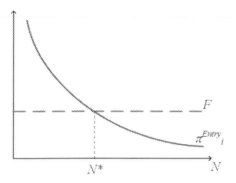

FIGURE 3.2 Equilibrium number of firms.

that is increasing in the available stock, S, but decreasing in the number of firms exploiting the resource, N.

We assume that the potential entrant must pay a fixed entry cost $F \geq 0$, which allows for the CPR to be open access ($F = 0$) or to require some fixed entry cost, such as licensing, capital, and technology investment. The potential entrant then joins the commons if and only if $\pi_i^{Entry} \geq F$, or

$$\frac{S}{(N+1)^2} \geq F.$$

Applying square roots on both sides, and rearranging, we obtain $\sqrt{S} \geq \sqrt{F}(N+1)$. Solving for N, we find the equilibrium number of firms

$$N^* = \left(\frac{S}{F}\right)^{1/2} - 1.$$

Note that N^* is positive as long as $S > F$, which intuitively means that the value of the stock is larger than the fixed entry cost; a reasonable assumption in most CPRs since F is relatively small. Figure 3.2 separately depicts the entry profit, $\pi_i^{Entry} = \frac{S}{(N+1)^2}$, which decreases in N, and the entry cost F, as well as their crossing point at the equilibrium number of firms N^*.

In addition, the equilibrium number of firms N^* is increasing in the available stock, as the CPR becomes more attractive and thus more firms enter, but decreasing in entry costs, as more firms are deterred from joining the commons. Graphically, an increase in S shifts the entry profit π_i^{Entry} upward, thus moving the crossing point rightward toward more firms entering the CPR, while an increase in F shifts the flat line in Figure 3.2 upward, implying that the crossing point moves leftward toward fewer firms joining the commons.

3.6.2   Socially Optimal Entry

We now identify the number of firms that maximize social welfare. Consider a welfare function

$$W = CS + PS - (N \times F),$$

where the last term denotes aggregate entry costs, and thus producer surplus PS does not include entry costs. Assuming a linear demand function $p(Q) = 1 - Q$, the social planner chooses the number of firms, N, that solves

$$\max_{N \geq 0} \; W = \underbrace{\int_0^{Q^*} (1-s)\, ds - N \times C(q_i^*, Q_{-i}^*)}_{CS+PS} - \underbrace{(N \times F)}_{\text{Entry costs}} \qquad (3.7)$$

$$= \int_0^{Q^*} (1-s)\, ds - N \frac{q^*(q^* + Nq^*)}{S} - (N \times F),$$

where $Q^* = Nq^*$ is the aggregate equilibrium appropriation, and $C(q_i^*, Q_{-i}^*) = \frac{q^*(q^* + (N-1)q^*)}{S}$ is the total cost for each firm. Therefore, the social planner's problem simplifies to

$$\max_{N \geq 0} \; W = \frac{N\left[2 - N(S-2)\right]S}{2(N+1)^2} - \frac{N^2 S}{(N+1)^2} - (N \times F).$$

Differentiating with respect to N, we find

$$\frac{S(1+N-NS)}{(N+1)^3} - \frac{2NS}{(N+1)^3} - F = 0.$$

Solving for N yields a highly nonlinear expression. However, evaluating the above first-order condition at $S = 10$, we obtain that the socially optimal number of firms is $N^{SO} = 0.8$ when $F = 1$ and decreases in F. For illustration purposes, Figure 3.3 depicts N^{SO} as a function of the entry cost, F, as well as the equilibrium number of

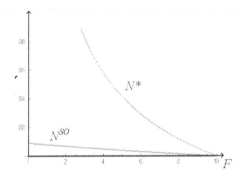

FIGURE 3.3 Equilibrium and socially optimal number of firms.

firms, N^*.[8] As a result, the equilibrium number of firms entering the CPR is socially excessive, $N^* > N^{SO}$, which occurs for all values of F.

Intuitively, when a firm enters into the CPR it only considers its own profit from doing so, π_i^{Entry}, but ignores the business-stealing effect that its entry implies for all existing firms, i.e., the individual appropriation of each firm $q^* = \frac{S}{N+1}$ decreases in N. The social planner, in contrast, considers both the additional profit that the firm brings to total welfare, but also the business-stealing effect, yielding a socially optimal number of firms, N^{SO}, that lies below the equilibrium number of firms if entry is unregulated, N^*.

3.6.3   No Entry Costs

In the special case in which entry costs are zero, $F = 0$, our above results imply that the equilibrium number of firms becomes $N^* = +\infty$. This finding could be also anticipated by observing Figure 3.2. If the horizontal line representing the fixed-entry cost F decreases until overlapping the horizontal axis, $F = 0$, the individual profit π_i^{Entry} does not cross F at any value of N, meaning that more firms keep entering the CPR since their net profits from doing so are still positive.

In contrast, the socially optimal number of firms is not necessarily infinite, even in a context with no entry costs. From problem

---

[8] The figure considers a stock $S = 10$, but similar results apply for other stock values. In addition, the entry cost in the horizontal axis considers only $F \leq 10$, since S must satisfy $S > F$ by definition.

(3.7) and its associated first-order condition evaluated at $F = 0$, we obtain that

$$\frac{S(1 + N - NS)}{(N + 1)^3} = \frac{2NS}{(N + 1)^3},$$

where the left side represents the increase in consumer surplus as more firms enter while the right side captures the decrease in producer surplus due to further entry (the business-stealing effect). This expression simplifies to

$$1 + N - NS = 2N,$$

and solving for N, yields a socially optimal number of firm $N^{SO} = \frac{1}{1+S}$. For instance, when $S = 10$, N^{SO} becomes $N^{SO} = \frac{1}{11} \simeq 0.09$ firms, as depicted in the vertical intercept of N^{SO} in Figure 3.3.

3.7   EXERCISES

3.1 Firms facing downward-sloping demand curve. Consider our analysis of equilibrium behavior in Section 3.3, where we assume that firms take the market price as given (and normalize it to $p = \$1$). Assume now that the incumbent faces a linear inverse demand curve $p(x) = 1 - bx$ in the first period, where x denotes the incumbent's first-period appropriation, and, similarly, firms face a linear inverse demand curve $p(Q) = 1 - bQ$ in the second period where Q represents second-period aggregate appropriation. In both periods, assume that parameter $b \geq 0$. (Note that when $b = 0$, the inverse demand collapses to $p = \$1$ in both periods, yielding the same results as in Section 3.3, whereas when $b > 0$ market price decreases as firms increase their appropriation.)

(a) *Second period.* Find every firm i's best response function, $q_i(q_j)$. How is $q_i(q_j)$ affected by an increase in parameter b? Interpret.

(b) Find every firm's second-period equilibrium appropriation $q_i^*(x)$, as a function of the incumbent's first-period appropriation x. How is $q_i^*(x)$ affected by an increase in parameter b? Interpret.

(c) *First period.* Find the incumbent's first-period equilibrium appropriation, x^*. For simplicity, assume no discounting, and parameter values $S = 2$ and $r = \frac{1}{2}$. Then, evaluate your results at $b = \frac{1}{2}$ and at $b = 1$. How is x^* affected by an increase in parameter b? Interpret.

3.2 Dynamic and static inefficiencies when firms face downward-sloping demand curve. Consider our analysis of equilibrium behavior in Exercise 3.1, and the socially optimal appropriation levels analyzed in Section 3.4. Identify the dynamic and static inefficiencies that emerge in this setting. How are your results affected by parameter b? Interpret.

3.3 Alternative second-period cost function. In this chapter, we considered a second-period cost function that produces tractable mathematical results about first- and second-period equilibrium appropriation. However, another well-known second-period cost function in the literature is

$$C_i(q_i, q_j) = \frac{q_i(q_i + q_j)}{S(1 + g) - x},$$

where $g \geq 0$ denotes the growth rate of the initial stock, S, and x represents the incumbent's first-period appropriation. Intuitively, when $g = 0$, the stock does not regenerate and the net stock available at the beginning of the second period is $S - x$, as captured by the denominator of the cost function. In contrast, when $g = \frac{x}{S}$, the stock is fully recovered, so the initial stock S is available again at the beginning of the second period. In this case, the second-period cost function is symmetric to that in the first period, simplifying to $\frac{q_i(q_i + q_j)}{S}$.

(a) *Second period.* Find every firm i's best response function, $q_i(q_j)$. How is $q_i(q_j)$ affected by an increase in the growth rate g? Interpret.

(b) Find every firm's second-period equilibrium appropriation $q_i^*(x)$, as a function of the incumbent's first-period appropriation x. How is $q_i^*(x)$ affected by an increase in the growth rate g? Interpret.

(c) *First period.* Find the incumbent's first-period equilibrium appropriation, x^*. How is x^* affected by an increase in the growth rate g? Interpret.

3.4 N firms competing in the second period. Consider our analysis of equilibrium behavior in Section 3.3, with only one incumbent in the first period and two firms in the second period. Let us expand our model to settings with $N \geq 2$ firms competing for the resource in the second period.

(a) *Second period.* Find every firm i's best response function, $q_i(q_j)$. How is $q_i(q_j)$ affected by an increase in the number of firms, N? Interpret.

(b) Find every firm's second-period equilibrium appropriation $q_i^*(x)$, as a function of the incumbent's first-period appropriation x. How is $q_i^*(x)$ affected by an increase in N? Interpret.

(c) *First period.* Find the incumbent's first-period equilibrium appropriation, x^*. How is x^* affected by an increase in N? Interpret.

3.5 **Finding socially optimal appropriation when N firms compete in the second period.** Consider the setting in Exercise 3.4.

(a) *Second period.* Find the socially optimal appropriation level in the second period, $q_i^{SO}(x)$. How is it affected by an increase in the number of firms, N?

(b) *First period.* Find the socially optimal appropriation level in the first period, x^{SO}. How is it affected by an increase in the number of firms, N?

(c) *Evaluating inefficiencies.* Use your results from Exercises 3.3 and 3.4 to find the static inefficiency, $SI = q^*(x) - q^{SO}(x)$, and the dynamic inefficiency, $DI = x^* - x^{SO}$. How are they affected by the number of firms operating in the second period, N? Show that both of these inefficiencies collapse to zero when $N = 1$.

3.6 **Only one firm exploiting the resource.** Consider your results in Exercises 3.3 and 3.4, but evaluate them at $N = 1$. That is, we consider a resource that is being exploited by a single firm in both periods.

(a) Find the firm's equilibrium appropriation level in the second period, and in the first period.

(b) Find the social optimum appropriation level assuming a welfare function $W = PS$. Show that no static or dynamic inefficiencies arise when a single firm exploits the resource. Why do you think all forms of inefficiencies cancel out?

(c) Find the social optimum appropriation level but now assuming a welfare function $W = PS + CS$. Show that there are now both static and dynamic inefficiencies. How do you reconcile these results with those from part (b) of the exercise?

3.7 **Two firms competing in both periods.** Consider our analysis of equilibrium behavior in Sections 3.3 and 3.4, with only one incumbent in the first period and two firms in the second period. Let us now assume that two incumbent firms, 1 and 2, operate in the first period and the *same two firms* keep operating in the second period.

(a) Repeat the equilibrium analysis of Section 3.3. How are first- and second-period equilibrium appropriation levels affected as a result of having one more firm operating in the first period?

(b) Repeat the socially optimal analysis of Section 3.4. How are first- and second-period socially optimal appropriation levels changed as a result of having one more firm operating in the first period?

(c) Use your results from parts (a) and (b) to find the static inefficiency, $SI = q^*(x) - q^{SO}(x)$, and the dynamic inefficiency, $DI = x^* - x^{SO}$, where x^* now denotes the first-period appropriation every firm i selects and x^{SO} represents the individual first-period appropriation selected by the social planner. How do each of these inefficiencies compare to those identified in Section 3.5? Are they larger or smaller? Interpret.

3.8 Welfare function that considers consumer surplus. Consider our analysis of socially optimal appropriation in Section 3.4, where we assumed that the social planner's welfare function was $W = PS$. Repeat the analysis assuming now that the social planner considers welfare function $W = CS + PS$. How are the results in that section affected?

3.9 Asymmetric discount factors. Consider our analysis of socially optimal appropriation in Section 3.4. Repeat the analysis assuming now that the incumbent firm's discount factor is δ_I while the regulator's is δ_R. How are the results in that section affected?

3.10 Socially excessive entry. Consider the setting in Section 3.6 about firms entering a CPR. Assume now that the social planner's welfare function is $W = PS$, that is, it only considers aggregate profits but ignores consumer surplus. For simplicity, let us assume specific values for the stock $S = 10$, and the fixed entry cost $F = 1$.

(a) Find the number of firms that enter the CPR in equilibrium, N^*. [*Hint*: Our analysis in Section 3.6.1 should still apply.]

(b) Find the socially optimal number of firms, N^{SO}. [*Hint*: Redo the analysis in Section 3.6.2 assuming that $W = PS$.]

(c) Show that equilibrium entry is socially excessive, that is, $N^{SO} < N^*$.

4 Entry Deterrence in the Commons

4.1 INTRODUCTION

In this chapter we relax one of our assumptions in Chapter 3, namely that the entrant joins the CPR in the second period. Importantly, we considered that the entrant exploits the CPR regardless of how depleted the resource becomes after the incumbent's first-period appropriation. However, in more realistic settings, the incumbent may strategically deplete the resource during the first period (choosing a relatively high x), deterring the potential entrant from joining the CPR. We examine the incumbent's strategic exploitation in this chapter.

Such an entry-deterring behavior is, however, costly for the incumbent, since entry deterrence may require the resource to be exploited more intensively than in the absence of entry threats. This intense exploitation decreases the incumbent's profits in the first period and leaves the CPR relatively depleted, thus also reducing its profits in the second period. As we show in this chapter, the incumbent may find it worthwhile to deter entry when the benefit from doing so (i.e., facing no competition during the second period) offsets its associated cost, but in other contexts the incumbent may find the entry-deterring costs too high, inducing the firm to accommodate entry.

Our analysis is based on Mason and Polasky (1994, 2002) and Espinola-Arredondo and Muñoz-Garcia (2013a). An example of entry-deterring behavior by an incumbent facing entry threats is that of the Hudson's Bay Company. As described in McLean (1849), this fur-trading company faced a threat from French traders considering entering the market, which responded by increasing its beaver harvests from 1736 to 1740, decreasing the estimated beaver population from 208,000 to 173,000. Other examples include the Navajo tribesmen increasing their cattle grazing communal meadows to deter other individuals from using this area, as reported in Johnson et al. (1980), or oil companies increasing their extraction rate to deter other companies from the same oil lease, as in Wiggins and Libecap (1985).

Technically, our setting is analogous to that in Gilbert and Vives (1986), which considers an oligopolistic market with N incumbent firms, each of them simultaneously and independently committing, in the first period of the game, to a given production level sold in the second period (once the potential entrant has decided whether or not to enter). In that setting, the potential entrant may be deterred if the incumbents' aggregate production (sold in the second period) is relatively large, as this leaves the potential entrant with a too small residual demand. In the model we examine next, the incumbent chooses a first-period appropriation that impacts the net stock available in the second period, thus reducing the incentives of the potential entrant to join the commons.

4.2 MODELING ENTRY DETERRENCE

Consider a CPR with the following time structure:

1. In the first stage, the incumbent chooses its appropriation level x.
2. After observing x, the potential entrant chooses whether to enter.
   (a) If entry does not occur, the incumbent selects its second-period appropriation q, while the entrant's profits from staying out are normalized to zero.
   (b) If entry ensues, the incumbent and entrant compete for the CPR, simultaneously and independently selecting their second-period appropriation q_1 and q_2.

We maintain similar assumptions as in Chapter 3, that is, firms take price as given, and normalized to $p = \$1$; the incumbent's first-period cost function is $C(x) = \frac{x^2}{S}$, where S denotes the initial stock; the incumbent's and entrant's second-period cost function is symmetric and given by

$$C(q_i, q_j, x) = \frac{q_i(q_i + q_j)}{S - (1 - r)x},$$

where $r \in [0, 1]$ represents the CPR's regeneration rate. (The intuition and comparative statics we discussed in Chapter 3 apply to these cost functions.)

Unlike in Chapter 3, however, we now consider that the potential entrant faces a fixed entry cost $F > 0$, which makes entry endogenous – a result of our model helping us predict under which parameter conditions the potential entrant chooses to enter – rather than exogenous to the model (i.e., an initial assumption of the model in Chapter 3).

Since this is a sequential-move game of complete information, we seek to find its Subgame Perfect Equilibrium (SPE). We find the SPE of this game by applying backward induction, so we start by analyzing firms' decisions in the second period, and then move on to study the first period.

4.2.1 Second-Period Appropriation – No Entry

If entry does not occur, the incumbent is the only firm exploiting the resource in the second period. In this setting, the incumbent chooses its second-period appropriation q that solves

$$\max_{q \geq 0} \pi^{2nd} = q - \frac{(q)^2}{S - (1 - r)x}.$$

When no entry occurs, $q_j = 0$, cost function $C(q_i, q_j, x) = \frac{q_i(q_i + q_j)}{S-(1-r)x}$ simplifies to $C(q_i, 0, x) = \frac{(q)^2}{S-(1-r)x}$. Differentiating with respect to q yields

$$1 - \frac{2q}{S - (1 - r)x} = 0.$$

Solving for q, we find the incumbent's second-period appropriation under no entry:[1]

$$q^{NE}(x) = \frac{S - (1 - r)x}{2},$$

---

[1] As usual, this appropriation is increasing in the net stock available at the beginning of the second period, $S - (1 - r)x$.

where superscript *NE* denotes "no entry." Therefore, the incumbent's second-period profit when entry does not occur, evaluated at $q^{NE}(x)$, is

$$\Pi_{NE}^{2nd} = q^{NE}(x) - \frac{\left(q^{NE}(x)\right)^2}{S-(1-r)x} = \frac{S-(1-r)x}{4}.$$

(profits under no entry)

4.2.2 Second-Period Appropriation – Entry

If entry ensues, the incumbent and entrant simultaneously and independently choose their second-period appropriation q_1 and q_2. That is, every firm $i = \{1,2\}$ chooses q_i to solve

$$\max_{q_i \geq 0} \pi_i^{2nd} = q_i - \frac{q_i\left(q_i+q_j\right)}{S-(1-r)x}.$$

(This setting is analogous to that in Section 3.3.1, but we reproduce it here for extra practice.) Differentiating with respect to q_i yields

$$1 - \frac{2q_i+q_j}{S-(1-r)x} = 0.$$

Solving for q_i, we obtain firm i's best response function

$$q_i(q_j) = \frac{S-(1-r)x}{2} - \frac{1}{2}q_j.$$

Firms' best response functions are then symmetric. In a symmetric equilibrium, all firms choose the same second-period appropriation, $q_i^* = q_j^* = q^*$, which reduces the best response function to

$$q^* = \frac{S-(1-r)x}{2} - \frac{1}{2}q^*.$$

Rearranging, we find $\frac{3}{2}q^* = \frac{S-(1-r)x}{2}$ and, solving for q^*, we obtain the second-period appropriation under entry

$$q^E(x) = \frac{S-(1-r)x}{3},$$

where superscript *E* denotes "entry." This appropriation is lower than the second-period appropriation that the incumbent chooses under no entry, that is, $q^E(x) < q^{NE}(x)$. However, aggregate second-period appropriation is larger with than without entry, that is,

$$Q^E(x) = 2q^E(x) = 2\frac{S - (1 - r)x}{3}$$

$$> \frac{S - (1 - r)x}{2} = q^{NE}(x) = Q^{NE}(x),$$

where we use $N = 2$ since there are only two firms in the industry if entry occurs (the incumbent and entrant).

We can now insert $q^E(X)$ into second-period profits, π_i^{2nd}, to find every firm i's second-period profits under entry

$$\Pi_E^{2nd} = q^E(x) - \frac{q^E(x)\left[q^E(x) + q^E(x)\right]}{S - (1 - r)x} = \frac{S - (1 - r)x}{9}.$$

(profits under entry)

As expected, the incumbent's second-period profit is higher under no entry, $\Pi_{NE}^{2nd} = \frac{S - (1 - r)x}{4}$, than under entry, $\Pi_E^{2nd} = \frac{S - (1 - r)x}{9}$, a condition that holds regardless of the net stock at the beginning of the second period, $S - (1 - r)x$.

4.2.3   Second-Period Appropriation – Enter or Not?

Expression $\Pi_E^{2nd} = \frac{S - (1 - r)x}{9}$ captures the profits of every firm, incumbent and entrant. It can then be used to understand the entrant's entry decision in the second stage. In particular, the entrant compares its profit from entering, $\Pi_E^{2nd} - F$, against its profit from staying out, zero; choosing to enter if and only if $\Pi_E^{2nd} - F \geq 0$, or more explicitly, if

$$\frac{S - (1 - r)x}{9} \geq F.$$

Solving for x, we find

$$x \leq \frac{S - 9F}{1 - r} = x_{ED} \qquad (x_{ED})$$

where the *ED* subscript denotes "entry deterrence." Figure 4.1 separately plots the entrant's profit from joining the CPR, Π_E^{2nd}, against its fixed entry cost, F. For all values of first-period appropriation to the right-hand side of the entry-deterring appropriation x_{ED}, the resource

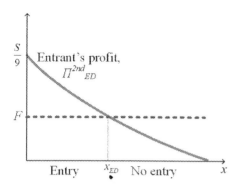

FIGURE 4.1 Entrant's decision: To enter or not to enter?

becomes so depleted that the potential entrant chooses to stay out. In this case, the incumbent's first-period appropriation successfully deters entry. In contrast, for values of x to the left-hand side of x_{ED}, the CPR is still sufficiently attractive for the entrant to join.

The minimal first-period appropriation that deters entry, x_{ED}, is decreasing in F. This can be graphically seen in Figure 4.1, since a higher entry cost F shifts the horizontal line upward, moving the crossing point x_{ED} leftward. Intuitively, as entry becomes more costly, the incumbent needs to exploit the resource *less intensively* during the first period if it seeks to deter entry. The opposite argument applies when the initial stock, S, increases, and/or when the resource regeneration rate, r, increases. In both cases, the CPR becomes more attractive for the entrant, requiring the incumbent to increase its first-period appropriation if it seeks to deter entry. As a result, the minimal first-period appropriation that deters entry, x_{ED}, increases.

For simplicity, we assume that entry costs are not extreme, $F < \frac{S}{9}$, which guarantees that the expression of x_{ED} is positive. This assumption can be rationalized by looking at the entrant's profit again, $\Pi_E^{2nd} = \frac{S-(1-r)x}{9}$, and evaluating it at the point where the incumbent does not appropriate any catches during the first period, $x = 0$, which yields $\frac{S}{9}$. From this perspective, condition $F < \frac{S}{9}$ says that the entrant has incentives to enter the CPR when the incumbent did not exploit the resource at all! Graphically, this condition can be understood as saying that the horizontal line depicting the entry cost F always originates below the vertical intercept of the entrant's profit function Π_E^{2nd}, which starts at $\frac{S}{9}$.

4.2.4 First-Period Appropriation – Entry Deterrence

The incumbent chooses the first-period appropriation x that maximizes the sum of its first- and second-period profits, separately considering the case in which its current appropriation deters entry (the values of x satisfying $x \geq x_{ED}$) and when it does not ($x < x_{ED}$).

Allowing Entry: When the incumbent chooses a first-period appropriation to the left-hand side of x_{ED} in Figure 4.1, it allows entry, thus making profit Π_E^{2nd} in the second period. The incumbent then solves

$$\max_{x < x_{ED}} \pi^{1st} + \delta\Pi_E^{2nd} = \underbrace{\left[x - \frac{x^2}{S}\right]}_{\pi^{1st}} + \delta\underbrace{\left[\frac{S - (1-r)x}{9}\right]}_{\Pi_E^{2nd}}.$$

This problem exactly coincides with Problem (3.3) in Chapter 3. From our analysis in that chapter, first-period appropriation is

$$x_E = \frac{S\left[9 - \delta(1-r)\right]}{18},$$

where subscript E indicates that this is the profit-maximizing first-period appropriation under "entry." Inserting x_E into the incumbent's objective function, we are able to find the overall profit that this firm earns from allowing entry, AE, as follows:

$$\Pi^{AE} = \left[x_E - \frac{x_E^2}{S}\right] + \delta\left[\frac{S - (1-r)x_E}{9}\right]$$

$$= \frac{S\left[81 + 18\delta(1+r) + \delta^2(1-r)^2\right]}{324}.$$

Entry Deterrence: When the incumbent chooses a first-period appropriation to the right-hand side of x_{ED} in Figure 4.1, it deters entry, thus making profit Π_{NE}^{2nd} in the second period. The incumbent then solves the following problem:

$$\max_{x \geq x_{ED}} \ \pi^{1st} + \delta\Pi_{NE}^{2nd} = \underbrace{\left[x - \frac{x^2}{S}\right]}_{\pi^{1st}} + \delta\underbrace{\left[\frac{S - (1-r)x}{4}\right]}_{\Pi_{NE}^{2nd}}.$$

A natural question at this point is whether the incumbent needs to exploit the resource beyond the minimal first-period appropriation that deters entry, x_{ED}, or just at x_{ED}. Differentiating with respect to x, we find that the discounted sum of profits monotonically decrease as x increases, since the first-order condition

$$1 - \frac{2x}{S} - \delta\frac{(1-r)}{4}$$

is unambiguously negative for all values of x, and for any parameter values S, δ, and r. Intuitively, the incumbent's profits decrease in x, which implies that when this firm seeks to deter entry, it chooses the minimal first-period appropriation that achieves this objective, x_{ED}.

Inserting $x = x_{ED}$ in the above objective function, we find that the overall profits from practicing entry deterrence, ED, are

$$\Pi^{ED} = \left[x_{ED} - \frac{x_{ED}^2}{S}\right] + \delta\left[\frac{S - (1-r)x_{ED}}{9}\right]$$

$$= \frac{9F\delta}{4} + \frac{(S - 9F)(9F - rS)}{S(1-r)^2}.$$

When Does the Incumbent Practice Entry Deterrence? After finding overall profits for the incumbent when it allows entry, Π^{AE}, and when it practices entry deterrence, Π^{ED}, we just need to compare them. The incumbent deters entry if $\Pi^{ED} \geq \Pi^{AE}$. For illustration purposes, we consider specific parameter values $\delta = 1$, $r = 1/4$, and $F = 1/100$, which simplifies $\Pi^{ED} \geq \Pi^{AE}$ to

$$\Pi^{ED} = \frac{89}{400} - \frac{9}{625S} - \frac{4}{9}S \geq \frac{185}{576}S = \Pi^{AE}.$$

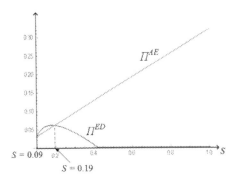

FIGURE 4.2 Entry deterrence/allowance regions.

Figure 4.2 separately depicts profit Π^{AE}, in the straight line starting at the origin, and profit Π^{ED}, which is concave in the initial stock. The figure considers that the initial stock S satisfies condition $F < \frac{S}{9}$, which can be rearranged as $S > 9F$. Since the figure also takes into account $F = 1/100$, this condition becomes $S > 9\frac{1}{100} \simeq 0.09$ in this context. This explains why the horizontal axis starts at $S = 0.09$ rather than at zero. Solving for S in profit condition $\Pi^{ED} \geq \Pi^{AE}$, we find $S \leq 0.19$, as depicted in Figure 4.2 by the crossing point between Π^{ED} and Π^{AE}.[2]

When $S \leq 0.19$, entry-deterring profit Π^{ED} lies above that of allowing entry, Π^{AE}, implying that the incumbent deters entry. Because the resource is relatively scarce, the incumbent can easily exploit the resource to make entry unattractive for the potential competitor. In contrast, when the stock is relatively abundant, $S > 0.19$, it is unprofitable for the incumbent to deplete the CPR enough to prevent entry, leading the incumbent to allow entry.

4.3   A GREATER DYNAMIC INEFFICIENCY

The strategic exploitation of the resource that the incumbent carries out to deter entry leads to a larger dynamic inefficiency than that we identified in Chapter 3. Specifically, when the incumbent finds

---

2   Solving the inequality $\Pi^{ED} \geq \Pi^{AE}$ for S, we find two roots, $S_1 = 0.097$ and $S_2 = 0.193$, so entry deterrence holds for every value of S satisfying $0.097 \leq S < 0.193$. However, only the second root, $S_2 = 0.193$, lies in the admissible range of the initial stock S described in the text (i.e., $S > 9F = 0.09$).

it optimal to practice entry deterrence, $\Pi^{ED} \geq \Pi^{AE}$, it chooses a first-period appropriation $x_{ED} = \frac{S-9F}{1-r}$, and the dynamic inefficiency becomes

$$DI = x_{ED} - x^{SO} = \frac{S - 9F}{1 - r} - \frac{S\left[9 - 2\delta(1 - r)\right]}{18}.$$

Comparing this inefficiency against that in Chapter 3, $DI = x^* - x^{SO}$, we see that the dynamic inefficiency is greater when the incumbent faces entry threats since $x_{ED} > x^*$, i.e., this firm needs to increase its first-period appropriation if it seeks to deter entry, whereas the socially optimal first-period appropriation x^{SO} is the same in both contexts. Formally, $x_{ED} - x^{SO} > x^* - x^{SO}$ since $x_{ED} > x^*$.

This inefficiency increase can, then, be attributed to the incumbent's strategic increase of its first-period appropriation to prevent entry, since in the setting we study in this chapter entry is endogenous while in Chapter 3 entry was exogenous, i.e., assumed to happen with certainty in the second period.

When the incumbent does not have incentives to practice entry deterrence, $\Pi^{ED} < \Pi^{AE}$, it chooses the same first-period appropriation as when entry happens with certainty, $x^* = \frac{S[9-\delta(1-r)]}{18}$, coinciding with our results in Chapter 3. Therefore, dynamic inefficiency DI coincides both when entry is endogenous and exogenous.

4.4   EXERCISES

4.1 Firms facing a downward-sloping demand curve. Consider the setting in this chapter, where we assumed that firms took the market price as given. Consider now that firms face a downward-sloping demand function $p(x) = 1 - bx$ in the first period, and $p(Q) = 1 - bQ$ in the second period, where parameter $b \geq 0$. In the case that $b = 0$, the price collapses to $p = \$1$ in both periods, yielding the same results as in this chapter, but otherwise firms should face fewer incentives to appropriate.

Repeat the analysis of Section 4.2. For simplicity, examine first-period appropriation assuming no discounting, and parameter values $S = 10$, $r = b = \frac{1}{2}$, and $F = \frac{1}{100}$.

4.2 Using a different second-period cost function. Chapters 3 and 4 consider a second-period cost function that produces tractable mathematical

results about first- and second-period equilibrium appropriation.
A different second-period cost function often used in the literature is

$$C_i(q_i, q_j) = \frac{q_i(q_i + q_j)}{S(1 + g) - x},$$

where $g \geq 0$ denotes the growth rate of the initial stock, S, and x
represents the incumbent's first-period appropriation. Intuitively, when
$g = 0$, the stock does not regenerate and the net stock available at the
beginning of the second period is $S - x$, as captured by the denominator
of the cost function. In contrast, when $g = \frac{x}{S}$, the stock is fully
recovered, so the initial stock S is available again at the beginning of the
second period. In this case, the second-period cost function is
symmetric to that in the first period, simplifying to $\frac{q_i(q_i + q_j)}{S}$.

Repeat the analysis of Section 4.2, evaluating under which values
of S the incumbent practices entry deterrence.

4.3 Using a different welfare function to measure inefficiencies. Assume
that the social planner considers a welfare function $W = CS + PS$. Our
analysis of Section 4.2 should be unaffected, since they only examine
firms' equilibrium behavior. However, our measurement of the dynamic
inefficiency in Section 4.3 is affected given that x^{SO} is now different.

Is the dynamic inefficiency $DI = x_{ED} - x^{SO}$ greater than when
the social planner considers welfare function $W = PS$? Interpret. For
simplicity, your analysis of first-period appropriation can assume no
discounting and parameter values $S = 10$, $r = \frac{1}{10}$, and $F = \frac{1}{100}$.

4.4 Asymmetric firms. Consider our analysis of Section 4.2. Assume now
that firms face a different cost function

$$C_1(q_1, q_2) = \frac{\alpha q_1(q_1 + q_2)}{S - (1 - r)x} \quad \text{and} \quad C_2(q_2, q_1) = \frac{q_2(q_1 + q_2)}{S - (1 - r)x}$$

where $\alpha \in [1/2, 1]$ denotes the incumbent's cost advantage. When $\alpha = 1$,
both firms face the same cost function, as in Section 4.2. However,
when $\alpha < 1$, the incumbent benefits from a lower cost than the
potential entrant.

(a) Repeat our analysis of Section 4.2, evaluating under which values of
S the incumbent practices entry deterrence. How are your findings
affected by parameter α? For illustration purposes, you may consider
no discounting and parameter values $r = \frac{1}{4}$ and $F = \frac{1}{100}$, at the end of
the calculations, as we did in the chapter. Then evaluate your

results at $\alpha = \frac{3}{4}$ and compare them against the case of $\alpha = 1$ analyzed in the chapter (firms are symmetric in their cost function).

(b) Find socially optimal appropriation in this setting (following the same steps as in Section 4.3), and evaluate the dynamic inefficiency $DI = x_{ED} - x^{SO}$. Compare your results with those in the chapter. How are your findings affected by parameter α?

4.5 **Two incumbent firms seeking to deter entry.** Consider again our analysis in Section 4.2, but assume now that two (rather than one) incumbent firms exploit the CPR during the first stage. Both incumbents are symmetric. Find for which values of S the incumbent practices entry deterrence, and compare your results with those in Section 4.2. [*Hint:* See Espinola-Arredondo and Muñoz-Garcia (2013a), which characterizes equilibrium behavior in the commons with N incumbents facing potential entry. Lemma 1 and Proposition 1 should be particularly helpful.]

5 Repeated Interaction in the Commons

5.1 INTRODUCTION

Previous chapters discussed games where firms (e.g., fishing companies or farmers sharing an aquifer) interact only once. These games are also known as "one-shot games" or "unrepeated games," and can help us model strategic settings in which players do not anticipate interacting again in future periods. In many settings, however, the same group of firms interact several times, facing the same game repeatedly. An interesting feature of repeated games is that they can help us rationalize players' cooperation, even when such cooperation could not be sustained in the unrepeated version of the game.

Section 5.2 presents a simple model of a CPR game, highlighting its similarities with the canonical prisoner's dilemma game. This tractable model helps us in our presentation of repeated interaction in finitely repeated games (Section 5.3) or infinitely repeated games (Section 5.4). Cooperative outcomes, understood as firms exploiting the resource below what they would do in an unrepeated game, cannot be sustained in the equilibrium of the finitely repeated game. Intuitively, firms anticipate that they will be appropriating as much as possible in the last period of interaction, and that such behavior will not be affected by previous history of play. In the previous-to-last period, they anticipate such exploitation in the subsequent period, which leads all firms to exploit the CPR at maximal levels on the previous-to-last period too. A similar argument extends to all previous periods until the first, implying that firms choose a high appropriation level during all periods; a big failure in our quest to use repeated games as a tool to promote cooperation in the commons!

Fortunately, Section 5.4 considers infinitely repeated games, showing that, in this case, firms may have incentives to cooperate by selecting lower appropriation levels if they assign a sufficiently large weight to their future profits.

5.2   MODELING REPEATED INTERACTION

Consider the CPR game in Matrix 5.1, where both firms simultaneously and independently choose between a high and a low appropriation level. Firm 1 selects a row, while firm 2 chooses a column. The first payoff in every cell corresponds to firm 1 and the second payoff to firm 2. When both firms choose Low appropriation, at the bottom right-hand corner of the matrix, both earn a payoff of a. If, instead, either firm unilaterally chooses a High appropriation, its payoff increases from a to b (where $b > a$), while that of its rival decreases to c (where $a > c$). Finally, if both firms choose a High appropriation (in the top left-hand corner of the matrix), they both earn a payoff of d, where $a > d > c$. In summary, payoffs satisfy $b > a > d > c$. For instance, $b = \$7$, $a = \$5$, $d = \$1$, and $c = \$0$ satisfy this payoff ranking.

Firm 2

		High approp.	Low approp.
Firm 1	High approp.	d, d	b, c
	Low approp.	c, b	a, a

Matrix 5.1 *CPR game as a prisoner's dilemma*

Finding Strictly Dominated Strategies: The game is strategically analogous to the common "prisoner's dilemma" game since both firms find High appropriation to be a strictly dominant strategy, making Low appropriation a strictly dominated strategy. To see this point, note that when firm 2 chooses High appropriation (in the left column), firm 1's payoff from also selecting High appropriation ($\$d$) is higher than when it chooses Low appropriation ($\$c$) since $d > c$ by definition. Similarly, when firm 2 selects Low appropriation (in the

right column), firm 1's payoff from choosing High appropriation (b)
is higher than when it chooses Low appropriation (a), where $b > a$
by assumption. In short, firm 1 finds it optimal to choose High
appropriation *regardless* of the strategy that firm 2 selects; what
we needed to show for High appropriation to be strictly dominant.
Since players are symmetric, a similar argument applies to firm 2,
which finds High appropriation to be strictly dominant as well. Since
rational players would never choose strictly dominated strategies
(Low appropriation for each firm), we can delete them from Matrix 5.1,
leaving us with a one-cell matrix containing only the High appropriation row and column. Therefore, the strategy profile (High, High)
survives strict dominance yielding a payoff pair (d, d).[1]

Finding Nash Equilibria: We can alternatively solve the game in
Matrix 5.1 by finding the best responses of both players, and then
identifying which strategy profile (i.e., which cell in the matrix)
implies that both players choose a best response to their opponent's
strategy. That is, we seek to find a mutual best response, as required
by the definition of the Nash Equilibrium (NE). Starting with the
best responses of firm 1, we find that, when firm 2 chooses High
appropriation (in the left column), firm 1 is better off responding with
High rather than Low appropriation since $d > c$. (We underline this
best response payoff, d, in the left column of Matrix 5.2.) A similar
argument applies when firm 2 chooses Low appropriation (in the right
column), where firm 1 is better off responding with High rather than
Low appropriation since $b > a$. We also underline this best response
payoff, b, in the right column of Matrix 5.2. Again, since players are
symmetric, a similar argument applies to firm 2.[2]

---

[1] For details on the application of strict dominance to more sophisticated games, see Tadelis (2013, chapter 4), and Muñoz-Garcia and Toro-Gonzalez (2019, chapter 1).

[2] As a practice, we include this analysis here. When firm 1 chooses High appropriation (in the top row), firm 2 responds with High appropriation since $d > c$, which we remark by underlining the d payoff in the top row corresponding to firm 2. When firm 1 chooses Low appropriation (in the bottom row), firm 2 responds with High appropriation since $b > a$, underlining the best response payoff of b in the bottom row.

Firm 2

		High approp.	Low approp.
Firm 1	High approp.	$\underline{d}, \underline{d}$	$\underline{b}, c$
	Low approp.	$c, \underline{b}$	a, a

Matrix 5.2 *CPR game – underlining best responses*

Once we underline both players' best response payoffs, we can see that there is only one cell where all payoffs are underlined (High, High), indicating that in this cell both firms play a best response to their opponent's strategies. In short, this strategy profile is an NE of the CPR game. This comes as no surprise, since this was the unique equilibrium prediction according to strict dominance, and when this occurs the NE of the game and the equilibrium that survives strict dominance must coincide.

Static Inefficiency: While stylized, Matrix 5.2 helps us illustrate the static inefficiency that arises in the NE of the CPR game. In particular, both firms choose High appropriation, each earning \$$d$ at the top left-hand corner of the matrix. However, they could both earn \$$a$ if they coordinated their appropriation decisions by both choosing Low appropriation at the bottom right-hand corner of the matrix. Interpreting "Low appropriation" as the socially optimal appropriation level (at least when the welfare function only considers producer surplus, $W = PS$) and "High appropriation" as the equilibrium that emerges in the game, we can understand their difference as the static inefficiency that arises when firms simultaneously and independently choose their appropriation decisions, with an individual profit loss of $a - d$ for each firm.

While our discussion has shown that the cooperative outcome (Low, Low) cannot be sustained in the equilibrium of the unrepeated game, the following sections explore under which conditions it can be sustained when the game is repeated, that is, when firms interact many times, playing the game of Matrix 5.1 in each round. For simplicity, our presentation abstracts from the dynamic inefficiencies that emerge in the CPR game by assuming that the resource fully regenerates across periods. A richer analysis should, however, consider that the resource does not fully regenerate, implying that both firms' appropriation decisions in period t are affected by the net stock available at the beginning of this period, which, in turn, depends on the stream of appropriation decisions by both players in all previous periods involving dynamic optimization techniques. For an excellent presentation of CPR in repeated environments, see Dockner et al. (2000, chapter 6).

5.3   FINITE REPETITIONS

Let us first consider that the game is repeated T periods, where T is a finite number (e.g., two times, or five hundred times, but not an infinite number of times). The time structure in this setting is the following:

1. *Period t.* Both firms choose their appropriation decision in period $t = \{1, 2, \ldots, T\}$, yielding an outcome (i.e., a cell in Matrix 5.1) for period t, which is perfectly observed by both firms.
2. *Period t + 1.* Observing the outcome of period t, both firms choose their appropriation decision in period $t + 1$, which yields an outcome for period $t + 1$.
3. ...
4. *Period T.* After observing the outcome of period $T - 1$, both firms choose their appropriation and the game ends.

This is, of course, a sequential-move game, since both firms, when considering their appropriation at period $t + 1$, perfectly observe the past history of appropriation decisions by both firms from period 1 until t. Given this history, both firms respond with their appropriation in period $t + 1$. To solve this sequential-move game of complete information, we only need to deploy the Subgame Perfect Equilibrium (SPE) solution concept we encountered in previous chapters (see Chapters 3 and 4) by applying backward induction. We therefore start by analyzing equilibrium appropriation decisions in the last period, T, for any previous history of appropriation decisions, as follows:

- *Period T.* Starting from the last round of play at $t = T$, we see that both firms' strictly dominant strategy is High appropriation, thus providing us with (High, High) as the NE of the last-period game.
- *Period T − 1.* In the previous-to-last period, $t = T − 1$, both firms anticipate that (High, High) will ensue in the subsequent stage, where both will be choosing High appropriation regardless of the outcome in period $T − 1$. As a consequence, each firm finds that High appropriation is a strictly dominant strategy. Therefore, strategy profile (High, High) is, again, the NE of the game in period $T − 1$.
- *Period T − 2.* A similar argument applies if we move one step up, to period $T − 2$, where both firms anticipate that (High, High) will be the equilibrium outcome in both subsequent periods, at $T − 1$ and T, thus choosing High appropriation at the current period $T − 2$, which yields (High, High) as the NE outcome in this period too.

Continuing with this argument, we find that (High, High) is the NE at *every* period t, from the beginning of the game at $t = 1$ to the last stage $t = T$. Therefore, the SPE of the game has both firms choosing High appropriation at every round of the game, regardless of the outcomes in previous rounds. Intuitively, the existence of a terminal period makes both firms anticipate that both will select High appropriation in that period, and since the last-stage outcome is unaffected by previous moves, firms in prior periods find no benefit from cooperating by choosing Low appropriation. As expected, this behavior can lead to the depletion of some natural resources.

In the next section, we explore whether such an unfortunate result can be avoided by allowing the game to be repeated an infinite number of times.

5.4   INFINITE REPETITIONS

Consider now an infinitely repeated version of the CPR game in Matrix 5.1. How can we operationalize an infinitely repeated game in reality, tying fishermen to their boats? Of course we can't; we just assume that, at any given moment, firms play one more round of the game with some probability p. To understand the effect of this probability, note that even if p is close to 1, the probability that players interact for a large number of rounds drops very rapidly. For instance, if $p = 0.9$, the probability that players interact for 10 rounds is $0.9^{10} \cong 0.34$, and the probability they continue playing for 100 rounds is extremely small, $0.9^{100} \cong 0.00002$. Nonetheless, this interaction is possible, so players could play for infinite rounds. As we know from previous sections, when the game is played once or a finite number of times the only equilibrium prediction is (High, High) in every single round of play. How can we sustain cooperation if the game is played an infinite number of times? By the use of a "Grim-Trigger Strategy" (GTS), such as the following:

Grim-Trigger Strategy (GTS):

1. In the first period $t = 1$, both firms cooperate (playing "Low appropriation" in the CPR game of Matrix 5.2).
2. In all subsequent periods $t > 1$,
   (a) Both firms continue to cooperate as long as they observe that both firms cooperated in all past periods.
   (b) If, instead, the firms observe some past cheating at any previous period (deviating from the GTS), they respond by playing "High appropriation" thereafter.

To show that the GTS can be sustained as an SPE of the infinitely repeated game, we need to show that both firms find the GTS optimal at every time period t. In addition, GTS must be optimal after any previous history of play, that is: (a) after no history of cheating; and (b) after some cheating episode. Let us separately analyze Cases (a) and (b) below.

Case (a): No cheating history. If no previous cheating occurs, the GTS dictates that both players cooperate in the next period, earning a payoff of a, yielding a stream of discounted payoffs

$$a + \delta(a) + \delta^2(a) + \cdots$$

where $\delta \in (0,1)$ represents their discount factor.[3] Factoring the a payoff out yields

---

[3] Intuitively, δ indicates how much the firm cares about future payoffs. When $\delta \to 1$, the firm assigns the same weight to future as to present payoffs, whereas when $\delta \to 0$ it assigns no importance to future payoffs. Alternatively, a high (low) discount factor δ can be interpreted as the firm's patience (impatience).

$$a + \delta(a) + \delta^2(a) + \cdots = a(1 + \delta + \delta^2 + \cdots),$$

which ultimately reduces to $a\frac{1}{1-\delta}$ since the term in parenthesis, $1 + \delta + \delta^2 + \cdots$, is an infinite geometric progression that can be simplified to $\frac{1}{1-\delta}$.[4] If, instead, a player cheats in the current period (playing High appropriation while its opponent chooses Low appropriation), its payoff increases from a to b, where $b > a$ by assumption.[5] However, its defection is detected by the other firm, which responds with High appropriation thereafter (recall that this is the punishment prescribed in Step 2b of the GTS), yielding a payoff of d thereafter, where $d < a$. As a result, its stream of discounted payoffs from cheating becomes

$$\underbrace{b}_{\text{Firm cheats}} + \underbrace{\delta(d) + \delta^2(d) + \cdots}_{\text{Punishment thereafter}},$$

which simplifies to

$$b + d(\delta + \delta^2 + \delta^3 + \cdots) = b + d\delta(1 + \delta + \delta^2 + \cdots)$$

$$= b + d\frac{\delta}{1-\delta}.$$

Therefore, after a history of cooperation, both firms keep cooperating, obtaining $d\frac{1}{1-\delta}$, rather than defecting, receiving $b + d\frac{\delta}{1-\delta}$, if

$$a\frac{1}{1-\delta} \geq b + d\frac{\delta}{1-\delta}.$$

Multiplying both sides by the denominator, $(1 - \delta)$, yields $a \geq b(1 - \delta) + d\delta$. Solving for δ, we obtain

$$\delta \geq \frac{b-a}{b-d}.$$

We interpret this result below. Now we consider incentives to cheat in Case (b).

---

[4] Recall that the infinite sum $1 + \delta + \delta^2 + \cdots$ can be expressed as $\delta^0 + \delta^1 + \delta^2 + \cdots$, or more compactly as $\sum_{t=0}^{\infty} \delta^t$. This is an infinite geometric series that can be written as $\frac{1}{1-\delta}$.

[5] Note that, in order to check if the GTS is optimal for both firms, we must maintain the other player selecting the GTS while the firm we consider is the only player deviating. That is, we test for "unilateral deviations." In this context, this means that the other firm keeps cooperating (choosing Low, as prescribed by the GTS) while the firm we consider deviates to High.

Case (b): Some cheating history. If one (or both) firms cheated in a previous period, the GTS prescribes that both firms should choose High appropriation thereafter, yielding a stream of discounted payoffs

$$d + \delta(d) + \delta^2(d) + \cdots = d(1 + \delta + \delta^2 + \cdots)$$
$$= d\frac{1}{1-\delta}.$$

If, instead, a firm unilaterally deviates from this punishment scheme (playing Low while its opponent chooses High), its stream of discounted payoffs becomes

$$\underbrace{c}_{\text{Firm deviates}} + \underbrace{\delta(d) + \delta^2(d) + \cdots}_{\text{Punishment thereafter}}.$$

Intuitively, this firm's payoff decreases from d to c during one period (since $c < d$ by assumption), when choosing Low while its opponent selects High. The choice of High by one firm triggers an infinite punishment by both firms, as prescribed by the GTS, yielding a payoff of d thereafter. This stream of payoffs reduces to

$$c + d(\delta + \delta^2 + \delta^3 + \cdots) = c + d\delta(1 + \delta + \delta^2 + \cdots)$$
$$= c + d\frac{\delta}{1-\delta}.$$

As a result, upon observing a defection to High appropriation, both firms prefer to stick to the GTS rather than deviating if

$$a\frac{1}{1-\delta} \geq c + d\frac{\delta}{1-\delta},$$

which simplifies to $(a - c)(1 - \delta) \geq (d - a)\delta$. Since $a > c$ and $d < a$ by definition, the left-hand (right-hand) side of this inequality is unambiguously positive (negative), implying that it holds for all values of δ. Intuitively, if your opponent chooses High appropriation thereafter, you do not have any incentives to unilaterally deviate toward a Low appropriation level, not even for one period!

Summary. Overall, we found that the only condition we require for cooperation to be sustained as an equilibrium of this infinitely repeated game (that is, for the GTS to be SPE of the game) was found in Case (a), namely

$$\delta \geq \frac{b-a}{b-d}.$$

In words, this condition states that firms cooperate for each round of the game (choosing Low appropriation) as long as they assign a sufficiently high weight to future payoffs. In particular, the numerator of the ratio we found, $b - a$, measures the instantaneous gain that a firm obtains by deviating from cooperation to defection, i.e., from Low to High appropriation. Informally, it evaluates the firm's incentives to cheat. In contrast, the denominator, $b - d$, measures the loss that the firm suffers thereafter because of its deviation.

Figure 5.1 illustrates the trade-off that a player faces when, upon observing that both firms chose Low appropriation levels in previous rounds, it must choose whether to continue cooperating (with a Low appropriation) or to cheat (with a High appropriation), as analyzed in Case (a). If the firm cooperates, its payoff remains at a all subsequent periods. If, instead, the firm cheats, its payoff increases from a to b today, but its defection is thereafter punished by the other firm, decreasing its payoff from b to d in all subsequent periods. Graphically, the instantaneous gain from cheating today is represented by the left-hand square, whereas the future loss from cheating is illustrated by the right-hand rectangle.

Figure 5.1 also helps us predict in which CPRs cooperation can more easily occur. For instance, if the instantaneous gain from choosing a High appropriation decreases (shallow left-hand square),

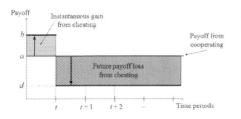

FIGURE 5.1 Incentives to cheat in repeated games.

the incentives to cheat also decrease. This may occur when the fishermen face relatively convex appropriation costs, limiting the unilateral increase in appropriation that an individual fisherman can choose when deviating from the cooperative agreement. A similar argument applies when cheating is detected immediately (e.g., one period after any fisherman defects) rather than requiring several periods to be detected by other fishermen; graphically entailing that the left-hand rectangle is narrow, rather than wide, thus shrinking the area that represents the firm's instantaneous gain from cheating.

Extensions. The end-of-chapter exercises consider variations of the above GTS, and how they can promote or hinder cooperation in the infinitely repeated game. First, we analyze a GTS where both firms temporarily revert to the NE of the unrepeated game, (High, High), as opposed to permanently reverting to the NE of the unrepeated game as we assumed in this section. For instance, the GTS could prescribe that, upon cheating, both firms choose a High appropriation level during T rounds (e.g., two periods) but return to cooperation once the punishment has been inflicted, i.e., after (High, High) has been played for T rounds. Relative to the setting with permanent reversion (i.e., infinite punishments), a temporary reversion increases the incentives to cheat, as a firm's defection is punished during a limited number of periods. Graphically, the future payoff loss from cheating (depicted in the right-hand rectangle of Figure 5.1) is narrower since the punishment phase only lasts T periods, thus making defection more attractive (see exercise 5.7). Second, we study the possibility that defection is detected with a positive probability, but not with certainty as we assumed in this chapter. This can happen when firms monitor each other's appropriation (e.g., observing a sample of other fishermen's catches at port), which is only a raw estimate of their actual appropriation level. In this setting, cheating also becomes more attractive since being detected choosing a High appropriation is less likely to occur than in the GTS we considered in this chapter (see exercise 5.8). Third, we examine if cooperation is more likely to occur when more firms exploit the commons (see exercise 5.5).[6]

5.5 EXPERIMENTAL STUDIES OF REPEATED INTERACTION IN THE COMMONS

5.5.1 *Experimental Design*

The above theoretical results have been recurrently tested in controlled experimental labs across several countries. The standard experimental session asks students (the experimental "subjects") to sit at computer terminals, often separated from each other to prevent them from seeing other individuals' responses. The experimenter then either reads the experiment instructions aloud or presents them on-screen for each participant to read. In a CPR game, the standard design provides the subject with a set of tokens, and asks them to distribute the tokens between two accounts: a public account (often named "account A" to avoid biases in favor/against public projects) and a private account (or "account B" to maintain the experiment being as neutral as possible). The tokens contributed to account A provide a benefit to all subjects who participate in the experiment, whether or not they deposited tokens in this account. Tokens contributed to account B, in contrast, only benefit the individual who deposited them in the account. The experimenter, of course, designs the return of each account so that it becomes a strictly dominant strategy to contribute to the private account (account B) alone, implying that depositing a positive amount of tokens in the public account is strictly dominated.

After reading the instructions, the experimenter often lets subjects ask questions and, in most experiments nowadays, subjects go through a trial run to gain some practice before the experiment starts.

---

[6] For a more advanced discussion of how to apply repeated games theory to CPRs, see Dutta and Sundaram (1993), Dockner et al. (2000, chapter 6), and Polasky et al. (2006).

Once it begins, instructions specify whether the CPR game will be played only once, twice, T times, or whether there is a positive probability p that the subject will play the game in the next period. The instructions also describe clearly if the payoff from each period is affected by players' behaviors in previous rounds (which is generally assumed, for simplicity, to not be the case), if the subject will be paired with a different individual or should continue playing with the same individual in subsequent rounds, whether other individuals received the same information they did, etc.

Finally, the game starts, and each individual selects how many tokens to deposit in account A and B, and is then informed about their payoff in that round (and, in some experiments, how other subjects deposited their tokens). If the game is repeated, the subject is then asked to submit their token deposits to accounts A and B, which may be different from those in period 1. Once the game ends, subjects collect the tokens earned in each round, and exchange them for money at the exit of the experimental lab, often around US\$20–\$50.

5.5.2   Experimental Results

After describing how CPR experiments work, a natural question is whether observed subject behavior coincides (or at least approaches) the theoretical predictions presented in this chapter. In finitely repeated games, experiments found that, generally, in the last round of interaction players behave "as if" they are in an unrepeated (one-shot) game, but cooperate in the first rounds of the game, i.e., deposit positive amounts in the public account. This behavior contradicts the theoretical prediction we discussed in Section 5.3, where firms choose a High appropriation level, thus not cooperating with each other in any round.

What about the infinitely repeated game? Since experimental subjects cannot play the game forever, individuals participating in the experiment were informed that they will play one more round of the game with some probability, e.g., $p = 80\%$. The common finding in this setting is that players' cooperation increases as they are more likely to interact in future rounds (e.g., p increases from 80%

to 90%). This result is consistent with our findings of cooperation being easier to sustain when players care more about the future, i.e., higher probability p is analogous to an increased discount factor δ. However, when players interact during many rounds, they start defecting more frequently. Anticipating that they may not interact in the future (since the probability they encounter each other again declines rapidly), they try to reap the gains from a unilateral defection in one of the last rounds of play.

For experimental studies considering complete information treatments where subjects are perfectly informed about all details of the CPR game, see Hackett et al. (1994), Ostrom (1994), Gardner et al. (1997), Herr et al. (1997), Keser and Gardner (1999), Walker et al. (2000), and Casari and Plott (2003). For experiments allowing for a stochastic component in subjects' payoff function, see Suleiman and Rapoport (1988), Suleiman et al. (1996), and Apesteguia (2006). For a discussion of the experimental literature on public goods, see Duffy and Ochs (2009) and Dal Bó and Fréchette (2011). For an introduction to the literature on experimental and behavioral economics, see Camerer (2003) and Angner (2016).

5.6   EXERCISES

5.1 Asymmetric payoffs. Consider the CPR game of Matrix 5.1, but assume that firm 1's payoffs are different from firm 2's. In particular, assume that firm i's payoffs are a_i, b_i, c_i, and d_i, where $b_i > a_i > d_i > c_i$.

    (a) What is the minimal discount factor sustaining cooperation if $b_1 - a_1 > b_2 - a_2$ and $b_1 - d_1 = b_2 - d_2$? Interpret.

    (b) What is the minimal discount factor sustaining cooperation if $b_1 - a_1 = b_2 - a_2$ and $b_1 - d_1 < b_2 - d_2$? Interpret.

5.2 Altering players' payoffs – I. Consider the CPR game of Matrix 5.1. Assume now that the payoff ranking changes to $a > b$, $d < c$, and $a > d$.

    (a) Identify each firm's strictly dominant strategies, if any.

    (b) Find the NE of the unrepeated game.

    (c) If the game is infinitely repeated, find the minimal discount factor sustaining the cooperative outcome (Low, Low) as an SPE of the game.

5.3 Altering players' payoffs – II. Consider the infinitely repeated CPR game of Section 5.4. Assume that a regulator sets a lump-sum tax t that firms pay when choosing a High appropriation, implying that Matrix 5.1 becomes:

Firm 2

		High approp.	Low approp.
Firm 1	High approp.	$d - t, d - t$	$b - t, c$
	Low approp.	$c, b - t$	a, a

(a) Find the NE of the game, and explain how it is affected by tax t.

(b) If the game is finitely repeated for two periods, can the cooperative outcome (Low, Low) be sustained as an SPE of the game? How are your results affected by t? Interpret.

(c) If the game is infinitely repeated, which is the minimal discount factor sustaining the cooperative outcome (Low, Low) as an SPE of the game? How are your results affected by t? Interpret.

5.4 Asymmetric discount factors. Consider the CPR game of Matrix 5.1, but assume that firm 1's discount factor is δ_1 while that of firm 2 is δ_2, where $\delta_1 > \delta_2$.

(a) What is the minimal discount factor supporting cooperation for each firm?

(b) Show that when firms are symmetric in their discount factors, $\delta_1 = \delta_2 = \delta$, your results coincide with those in Section 5.4.

(c) How are your results affected by an increase in either firm's discount factor?

5.5 N firms exploiting the commons. Consider the CPR game of Matrix 5.1. Let us now extend it to $N \geq 2$ firms. For simplicity, assume that if all firms choose Low appropriation, every firm earns $\$a$; if all firms choose High appropriation, they all earn $\$d$; and if one or more firms choose High appropriation while at least one of its rivals chooses Low appropriation, the firm/s selecting a High appropriation earn $\$b$ while the firm/s choosing Low appropriation earn $\$c$.

(a) What is the minimal discount factor supporting cooperation?

(b) How is the minimal discount factor you found in part (a) affected by the number of firms, N? Interpret.

(c) Show that when only $N - 2$ firms exploit the commons, you obtain the same results as in Section 5.4.

5.6 **Firms facing a continuous action space.** This chapter assumes, for simplicity, that firms could only choose between two different appropriation levels: High or Low. In this exercise, we generalize that setting showing that a similar approach applies. Consider the CPR with two firms we studied in Section 2.3 (see Chapter 2) where, in the unrepeated version of the game, firm i solves

$$\max_{q_i \geq 0} \quad q_i - \frac{q_i(q_i + q_j)}{S}.$$

We next separately find each of the elements needed to identify the minimal discount factor sustaining cooperation in the infinitely repeated version of the game.

(a) Find firm i's equilibrium appropriation in the NE of the unrepeated game. Evaluate firm i's profits in this setting. (Section 2.3 should facilitate your calculations.)

(b) If both firms seek to maximize their joint profits, find the appropriation each of them should choose, and evaluate their profits in this setting. (Section 2.4 should facilitate your calculations.)

(c) If firm j chooses the cooperative appropriation level found in part (b) but firm i does not, which is firm i's optimal deviation that maximizes its profits? Find firm i's and j's profits in this case.

(d) Consider a GTS like that in this chapter: Every firm starts cooperating (i.e., choosing the appropriation you found in part (b)), and continues to do so until one firm deviates. If firm i detects a firm deviating, it reverts to the NE of the unrepeated game – found in part (a) – thereafter. Comparing your results from part (b), where firms cooperate, against those in part (c) and (a), where firm i cheats and triggers an infinite punishment, find which is the minimal discount factor that sustains cooperation. Interpret your results.

5.7 **Temporary punishments.** Consider the CPR game of Matrix 5.1. We now study a GTS where firms, upon observing a firm defecting to High appropriation, respond by defecting to High appropriation during $T \geq 1$ periods (rather than thereafter, as assumed in this chapter).

Under which parameter conditions can cooperation be sustained? [*Hint*: At the end of your analysis, solve for the minimal number of punishment periods that sustains cooperation, rather than solving for the minimal discount factor.]

5.8 **Probabilistic cheating detection.** Consider the CPR game in Matrix 5.1, but assume now that, after either firm defects to High appropriation, its rival detects the deviation with probability $p \in [0, 1]$. Intuitively, when $p = 0$ firms are not detected cheating (e.g., rivals cannot observe any information about other firms' catches) while when $p = 1$ a firm's cheating is detected with certainty. For simplicity, consider that firm i cannot interpret that its rival j chose High appropriation if it actually chose Low appropriation.

(a) What is the minimal discount factor supporting cooperation?

(b) How is the minimal discount factor you found in part (a) affected by the probability of detection, p? Interpret.

(c) Show that when the probability of detection is perfect, $p = 1$, your results in part (a) coincide with those in Section 5.4.

6   Commons under Incomplete Information

Previous chapters assumed that firms perfectly observe all relevant information necessary to operate in the CPR, such as the available stock or the cost externality that they suffer from their rivals' appropriation. Firms interacted in a complete information game, either simultaneously or sequentially, facing no uncertainty about their own profit function or their rivals'. While such a model can be justified in commons where several firms have operated for long periods, and where technologies are well-known, it may not be a good description of CPRs where all (or some) firms have started to operate and/or have limited experience exploiting a similar resource. In that setting, firms face uncertainty about how abundant the resource is, since their technology does not provide a precise estimate of the stock, but instead a distribution of possible stocks, each with an associated probability (i.e., a probability distribution over stocks).

This chapter explores settings where all firms face uncertainty about the available stock, and must choose their appropriation decisions without observing the exact stock. Firms may, of course, have estimates of this stock, but do not know it with certainty. In this context, firms maximize their expected profits, taking into account the probability associated with each stock level. We find equilibrium appropriation in this setting, and compare it against that arising under complete information, identifying in which cases firms exploit the resource more or less intensively when they operate under uncertainty than otherwise.

We then study another context of incomplete information where, rather than having all firms being uninformed about the stock, only one firm is uninformed while its rival – having more experience exploiting the CPR – observes the available stock. This creates an information asymmetry that the privately informed firm may exploit to its benefit. Similarly, as in our previous discussion, we find equilibrium appropriation in this setting, which involves a stock-dependent appropriation for the informed firm but a stock-independent appropriation for the uninformed firm. Intuitively, the informed (uninformed) firm can (cannot) condition its exploitation decision on the stock level since it can (cannot, respectively) observe the available stock. We also compare equilibrium appropriation under complete and incomplete information, and evaluate if the static inefficiencies we found in Chapter 2 are ameliorated or augmented by the presence of incomplete information. We finish the chapter with a review of the literature testing CPRs under incomplete information in controlled experiments.[1]

6.2 SYMMETRICALLY UNINFORMED FIRMS – EVERYONE IS IN THE DARK

Consider our setting with N firms exploiting a CPR from Section 2.3 (see Chapter 2), where every firm i must simultaneously and independently choose its appropriation level x_i. However, let us now assume that all firms face a common uncertainty: They cannot observe the available stock, S, but know that it is high S_H with probability p or low S_L with probability $1 - p$, where $p \in [0, 1]$. The unobservability of the stock can be rationalized as poor technology or higher variations of the stock due to weather conditions. For simplicity, we assume that firms interact only once.

In that setting, every firm faces the following expected profit-maximization problem:

---

[1] For experimental studies testing how appropriation levels are affected by uncertainty, see Walker and Gardner (1992), Hackett et al. (1994), Budescu, Rapoport and Suleiman (1995), Gardner et al. (1997), Herr et al. (1997), Keser and Gardner (1999), Walker et al. (2000), Casari and Plott (2003), and Apesteguia (2006), among others.

$$\max_{x_i \geq 0} \quad p \underbrace{\left(x_i - \frac{x_i(x_i + X_{-i})}{S_H} \right)}_{\text{Profit if stock is high}} + (1-p) \underbrace{\left(x_i - \frac{x_i(x_i + X_{-i})}{S_L} \right)}_{\text{Profit if stock is low}}.$$

Intuitively, firm i chooses its appropriation level x_i without being able to condition its choice on the stock of the resource. The solution to this game yields a Bayesian Nash Equilibrium (BNE) of the incomplete information game.[2]

Differentiating with respect to x_i, and solving for x_i, we obtain the best response function

$$x_i(X_{-i}) = \frac{S_H S_L}{2\left[pS_L + (1-p)S_H \right]} - \frac{1}{2} X_{-i}, \qquad \text{(BRF)}$$

which, as usual, decreases in the aggregate appropriation by all firm i's rivals, X_{-i}. As a confirmation that our results go in the right direction, note that when $p = 1$ the above best response function collapses to $\frac{S_H}{2} - \frac{1}{2}X_{-i}$, as in the complete-information setting analyzed in Chapter 2 when all firms know that the stock is high; whereas when $p = 0$ it simplifies to $\frac{S_L}{2} - \frac{1}{2}X_{-i}$, as in the complete-information game where firms observe a low stock.

In a symmetric equilibrium, appropriation levels satisfy $x_i^* = x_j^* = x^*$, which entails $X_{-i}^* = (N-1)x^*$. Inserting this property in the above best response function, we find

$$x^* = \frac{S_H S_L}{2\left[pS_L + (1-p)S_H \right]} - \frac{1}{2}(N-1)x^*.$$

Rearranging and solving for x^*, we find the equilibrium appropriation level

$$x^* = \frac{S_H S_L}{(N+1)\left[pS_L + (1-p)S_H \right]}.$$

We can easily check that when $p = 1$ equilibrium appropriation x^* reduces to $x_H = \frac{S_H}{N+1}$, where the H subscript denotes that all

---

[2] For references, see Tadelis (2013, chapter 12) or Muñoz-Garcia and Toro-Gonzalez (2019, chapter 7).

firms know that the stock is high; while when $p = 0$ it collapses to $x_L = \frac{S_L}{N+1}$, where the L subscript indicates that all firms observe a low stock.

6.2.1 Comparing Equilibrium Appropriation in Different Information Contexts – I

We can now compare equilibrium appropriation under incomplete information, x^*, against its complete-information counterparts, x_H and x_L. First, we find that

$$
x_H - x^* = \frac{S_H}{N+1} - \frac{S_H S_L}{(N+1)\left[pS_L + (1-p)S_H\right]}
$$

$$
= \frac{S_H\left(1 - \frac{S_L}{pS_L + (1-p)S_H}\right)}{N+1},
$$

which is positive if $1 - \frac{S_L}{pS_L + (1-p)S_H} > 0$, or rearranging, $S_L < pS_L + (1-p)S_H$, which simplifies to $S_L < S_H$, a condition that holds by definition. Therefore, we can conclude that $x_H > x^*$. Intuitively, every firm exploits the resource more intensively when informed about the stock being high with certainty than when facing some uncertainty about the stock's value.[3]

We can similarly compare the equilibrium appropriation under incomplete information, x^*, against that in the complete-information context where all firms observe a low stock, x_L, finding a difference

$$
x_L - x^* = \frac{S_L}{N+1} - \frac{S_H S_L}{(N+1)\left[pS_L + (1-p)S_H\right]}
$$

$$
= -\frac{p(S_H - S_L)S_L}{(N+1)\left[pS_L + (1-p)S_H\right]},
$$

which is clearly negative since $S_H > S_L$ and $p \in [0,1]$. Hence, we found that $x_L < x^*$, meaning that every firm appropriates fewer units of the resource when informed that the stock is low (with certainty) than when facing uncertainty about the stock.[4]

---

[3] Needless to say, when $p = 1$, the above difference $x_H - x^*$ collapses to zero.

[4] When firms are sure of dealing with a low-stock CPR, $p = 0$, the above difference $x_L - x^*$ collapses to zero.

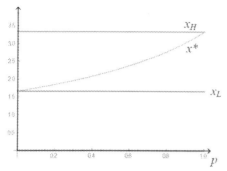

FIGURE 6.1 Equilibrium appropriation under complete and incomplete information.

Overall, equilibrium appropriation under incomplete information, x^*, lies in between firms' complete-information appropriation when they observe the stock

$$x_H > x^* > x_L.$$

Figure 6.1 depicts appropriation levels x^H, x^*, and x^L as a function of probability p, illustrates that $x^* = x_L$ when $p = 0$, that x^* increases in the probability that the stock is high, and x^* converges to x_H when $p = 1$. For illustration purposes, Figure 6.1 considers $S_H = 10$, $S_L = 5$, and $N = 2$ firms, yielding $x_H = \frac{10}{3} \simeq 3.33$, $x_L = \frac{5}{3} \simeq 1.66$, and $x^* = \frac{10}{6-3p}$. We can then expect that in CPRs in which firms operate under incomplete information about the stock, but where the stock is actually high (low), firms appropriate the resource less (more) intensively than when they are fully informed.

6.2.2 Comparative Statics

We can briefly analyze how equilibrium appropriation under incomplete information, x^*, is affected by a change in parameters. First, it decreases in the number of firms competing for the commons, N. Second, it increases in the high stock value, S_H, since

$$\frac{\partial x^*}{\partial S_H} = \frac{pS_L^2}{(N+1)\left[pS_L + (1-p)S_H\right]^2} > 0$$

and in the low stock value, S_L, given that

$$\frac{\partial x^*}{\partial S_L} = \frac{(1-p)S_H^2}{(N+1)\left[pS_L + (1-p)S_H\right]^2} > 0$$

and also in the probability that the stock is high, p, since

$$\frac{\partial x^*}{\partial p} = \frac{S_H(S_H - S_L)S_L}{(N+1)\left[pS_L + (1-p)S_H\right]^2} > 0.$$

In words, equilibrium appropriation x^* increases as the stock becomes more abundant, either S^H or S^L. This appropriation is also increasing in the probability that the stock is high, as discussed in Subsection 6.2.1 and illustrated in Figure 6.1.

6.3   ASYMMETRICALLY   UNINFORMED   FIRMS   –   ONLY SOME FIRMS ARE IN THE DARK

Section 6.2 considered that all firms were uninformed about the stock level. However, what if only one of the firms is uninformed? In such a setting, we can also apply the solution concept of BNE: The privately informed firm conditions its appropriation on the stock (as this firm observes the stock), while the uninformed firm does not condition its appropriation strategy on the stock (since this firm cannot observe it). For simplicity, this section considers only two firms.

To find the BNE in this setting, a common trick is to follow these three steps:

1. First, find the best response function of the privately informed player (one when this firm observes a high stock, and another when it observes a low stock).
2. Second, find the best response function of the uninformed player (which is only one since this firm cannot condition it on the stock's value).
3. Third, use the three best response functions we found to solve a system of three equations with three unknowns, x_H, x_L, x_U, representing, respectively, the appropriation level of the informed firm when observing a high stock, a low stock, and the appropriation level of the uninformed firm.

Privately Informed Firm – High Stock: When the privately informed firm (firm i) observes a high stock, it chooses x_H to solve

$$\max_{x_i \geq 0} x_i - \frac{x_i(x_i + x_U)}{S_H}.$$

Note that we wrote x_U in the position of x_j to emphasize that firm j is uninformed about the stock, so subscript U in this section denotes "uninformed."

Differentiating with respect to x_i, and solving for x_i, we find the best response function of the privately informed firm observing a high stock, BRF_H,

$$x_H(x_U) = \frac{S_H}{2} - \frac{1}{2}x_U \qquad (\text{BRF}_H)$$

which, as expected, is increasing in the stock, S_H, but decreasing in the appropriation decision of the uninformed firm, x_U.

Privately Informed Firm – Low Stock: When the privately informed firm (firm i) observes, instead, a low stock, a similar argument applies. In this case, the firm solves

$$\max_{x_i \geq 0} \ x_i - \frac{x_i(x_i + x_U)}{S_L},$$

which is now evaluated at the low stock, S_L.

Differentiating with respect to x_i, and solving for x_i, we find the best response function of the privately informed firm observing a low stock, BRF_L,

$$x_L(x_U) = \frac{S_L}{2} - \frac{1}{2}x_U, \qquad (\text{BRF}_L)$$

which, as in the previous case, is increasing in the stock, S_L, but decreasing in the appropriation decision of the uninformed firm, x_U.

Uninformed Firm: The firm that does not observe the stock level (firm j) solves an expected profit-maximization problem analogous to that in Section 6.2, that is,

$$\max_{x_j \geq 0} \ \underbrace{p\left(x_j - \frac{x_j(x_j + x_H)}{S_H}\right)}_{\text{Profit if stock is high}} + \underbrace{(1-p)\left(x_j - \frac{x_j(x_j + x_L)}{S_L}\right)}_{\text{Profit if stock is low}}.$$

Importantly, note that the profits when the stock is high are evaluated at the appropriation level of the privately informed firm, x_H, while those when the stock is low are evaluated at this firm's appropriation in this setting, x_L. This did not occur in the maximization problem we described in Section 6.2, since no firm could condition its appropriation decisions on the stock's level; all firms were operating in the dark. In contrast, now the uninformed firm anticipates that, when the stock is high, the informed firm will choose a different appropriation level than when the stock is low.

Differentiating with respect to x_j, and solving for x_j, we find the best response function of the uninformed firm, BRF_U, which is a function of the appropriation decisions of the privately informed firm when the stock is high, x_H, and when the stock is low, x_L, as follows:

$$x_U(x_H, x_L) = \frac{S_H\left[S_L - (1-p)x_L\right] - px_H S_L}{2\left[pS_L + (1-p)S_H\right]},$$

which can alternatively be expressed as

$$x_U(x_H, x_L) = \underbrace{\frac{S_H S_L}{2\left[pS_L + (1-p)S_H\right]}}_{\text{Vertical intercept}} - \underbrace{\frac{pS_L}{2\left[pS_L + (1-p)S_H\right]}x_H}_{\text{Slope for } x_H}$$

$$- \underbrace{\frac{(1-p)S_H}{2\left[pS_L + (1-p)S_H\right]}x_L}_{\text{Slope for } x_L}. \qquad (\text{BRF}_U)$$

Combining All Best Responses: We can now combine the two best response functions for the informed firm – one when it observes that the stock is high, $x_H(x_U)$, and another when it observes a low stock, $x_L(x_U)$ – and the best response function of the uninformed firm, $x_U(x_H, x_L)$. Inserting $x_H(x_U)$ and $x_L(x_U)$ into $x_U(x_H, x_L)$ yields

$$x_U = \frac{S_H S_L}{4\left[pS_L + (1-p)S_H\right]} + \frac{1}{4}x_U,$$

which, solving for x_U, entails the equilibrium appropriation for the uninformed firm

$$x_U^* = \frac{S_H S_L}{3\left[pS_L + (1-p)S_H\right]}.$$

We can now insert x_U^* into best response function $x_H(x_U)$ to obtain the equilibrium appropriation for the informed firm when it observes a high stock, as follows:

$$x_H^* = x_H(x_U^*) = \frac{S_H}{2} - \frac{1}{2} \overbrace{\frac{S_H S_L}{3\left[pS_L + (1-p)S_H\right]}}^{x_U^*}$$

$$= \frac{S_H}{2}\left(1 - \frac{S_L}{3\left[pS_L + (1-p)S_H\right]}\right).$$

Operating similarly, we can insert x_U^* into best response function $x_L(x_U)$ to find the equilibrium appropriation for the informed firm when it observes a low stock, as follows:

$$x_L^* = x_L(x_U^*) = \frac{S_L}{2} - \frac{1}{2}\overbrace{\frac{S_H S_L}{3\left[pS_L + (1-p)S_H\right]}}^{x_U^*}$$

$$= \frac{S_L}{2}\left(1 - \frac{S_H}{3\left[pS_L + (1-p)S_H\right]}\right).$$

In summary, the BNE of this game is (x_H^*, x_L^*, x_U^*). For illustration purposes, Figure 6.2 evaluates the above BNE triplet at the same parameter values as Figure 6.1, $S_H = 10$ and $S_L = 5$, yielding

$$(x_U^*, x_H^*, x_L^*) = \left(\frac{10}{6-3p}, 5 - \frac{5}{3(2-p)}, \frac{5}{2} - \frac{5}{3(2-p)}\right).$$

Our result illustrates two interesting points:

- The uninformed firm exploits the resource at the same rate as the privately informed firm when $p = 0$ (that is, when the uninformed firm is actually informed of facing a low-stock CPR), increases its appropriation as the probability of facing a high stock, p, increases, and appropriates the same amount as the privately informed firm facing a high-stock resource (which occurs when $p = 1$).
- The privately informed firm, both when facing a high and a low stock, decreases its appropriation as the uninformed firm assigns a higher probability to facing a high-stock CPR. Intuitively, the privately informed firm anticipates that its uninformed rival will increase its appropriation as p increases, leading the former to decrease its own exploitation of the resource.

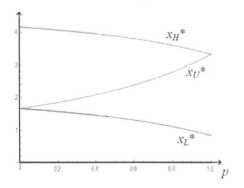

FIGURE 6.2 Equilibrium appropriation.

6.3.1 Comparing Equilibrium Appropriation in Different Information Contexts – II

Uninformed Firm: We start by comparing the equilibrium appropriation that the firm chooses under complete information, $x_H = \frac{S_H}{N+1} = \frac{S_H}{3}$, and in the above incomplete information setting where this firm is uninformed, x_U^* (as identified in Section 6.3), to obtain

$$x_H - x_U^* = \frac{S_H}{3} - \frac{S_H S_L}{3\left[pS_L + (1-p)S_H\right]}$$

$$= \frac{S_H}{3}\left(1 - \frac{S_L}{\left[pS_L + (1-p)S_H\right]}\right),$$

which is positive.[5] Therefore, $x_H > x_U^*$, meaning that the uninformed firm exploits the resource less intensively than when it knew with certainty that the stock is high. Doing a similar comparison when the stock is low, we find

$$x_L - x_U^* = \frac{S_L}{3} - \frac{S_H S_L}{3\left[pS_L + (1-p)S_H\right]}$$

$$= -\frac{pS_L\left(S_H - S_L\right)}{3\left[pS_L + (1-p)S_H\right]},$$

---

[5] We encountered a similar result in Section 6.2. To see this point, note that this expression is positive if $1 - \frac{S_L}{pS_L+(1-p)S_H} > 0$ holds, or rearranging, $S_L < pS_L + (1-p)S_H$, which simplifies to $S_L < S_H$, a condition that holds by definition.

which is negative, implying that $x_L < x_U^*$. In words, the uninformed firm appropriates more units than when it knew with certainty that the stock was low. Overall, the uninformed firm exploits the resource more intensively than when it is informed that the stock is low, but less intensively than when it is informed that it is high, $x_H > x_U^* > x_L$.

Informed Firm – High Stock: We can similarly compare the equilibrium appropriation that the firm informed about a high stock chooses under complete information, $x_H = \frac{S_H}{3}$, and in the above incomplete information setting, x_H^* (as identified in the previous Section 6.3), we obtain

$$x_H - x_H^* = \frac{S_H}{3} - \frac{S_H}{2}\left(1 - \frac{S_L}{3\left[pS_L + (1-p)S_H\right]}\right)$$
$$= -\frac{S_H(S_H - S_L)(1-p)}{6\left[pS_L + (1-p)S_H\right]},$$

which is clearly negative, thus implying that $x_H < x_H^*$. In words, the privately informed firm that observes a high stock exploits the resource more intensively when it knows that its rival is uninformed about the stock value than when its rival is informed about it. Intuitively, the former anticipates that the latter appropriates less when being uninformed, thus letting the informed firm increase its appropriation. Mathematically, this occurs because appropriation decisions are strategic substitutes, i.e., they enter negatively in all three best response functions described in Section 6.3. As a result, a lower appropriation by one firm is followed by other firms increasing their own exploitation of the CPR.

Informed Firm – Low Stock: Finally, we can run a similar comparison for the privately informed firm, but when it observes a low stock, yielding

$$x_L - x_L^* = \frac{S_L}{3} - \frac{S_L}{2}\left(1 - \frac{S_H}{3\left[pS_L + (1-p)S_H\right]}\right)$$
$$= \frac{pS_L(S_H - S_L)}{6\left[pS_L + (1-p)S_H\right]}.$$

which is clearly positive, entailing that $x_L > x_L^*$. Intuitively, this means that the privately informed firm observing a low stock appropriates fewer units when it knows that its rival is uninformed than otherwise. This result follows the opposite argument to when the stock is high: the informed firm can anticipate that its rival exploits the resource more intensively when operating under uncertainty about the stock's value than when it knows that the stock is low. As a consequence, the informed firm responds by reducing its own appropriation.

More or Less Intense Overall Exploitation?: From our results, we found that the informed firm exploits the resource more intensively when it observes that the stock is high than when it is uninformed about it, while the uninformed firm appropriates it less intensively. Comparing the decrease in the informed firm's appropriation, $x_H - x_H^*$, against the increase in the uninformed firm's appropriation, $x_H - x_U^*$, we obtain

$$\underbrace{\left(x_H - x_H^*\right)}_{-} - \underbrace{\left(x_H - x_U^*\right)}_{+} = x_U^* - x_H^*$$

$$= -\frac{(1-p)S_H\,(S_H - S_L)}{2\left[pS_L + (1-p)S_H\right]},$$

which is negative. Therefore, the decrease in the uninformed firm's appropriation, $x_H - x_U^*$, offsets the increase in the informed firm's appropriation, $x_H - x_H^*$, ultimately implying that overall appropriation of the resource decreased.

When the stock is low, the informed firm exploits the resource less intensively than under complete information, but the uninformed firm appropriates it more intensively. Overall, we find that

$$\underbrace{\left(x_L - x_L^*\right)}_{+} - \underbrace{\left(x_L - x_U^*\right)}_{-} = x_U^* - x_L^*$$

$$= \frac{pS_L\,(S_H - S_L)}{2\left[pS_L + (1-p)S_H\right]},$$

which is clearly positive. In this case, the increase in the uninformed firm's appropriation offsets the decrease in the informed firm's exploitation, leading to an overall increase in the CPR's appropriation. In summary, we then found that, when only one firm is informed about the stock of the resource, and the stock is actually abundant (scarce) overall appropriation is lower (higher) than under complete information. Paradoxically, conservation is more intense when the CPR is abundant, but exploitation becomes particularly severe when the resource is scarce.

6.3.2   Efficiency Properties

Under complete information, as firms interact for only one period, they overexploit the CPR; see Chapter 2 for more details. Under incomplete information, we have just demonstrated that overall appropriation is smaller than under complete information when the resource is abundant, but greater when it is scarce. Therefore, when the stock is high, our results predict that incomplete information ameliorates the static inefficiencies identified in Chapter 2, while when the stock is low, incomplete information augments those inefficiencies.

6.4   EXERCISES

6.1   Socially optimal appropriation. Consider the setting in Section 6.2.

(a) Assuming that the social planner has a welfare function $W = PS$, find the socially optimal appropriation for each firm, x^{SO}, and evaluate the static inefficiency, $x_i^* - x^{SO}$. Is this inefficiency greater than that under complete information?

(b) Assuming that the social planner has a welfare function $W = CS + PS$, find the socially optimal appropriation for each firm, x^{SO}, and evaluate the static inefficiency, $x_i^* - x^{SO}$. Is this inefficiency greater than that under complete information?

6.2   Twoperiods facing uncertainty. Consider the setting in Section 6.2, but extended to a two-period game. As in Chapter 3, consider that the stock regenerates at a rate r, and assume that firms are uninformed about the stock during both periods. To facilitate your calculations, assume parameter values $S_H = 10$ and $S_L = 5$.

6.3   Two-period interaction, but only one of them facing uncertainty.
Consider the setting in Section 6.2, but extended to a two-period game.
Consider a regeneration rate r and assume that firms are uninformed
about the stock only during the first period, but are informed before the
second period starts. To facilitate your calculations, you may assume
parameter values $S_H = 10$ and $S_L = 5$.

6.4   Allowing for market power – Symmetrically uninformed players.
Consider the setting in Section 6.2, but allow for players to face a linear
inverse demand function $p(X) = 1 - X$, where X denotes aggregate
appropriation. Repeat our analysis and compare your results. How are
the equilibrium appropriation decisions affected by market power?
To facilitate your calculations, assume parameter values $S_H = 10$ and
$S_L = 5$.

6.5   Allowing for market power – Asymmetrically informed players.
Consider the setting in Section 6.3, but allow for players to face a linear
inverse demand function $p(X) = 1 - X$, where X denotes aggregate
appropriation. Repeat our analysis and compare your results. How are
the equilibrium appropriation decisions for the privately informed firm
and for the uninformed firm affected by market power? To facilitate
your calculations, assume parameter values $S_H = 10$ and $S_L = 5$.

7   Signaling in the Commons

7.1   INTRODUCTION

In this chapter, we continue our analysis of equilibrium behavior in settings where firms operate under incomplete information. We now examine CPRs that have been exploited by a single firm (the incumbent) and subject to entry threats by a potential entrant. The incumbent, after years of experience appropriating the resource, has access to more accurate information about the available stock than the potential entrant. However, the latter can observe the appropriation decisions of the incumbent, using them as signals that can help the potential entrant infer the stock. We analyze equilibria where the incumbent chooses a different appropriation for each stock level, and thus appropriation is an informative signal of the unobserved stock, i.e., separating equilibria. We then study equilibria where the incumbent selects the same appropriation level regardless of the stock they face. In this context, the entrant cannot infer the available stock upon observing the incumbent's appropriation. This type of equilibria are known as "pooling equilibria" since an incumbent facing different levels of stock pools into the same appropriation level, which conceals the underlying stock from the entrant.

For each of these equilibria, we investigate how their equilibrium appropriation levels differ from those arising under complete information, and evaluate how far away they are from the social optimum. This helps us understand if the static and dynamic inefficiencies that emerge under complete information (see Chapters 2–4) become emphasized when firms operate under incomplete information and face entry threats. We show that, while in some cases this information setting may lead to more severe inefficiencies, in other contexts firms' incentives under incomplete information may induce them to alleviate part of the inefficiencies arising under complete information. In these situations, the uncertainty that the potential entrant faces about the available stock yields a welfare-improving outcome.

At the end of the chapter, we consider a regulatory agency that does not observe the available stock, thus being as poorly informed as the potential entrant, and evaluate under which conditions this agency may have incentives to invest in acquiring information about the stock value, subsequently distributing this information in media outlets, making the entrant informed; and in which cases it prefers, instead, to remain uninformed.

7.2 MODELING SIGNALS IN THE COMMONS

Consider an incomplete information setting where the incumbent firm has access to better information about the stock than the potential entrant. This can be rationalized on this firm's longer experience exploiting the resource, or on asymmetric technologies between the incumbent and entrant.

The sequential-move game has the following time structure, also depicted in Figure 7.1 for illustration purposes:

1. *Stock realization.* Nature determines the realization of the stock, either high, S_H, with probability p, or low, S_L, with probability $1 - p$, where $S_H > S_L$ and $p \in (0, 1)$. The incumbent privately observes this realization but the entrant does not. The entrant, however, knows the rules of this game, which entails that it knows the probability of each stock occurring, p and $1 - p$.

2. *First-period appropriation.* In the first period, the incumbent chooses an appropriation level x.

3. *Belief updating.* Observing the incumbent's first-period appropriation level x, the entrant forms beliefs about the initial stock, S. Let $\mu(S|x)$ denote the entrant's posterior belief about the initial stock being high after observing x.

4. *Entry decision.* Given the above beliefs, the entrant decides whether to enter the CPR or not.
   (a) If entry does not occur, the incumbent remains the only firm exploiting the resource in the second period.
   (b) If entry ensues, both the incumbent and entrant compete for the CPR.

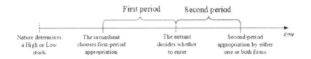

FIGURE 7.1 Time structure of the signaling game.

As in previous chapters, consider that firms face a given market price $p = \$1$ and the same cost functions as defined before (for a detailed explanation, see Chapters 3–4). This will help us compare our equilibrium appropriation under incomplete information (which we find in Sections 7.3 and 7.4) against that in the complete information model of entry deterrence in Chapter 4, letting us measure how the incumbent's behavior changes when this firm deals with a potential entrant that does not know the exact amount of stock available. For simplicity, we assume that, if the entrant was perfectly informed about the stock, it would enter (not enter) when the stock is high (low, respectively). This allows for information about the stock to play an entry-deterring role, which the incumbent may exploit to prevent entry.

Players then interact in a sequential-move game of incomplete information, where the incumbent uses first-period appropriation to convey or conceal information about the available stock from the potential entrant, thus inducing the latter to enter or not in to the CPR. In this type of game, we use the Perfect Bayesian Equilibrium (PBE) solution concept, which entails that:

(a) Every firm finds its appropriation profit maximizing, given the point of the game at which the firm is called on to move, and given the information that the firm observes at that point; and

(b) The potential entrant updates its beliefs about the stock using Bayes' rule, whenever possible.

We elaborate on players' beliefs, and how they update them, in the next Section 7.2.1.

7.2.1 Prior and Posterior Beliefs

Bayes' rule essentially helps the uninformed player (the potential entrant in this context) use the first-mover's actions (i.e., first-period appropriation x) to increase or decrease the probability of dealing with a high-stock CPR. For instance, if the incumbent chooses a stock-dependent first-period appropriation (e.g., $x_L = 2$ tons when the stock is low, but $x_H = 10$ tons when the stock is high), the entrant can perfectly infer the stock's level by just observing the incumbent's first-period appropriation.

Separating Equilibria: This belief updating happens in "separating equilibria," where the word "separating" highlights the idea that each type of incumbent separates from each other by choosing a different first-period appropriation. They are also known as "informative equilibria" since they convey information to the uninformed player.

In this setting, Bayes' rule helps us update the entrant's posterior belief of facing a high stock, S_H, from the prior probability p to $\mu(S_H|x)$, as follows:

$$\mu(S_H|x) = \frac{p \times \alpha_H}{(p \times \alpha_H) + \left[(1-p) \times \alpha_L\right]}, \qquad \text{(posterior belief)}$$

where α_k denotes the probability that the incumbent facing a k-type stock chooses a first-period appropriation of exactly x units, and $k = \{H, L\}$. Hence, when only the high-stock incumbent chooses such a first-period appropriation, these probabilities become $\alpha_H = 1$ and $\alpha_L = 0$, simplifying the posterior belief to

$$\mu(S_H|x) = \frac{p \times 1}{(p \times 1) + \left[(1-p) \times 0\right]} = \frac{p}{p} = 1.$$

Intuitively, if only the high-stock incumbent chooses this level of x, the entrant can put full probability, $\mu(S_H|x) = 1$, on facing this type of incumbent. In other words, the incumbent, by choosing a different first-period appropriation depending on the stock, *signals* (or conveys) information about this stock to the potential entrant.

Pooling Equilibria: If, in contrast, the incumbent selects a stock-independent first-period appropriation (e.g., $x = 5$ tons both when the stock is high and low), the entrant cannot infer the available stock after observing the incumbent's appropriation. This occurs in "pooling equilibria," where the adjective "pooling" emphasizes the feature that both types of incumbent pool by choosing the same first-period appropriation. They are also known as "uninformative equilibria" since no information is conveyed to the uninformed player.

In this context, Bayes' rule does not help the entrant change its posterior belief about the stock being high, p. To see this, note that both types of incumbent choose x, entailing probabilities $\alpha_H = \alpha_L = 1$, which yields a posterior

$$\mu(S_H|x) = \frac{p \times 1}{(p \times 1) + \left[(1-p) \times 1\right]} = \frac{p}{1} = p.$$

In words, this says that, upon observing the incumbent's first-period appropriation, x, the entrant cannot refine its beliefs about the incumbent's type since x does not reveal any information about the available stock. Alternatively, by choosing the same first-period appropriation, the incumbent *conceals* the state of the stock from the potential entrant.

Off-the-Equilibrium beliefs: But why did point (b) of the PBE definition finish with the "...whenever possible" clause? This is to account for the possibility of first-period appropriation levels that are not selected by any type of incumbent in equilibrium, i.e., off-the-equilibrium appropriation levels. Indeed, if a first-period appropriation x is not chosen by either type of incumbent, the above probabilities become $\alpha_H = \alpha_L = 0$, entailing a posterior probability

$$\mu(S_H|x) = \frac{p \times 0}{(p \times 0) + \left[(1-p) \times 0\right]} = \frac{0}{0}.$$

This is, of course, an undefined result, implying that Bayes' rule cannot be applied to off-the-equilibrium appropriation levels. In these cases, for generality, we could leave the entrant's beliefs unrestricted, thus allowing for any probability $\mu(S_H|x) \in (0,1)$. However, for presentation purposes, we assume here that $\mu(S_H|x) = 1$, making the CPR more attractive for the entrant, and reducing the incumbent's incentives to deviate toward x.

Section 7.3 investigates the separating equilibrium, while Section 7.4 focuses on the pooling equilibrium. Our approach follows the Milgrom and Roberts (1982) limit pricing model. In our setting, however, first-period actions (appropriation) affect second-period profits for both incumbent and entrant since appropriation depletes a portion of the resource, as opposed to their article where second-period profits are unaffected by first-period prices or output.

7.3   SEPARATING EQUILIBRIUM

Consider that the incumbent chooses a first-period appropriation x_H when the stock is high, S_H, but an appropriation x_L when the stock is low, S_L, where $x_H > x_L$. In this context, the entrant's beliefs are $\mu(S_H|x_H) = 1$ after observing x_H, $\mu(S_H|x_L) = 0$ after observing x_L, and $\mu(S_H|x) = 1$ after observing any off-the-equilibrium appropriation $x \neq x_H, x_L$. Therefore, the entrant stays out of the CPR after observing a first-period appropriation x_L, but enters otherwise. Anticipating this response by the potential entrant, the incumbent chooses its first-period appropriation as follows. For presentation purposes, we separately analyze the incumbent who faces a high or a low stock.

High-Stock Incumbent: The incumbent chooses the same first-period appropriation as in a complete information setting with subsequent entry, denoted by $x^* = \frac{S_H[9-\delta(1-r)]}{18}$ in Chapter 4. To clarify that we deal with the high-stock incumbent, we relabel x^* as x_H, which yields an overall profit

$$\Pi_H^{AE} = \underbrace{\left[x_H - \frac{x_H^2}{S_H} \right]}_{\text{First-period profit}} + \delta \underbrace{\left[\frac{S_H - (1-r)x_H}{9} \right]}_{\text{Second-period profit with entry}},$$

where the AE superscript in Π_H^{AE} denotes "allow entry" while the H subscript represents the incumbent's type (note that the above expression is evaluated at stock $S = S_H$ everywhere). Intuitively, by choosing first-period appropriation x_H the incumbent maximizes its discounted stream of profits (good news!) but does not deter entry (bad news!). To prevent entry, the incumbent could deviate toward the low-stock incumbent's appropriation level, x_L, inducing the entrant to believe that the stock is low. (We haven't found the specific value of this appropriation x_L, so at this point it is our unknown variable. We solve for x_L at the end of Section 7.3.) Choosing x_L yields an overall profit

$$\Pi_H^{ED} = \underbrace{\left[x_L - \frac{x_L^2}{S_H} \right]}_{\text{First-period profit}} + \delta \underbrace{\left[\frac{S_H - (1-r)x_L}{4} \right]}_{\text{Second-period profit without entry}},$$

where the ED superscript in Π_H^{ED} denotes "entry deterrence." In words, the incumbent chooses a suboptimal first-period appropriation but deters entry. Therefore, for the high-stock incumbent to choose x_H in the separating equilibrium, rather than choosing the same appropriation level as the low-stock incumbent (i.e., pooling with this type of firm), the overall profits from allowing entry must exceed those from deterring entry, that is, $\Pi_H^{AE} \geq \Pi_H^{ED}$. Expanding this inequality, and rearranging terms so first-period profits are all on the left-hand side while second-period profits are on the right-hand side, we obtain

$$\underbrace{\left[x_H - \frac{x_H^2}{S_H} \right] - \left[x_L - \frac{x_L^2}{S_H} \right]}_{\text{First-period profit gain}}$$

$$\geq \delta \underbrace{\left[\frac{S_H - (1-r)x_L}{4} - \frac{S_H - (1-r)x_H}{9} \right]}_{\text{Second-period profit loss}}, \qquad (\text{IC}_H)$$

which is often known as an "incentive compatibility" condition of the high-stock incumbent, or IC_H. In words, the first-period profit gain – choosing x_H yields a larger profit than x_L – exceeds the second-period loss from attracting entry, which occurs when the incumbent chooses x_H but does not when it selects x_L.[1] Alternatively, first-period appropriation x_L, despite deterring entry, must be unprofitable to mimic for the high-stock incumbent.

---

[1] Incentive compatibility condition IC_H also guarantees that the high-stock incumbent does not have incentives to deviate toward any off-the-equilibrium appropriation, $x \neq x_H \neq x_L$. For a proof of this result, see Espinola and Muñoz-Garcia (2011, proposition 1).

Low-Stock Incumbent: A similar argument applies to the low-stock incumbent. If it chooses the first-period appropriation that this separating equilibrium prescribes, x_L, it deters entry, yielding overall profit

$$\Pi_L^{ED} = \underbrace{\left[x_L - \frac{x_L^2}{S_L} \right]}_{\text{First-period profit}} + \delta \underbrace{\left[\frac{S_L - (1-r)x_L}{4} \right]}_{\text{Second-period profit without entry}},$$

where the ED superscript in Π_L^{ED} denotes "entry deterrence" while the L subscript represents the incumbent's low stock. If, instead, the incumbent deviates toward the appropriation level of the high-stock incumbent, x_H, it attracts entry. Conditional on entry, however, x_H does not yield the highest profit. The first-period appropriation that, conditional on entry, maximizes the low-stock incumbent's overall profits solves

$$\max_{x \geq 0} \underbrace{\left[x - \frac{x^2}{S_L} \right]}_{\text{First-period profit}} + \delta \underbrace{\left[\frac{S_L - (1-r)x}{9} \right]}_{\text{Second-period profit with entry}},$$

yielding $x_{L,E} = \frac{S_L[9 - \delta(1-r)]}{18}$. We denote such appropriation as $x_{L,E}$ to distinguish it from x_L (our only unknown in this problem). Choosing $x_{L,E}$, the low-stock incumbent attracts entry and earns

$$\Pi_L^{AE} = \underbrace{\left[x_{L,E} - \frac{x_{L,E}^2}{S_L} \right]}_{\text{First-period profit}} + \delta \underbrace{\left[\frac{S_L - (1-r)x_{L,E}}{9} \right]}_{\text{Second-period profit with entry}}.$$

Therefore, the low-stock incumbent chooses first-period appropriation x_L, deterring entry, rather than $x_{L,E}$, attracting entry, as required in this separating equilibrium, if and only if $\Pi_L^{ED} \geq \Pi_L^{AE}$. Expanding this inequality, and rearranging first- and second-period profits, yields the incentive compatibility condition for the low-stock incumbent, IC_L,

$$\underbrace{\left[x_{L,E} - \frac{x_{L,E}^2}{S_L}\right] - \left[x_L - \frac{x_L^2}{S_L}\right]}_{\text{First-period profit gain}}$$

$$\leq \delta \underbrace{\left[\frac{S_L - (1-r)x_L}{4} - \frac{S_L - (1-r)x_{L,E}}{9}\right]}_{\text{Second-period profit loss}}, \qquad \text{(IC}_L\text{)}$$

which, in words, says that the first-period profit gain (of choosing $x_{L,E}$ rather than x_L) does not compensate for the second-period profit loss that the firm experiences when attracting entry; the opposite profit ranking as for the high-stock incumbent.

Solving for x_L To find our only unknown, x_L, we need to simultaneously solve for it in IC$_H$ and IC$_L$, which will give us an upper and lower bound for xL. For illustration purposes, we assume parameter values $S_H = 10$, $S_L = 5$, and $\delta = 1$. Solving in this context for x_L in IC$_H$, we obtain

$$x_L \geq \frac{5\left[9 + 3r + (9r^2 + 54r + 161)\right]}{25}.$$

Similarly, solving for x_L in IC$_L$ yields

$$x_L \leq \frac{5\left[27 + 9r + \sqrt{5}\,(85 + r\,(46 + 13r))\right]}{36}.$$

Therefore, the first-period appropriation x_L must lie in the interval

$$x_L \in \left[\frac{5\left[9 + 3r + (9r^2 + 54r + 161)\right]}{25},\right.$$

$$\left.\frac{5\left[27 + 9r + \sqrt{5}\,(85 + r\,(46 + 13r))\right]}{36}\right].$$

Since all appropriation levels in this range convey the low stock to the potential entrant, deterring entry, this type of incumbent chooses the highest of them

$$x_L = \frac{5\left[27 + 9r + \sqrt{5}\,(85 + r\,(46 + 13r))\right]}{36}$$

since by doing so it deviates the least from its complete-information appropriation decision.

Using the jargon of signaling games, the low-stock incumbent chooses the "least-costly separating equilibrium," also known as the "Riley outcome." In addition, this appropriation level survives the Cho and Kreps' (1987) Intuitive Criterion; see Espinola and Muñoz-Garcia (2011) for further details.[2] Intuitively, all other separating appropriation levels would also convey the low stock to the potential entrant, deterring entry, but would entail an unnecessarily severe underexploitation of the resource, thus reducing the incumbent's profit.

7.3.1   Separating Effort

The difference between the first-period appropriation that the low-stock incumbent selects under complete information,[3] $x_{L,NE} = \frac{S_L[4-\delta(1-r)]}{8}$, and that in the separating equilibrium, x_L, represents the "separating effort" that the incumbent exerts to convey the low stock to the potential entrant and thus deter entry. Since $S_L = 5$, and $\delta = 1$, $x_{L,NE}$ simplifies to $x_{L,NE} = \frac{5[4-(1-r)]}{8} = \frac{5(3+r)}{8}$ in this context, implying that the separating effort becomes

$$\text{Separating effort} = x_{L,NE} - x_L$$

$$= \frac{5\,(3+r)}{8}$$

$$- \frac{5\left[27 + 9r + \sqrt{5}\,(85 + r\,(46 + 13r))\right]}{36}$$

$$= \frac{5\left[27 + 9r + 2\left[85 + r\,(46 + 13r)\right]^{1/2}\right]}{27},$$

---

[2] For other applications of signaling games to CPRs, see Polasky and Bin (2001).
[3] Recall that under complete information, the potential entrant observes the low stock, and does not enter into the CPR. Conditional on no entry, the incumbent's second period profits are $\frac{S_L-(1-r)x}{4}$; see Chapter 4 for further details. Therefore, the incumbent's optimal first-period appropriation under complete information maximizes $(x - \frac{x^2}{S_L}) + \delta\frac{S_L-(1-r)x}{4}$. Differentiating with respect to x, we obtain $1 - \frac{2x}{S_L} - \frac{\delta(1-r)}{4} = 0$, which, solving for x, yields a first-period appropriation $x_{L,NE} = \frac{S_L[4-\delta(1-r)]}{8}$.

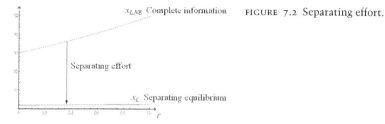

FIGURE 7.2 Separating effort.

which is positive for all regeneration rates $r \in [0, 1]$. Figure 7.2 depicts the complete information appropriation, $x_{L,NE}$, the separating equilibrium appropriation, x_L, and the separating effort, $x_{L,NE} - x_L$. Recall that the low-stock incumbent exerts this separating effort to separate from the high-stock incumbent, who has incentives to mimic the low-stock firm to deter entry. By underexploiting the CPR – that is, choosing an appropriation level x_L lower than $x_{L,NE}$ – the low-stock incumbent makes mimicking unprofitable for the high-stock incumbent.

In addition, this separating effort increases in the regeneration rate r since

$$\frac{\partial \left(x_{L,NE} - x_L \right)}{\partial r} = \frac{5}{72} \left(9 + \frac{\sqrt{5} \, (46 + 26r)}{[85 + r \, (46 + 13r)]^{1/2}} \right)$$

is positive for all $r \in [0, 1]$. Intuitively, as a larger share of the resource regenerates across periods, the CPR becomes more attractive, and the high-stock incumbent has stronger incentives to mimic the low-stock incumbent to deter entry. As a response, the low-stock incumbent must underexploit the CPR more intensively so the high-stock incumbent no longer has incentives to mimic its choice of appropriation level x_L. Figure 7.2 depicts this result, where the separating effort that the low-stock incumbent exerts expands as the regeneration rate, r, increases.

This is an interesting result, because the separating effort can be interpreted as the "strategic conservation effort" that the incumbent facing a low stock exerts to prevent entry. Our results, hence, indicate that this conservation effort increases as the regeneration rate of the resource, r, increases, thus suggesting that CPRs with high regeneration rates should exhibit relatively substantial conservation efforts while those with low regeneration rates should have a low conservation effort.

7.3.2 Efficiency Properties

Our findings also help us evaluate the efficiency properties of the separating equilibrium. When the initial stock is high, the incumbent chooses the same appropriation as under complete information, x_H. However, this appropriation is socially excessive since the incumbent ignores the dynamic inefficiency that its first-period appropriation imposes on the entrant's second-period profits; see Chapter 4 for details. Therefore, under a high stock, the same inefficiencies emerge under complete and incomplete information.

When the initial stock is low, however, the incumbent underexploits the resource relative to complete information, i.e., $x_L < x_{L,NE}$. Under complete information no inefficiencies arise, as the incumbent is the only firm operating in both periods, thus internalizing the effects of its appropriation. In the separating equilibrium, however, the underexploitation that emerges gives rise to a new form of inefficiency, i.e., a socially insufficient appropriation of the CPR, stemming from the incomplete information environment where firms interact. The behavior identified by the separating equilibrium, that is, an underexploitation of the resource relative to the social optimum, has been reported in fishing grounds like those of the Silver hake in the North Atlantic and blackfin tuna in the Caribbean. While such underexploitation can stem from technological reasons or a low demand for the product, our results indicate that incomplete information would further decrease appropriation, enlarging inefficiencies.

In this context, if regulatory authorities are perfectly informed about the available stock, our results suggest that they should strategically distribute this information among potential entrants (e.g., publicizing the low stock in different media outlets). This information dissemination would transform the structure of firms' interaction, from an incomplete information game, where entry is deterred via underexploiting the resource, to a complete information game, where entry does not occur and appropriation is socially optimal. A natural question is, however, if we can assume that regulatory agencies have access to the same information about the available stock as incumbents operating in the CPR or, instead, are as poorly informed as the potential entrant. Section 7.5 examines this setting.

7.4   POOLING EQUILIBRIUM

In this equilibrium, both types of incumbent choose the same first-period appropriation – that corresponding to the low-stock incumbent under complete information, $x_{L,NE}$. In this setting, the potential entrant posterior belief $\mu(S_H|x)$ coincides with its prior p, i.e., the probability that the stock is high. Intuitively, the observation of the incumbent's appropriation decision does not help the entrant restrict its beliefs about the available stock. In other words, the pooling appropriation level $x_{L,NE}$ conceals information about the stock from the entrant, as opposed to what happened in the separating equilibrium where first-period appropriation conveyed information about the stock to the entrant. As we did in the separating equilibrium, we next separately analyze the incentives of each type of incumbent to choose $x_{L,NE}$.

Low-Stock Incumbent: By selecting the same appropriation level as under complete information, $x_{L,NE}$, this type of incumbent deters entry. Importantly, this appropriation level maximizes the incumbent's overall profit conditional on no entry in the next period, thus becoming a rather attractive option. If, instead, the low-stock incumbent deviates to any other appropriation level, $x \neq x_{L,NE}$, entry ensues, yielding an unambiguously lower overall profit. In short, this type of incumbent does not have incentives to deviate from appropriation $x_{L,NE}$.

High-Stock Incumbent: By selecting appropriation level $x_{L,NE}$, this type of incumbent also deters entry, earning overall profit

$$\Pi_H^{ED} = \underbrace{\left[x_{L,NE} - \frac{x_{L,NE}^2}{S_H} \right]}_{\text{First-period profit}} + \delta \underbrace{\left[\frac{S_H - (1-r)x_{L,NE}}{4} \right]}_{\text{Second-period profit without entry}} .$$

If, instead, the high-stock incumbent deviates to any other appropriation level, $x \neq x_{L,NE}$, entry occurs. In that setting, the incumbent solves

$$\max_{x \geq 0} \underbrace{\left[x - \frac{x^2}{S_H} \right]}_{\text{First-period profit}} + \delta \underbrace{\left[\frac{S_H - (1-r)x}{9} \right]}_{\text{Second-period profit with entry}} ,$$

which yields $x_{H,E} = \frac{S_H[9 - \delta(1-r)]}{18}$, thus coinciding with its first-period appropriation under complete information. Evaluating this problem at $x_{H,E}$, we obtain

$$\Pi_H^{AE} = \underbrace{\left[x_{H,E} - \frac{x_{H,E}^2}{S_H} \right]}_{\text{First-period profit}} + \delta \underbrace{\left[\frac{S_H - (1-r)x_{H,E}}{9} \right]}_{\text{Second-period profit with entry}} .$$

Therefore, the high-stock incumbent chooses appropriation $x_{L,NE}$, deterring entry, rather than $x_{H,E}$, which attracts entry, if and only if overall profits satisfy $\Pi_H^{ED} \geq \Pi_H^{AE}$. Expanding this inequality and rearranging terms yields the incentive compatibility condition

$$\left[x_{L,NE} - \frac{x_{L,NE}^2}{S_H} \right] - \left[x_{H,E} - \frac{x_{H,E}^2}{S_H} \right]$$
$$\geq \delta \left[\frac{S_H - (1-r)x_{H,E}}{9} - \frac{S_H - (1-r)x_{L,NE}}{4} \right].$$

Continuing with our numerical example in Subsection 7.3.1, $S_H = 10$, $S_L = 5$, and $\delta = 1$, this inequality simplifies to

$$\left[x_{L,NE} - \frac{x_{L,NE}^2}{10} \right] - \left[x_{H,E} - \frac{x_{H,E}^2}{10} \right]$$
$$\geq \frac{10 - (1-r)x_{H,E}}{9} - \frac{10 - (1-r)x_{L,NE}}{4}.$$

And inserting these parameter values into the equilibrium appropriation levels, we obtain that

$$x_{L,NE} = \frac{S_L\left[4 - \delta(1 - r)\right]}{8} = \frac{5(3 + r)}{8}, \text{ and}$$

$$x_{H,E} = \frac{S_H\left[9 - \delta(1 - r)\right]}{18} = \frac{5(8 + r)}{9}.$$

Therefore, the above inequality becomes

$$\frac{6,075(3 + r)^2 - 1,600\left[19 + r(16 + r)\right]}{51,840} \geq 0,$$

which holds for all admissible regeneration rates $r \in [0,1]$. Therefore, the high-stock incumbent has incentives to decrease its first-period appropriation, from $x_{H,E}$ under complete information that attracts entry, to $x_{L,NE}$ under incomplete information that deters entry.

For more general parameter values, the pooling equilibrium can be sustained as long as the lowstock that the high-stock incumbent seeks to mimic is not significantly lower than its high stock, that is, S_L satisfies

$$S_L > S_H - \frac{\sqrt{5}\left[(3 + r)^2 \, (85 + r(46 + 13r)) \, S_H^2\right]^{1/2}}{9 \, (3 + r)^2}.$$

Our ongoing numerical example, $S_H = 10$ and $S_L = 5$, satisfies this property. Indeed, evaluating this inequality at these parameter values, we obtain

$$5 > 10 - \frac{10\sqrt{5}\left[(3 + r)^2 \, (85 + r(46 + 13r))\right]^{1/2}}{9 \, (3 + r)^2},$$

which holds for all regeneration rates $r \in [0,1]$.

Examples: This type of behavior has been observed in seven coastal communities in Loreto (Mexico) where fishermen reduced their appropriation when new firms showed an interest in exploiting the fishing ground. In this type of small-scale fishery, it is reasonable to assume that local fishermen have more accurate information about the available stock, as in the model we consider in this chapter, than fishermen operating at different locations. Under-exploitation has also been observed in other fishing grounds, such as those of the yellowfin sole in the Pacific Northwest, the blackfin tuna and diamond black squid in the Caribbean region, and the Argentine anchovy in the Southern Atlantic; see Haughton (2002) and Food and Agriculture Organization (2005).

7.4.1 Pooling Effort

The decrease in exploitation that the high-stock incumbent exerts to mimic the low-stock firm, and thus deter entry, can be interpreted as its "pooling effort." Specifically, this effort is measured by the difference

$$
\begin{aligned}
\text{Pooling effort} &= x_{H,E} - x_{L,NE} \\
&= \frac{S_H\left[9 - \delta(1-r)\right]}{18} - \frac{S_L\left[4 - \delta(1-r)\right]}{8} \\
&= \frac{4S_H\left[9 - \delta(1-r)\right] - 9S_L\left[4 - \delta(1-r)\right]}{72}.
\end{aligned}
$$

As for the separating effort, this pooling effort suggests a strategic conservation that the high-stock incumbent exerts seeking to deter potential entrants. Figure 7.3 plots the appropriation level that the high-stock incumbent chooses under complete information, $x_{H,E}$, the appropriation it selects under the pooling equilibrium, $x_{L,NE}$, and the pooling effort, $x_{H,E} - x_{L,NE}$. For illustration purposes, the figure evaluates these appropriation levels at the same parameter

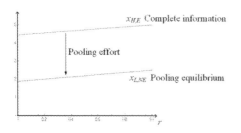

FIGURE 7.3 Pooling effort.

values as previous figures, $S_H = 10$, $S_L = 5$, and $\delta = 1$, which yield $x_{H.E} = \frac{5(8+r)}{9}$ and $x_{L.NE} = \frac{5(3+r)}{8}$, and a separating effort of $\frac{5(37-r)}{72}$.

Let us now evaluate how pooling effort is affected by changes in the parameter values (that is, let us do some comparative statics). The pooling effort is:

1. Increasing in the high stock S_H, as the incumbent needs to decrease its first-period appropriation more significantly to mimic the low-stock firm;
2. Decreasing in S_L, since the incumbent lowers its appropriation to a smaller extent.
3. Differentiating the pooling effort with respect to the discount factor δ we find

$$\frac{\partial \left(x_{H.E} - x_{L.NE}\right)}{\partial \delta} = -\frac{(4S_H - 9S_L)(1-\delta)}{72},$$

which is positive if $4S_H < 9S_L$, that is, if $S_H < \frac{9}{4}S_L$, meaning that the high-stock value is not extremely higher than the low-stock value. (This was the case, for instance, in our ongoing numerical example where $S_H = 10$ and $S_L = 5$, since $10 < \frac{9}{4}5 = 11.25$.) In this setting, pooling effort increases in the discount factor δ, indicating that the high-stock incumbent cares more about its future profits during the second period, and thus has stronger incentives to deter entry by undergoing a costly underexploitation of the resource today.

4. Differentiating the pooling effort with respect to the regeneration rate, r, we obtain

$$\frac{\partial \left(x_{H.E} - x_{L.NE}\right)}{\partial r} = \frac{\delta(4S_H - 9S_L)}{72},$$

which is negative if the above condition, $S_H < \frac{9}{4}S_L$, holds, suggesting that the pooling effort is decreasing in the regeneration rate, r. Intuitively, the high-stock firm is less willing to mimic the low-stock incumbent when the CPR regenerates faster. In that setting, the commons becomes more attractive, even if the high-stock incumbent shares it with another firm, entailing that the former has fewer incentives to undergo a (costly) pooling effort during the first period to deter entry in the next period.

7.4.2 Efficiency Properties

Under complete information, the high-stock incumbent overexploits the resource in the first period (dynamic inefficiency) and in the second (once entry occurs, where a static inefficiency arises). Under incomplete information, entry is deterred, thus eliminating the emergence of the static inefficiency during the second period. However, in the first period, the incumbent chooses a first-period exploitation below that under complete information, but not necessarily at the socially optimal level.

In this setting, we cannot identify a precise efficiency result: If eliminating the second-period static inefficiency offsets the first-period dynamic inefficiency, overall welfare increases relative to the complete information environment. Otherwise, welfare would be lower under incomplete than complete information.[4] Interestingly, in the first case, our results would suggest that regulatory agencies perfectly informed about the available stock should *not* disseminate information to potential entrants, since the incomplete-information setting is welfare superior. In the second case, in contrast, distributing information about the available stock becomes welfare enhancing.

7.5   WHAT IF THE REGULATOR IS UNINFORMED?

Our previous policy implications, both in separating and pooling equilibria, assume that the regulator is as perfectly informed about the available stock as the incumbent. This can occur in CPRs where the regulator closely monitors appropriation levels for decades and has access to similar technology as the incumbent. The potential entrant, in contrast, has little experience in the CPR (or in similar CPRs) thus not being able to observe the available stock as accurately as the incumbent and regulator.

In other settings, however, the regulator may have just started to monitor the incumbent's appropriation level, or may not have access to the same type of technology as the incumbent. In some contexts, the regulator may actually be as poorly informed as the potential entrant, implying that they cannot choose to strategically disseminate information about the available stock to the entrant,

---

[4] We do not discuss efficiency results for the low-stock incumbent since this type of firm chooses the same appropriation level across both information contexts.

since they do not have more information than the entrant! Espinola-Arredondo (2013b) investigate the regulator's role in this setting, which we describe in this section.

Separating Equilibrium: In the separating equilibrium analyzed in Section 7.3, first-period appropriation is lower than under complete information (recall that the low-stock incumbent underexploits the CPR to reveal its type to the potential entrant), $x_L < x_{L,NE}$. However, the increase in second-period appropriation, $q_L(x_L) > q_L(x_{L,NE})$, is relatively larger, yielding an overall increase in the exploitation of the resource, that is,

$$x_L + q_L(x_L) > x_{L,NE} + q_L(x_{L,NE}).$$

This result suggests the separating equilibrium gives rise to two welfare effects: (1) an increase in consumer surplus, since overall appropriation is larger; and (2) a reduction in the incumbent's profits, given that the firm needs to underexploit the commons to deter entry. When the first (positive) effect dominates the second (negative) effect, overall welfare is greater in the separating equilibrium than under complete information.

Pooling Equilibrium: In the pooling equilibrium discussed in Section 7.4, first- and second-period appropriation is lower than under complete information.[5] Overall exploitation is then smaller in the pooling equilibrium than under complete information, yielding the opposite welfare effects than in the separating equilibrium: (a) a decrease in consumer surplus given that overall exploitation is now smaller; and (b) an increase in the incumbent's profits, since otherwise this firm would not be underexploiting the resource to deter entry. When the second (positive) effect in (b) dominates the first (negative) effect in (a), the pooling equilibrium yields a greater welfare than under complete information.

---

[5] Formally, $x_{H,NE} < x_{H,E}$ in the first period, and $q_H(x_{H,NE}) < q_H(x_{H,E}) + q_H(x_{H,E})$ in the second period. In the pooling equilibrium, we only consider the incumbent's second-period appropriation since this firm successfully deters entry, while under complete information we account for both the incumbent's and the entrant's second-period appropriation since entry ensues.

7.5.1 *Welfare Comparisons*

Combining our welfare comparisons in the separating and pooling equilibria, and recalling that the regulator is uninformed about the value of the stock, different cases emerge:

1. *Both types of equilibria generate a lower welfare than under complete information.* This means that firms' strategic appropriation under incomplete information yields an unambiguous welfare loss *regardless* of the value of the stock. In this context, regulatory authorities have incentives to incur the cost of researching the available stock, and subsequently publicizing this information in media outlets, thus changing the structure of the game from incomplete to complete information.

2. *Both types of equilibria generate a greater welfare than under complete information.* In this case, firms' appropriation under incomplete information yields an unambiguous welfare gain *regardless* of the value of the stock. Unlike in the first case, the regulator now does not have incentives to investigate the available stock and distribute that information among potential entrants. Instead, keeping them in the dark is welfare superior!

3. *Only the separating (pooling) equilibrium yields a welfare gain.* In this setting, firms' strategic appropriation under incomplete information generates a greater welfare than under complete information, but only when the stock is low (high, respectively). The regulator can carry out research on the available stock, disseminating its findings only when the stock is scarce (abundant).[6]

7.6   EXERCISES

7.1 Separating equilibrium when the potential entrant enjoys a cost advantage. Consider the separating equilibrium we found in Section 7.3. Assume now that the potential entrant enjoys a cost advantage relative to the incumbent, so its cost function is $C_2(q_1, q_2) = \alpha \frac{q_2(q_1+q_2)}{S-(1-r)x}$, where $\alpha \in [1/2, 1]$ measures this firm's cost advantage. Intuitively, if $\alpha = 1$ the potential entrant does not benefit from a cost advantage, but otherwise it does.

---

[6] This strategy is, however, problematic, since the absence of information dissemination from the regulator would also reveal the stock's value to the potential entrant if this firm knows that the regulator conducted research on the stock. To prevent this possibility, the regulator's research should not be publicly known.

Repeating the analysis in Section 7.3, identify the incentive compatibility condition for the high-stock incumbent and for the low-stock incumbent. Then use these two conditions to find the appropriation level that each type of incumbent chooses in the separating equilibrium. For simplicity, you can consider the same parameter values as in the chapter, namely, no discounting, $S_H = 10$, and $S_L = 5$.

(a) How are your equilibrium results affected by parameter α? Interpret your results.

(b) Show that when $\alpha = 1$ your results coincide with those in Section 7.3.

7.2 **Pooling equilibrium when the potential entrant enjoys a cost advantage.** Repeat your analysis in Exercise 7.1, but now identifying the pooling equilibrium.

7.3 **Considering a different second-period cost function.** Chapters 3, 4, and 7 considered a second-period cost function that yields tractable first- and second-period equilibrium appropriation. Another second-period cost function used in the literature is

$$C_i(q_i, q_j) = \frac{q_i(q_i + q_j)}{S(1 + g) - x},$$

where $g \geq 0$ denotes the growth rate of the initial stock, S, and x represents the incumbent's first-period appropriation. Intuitively, when $g = 0$, the stock does not regenerate and the net stock available at the beginning of the second period is $S - x$, as captured by the denominator of the cost function. In contrast, when $g = \frac{x}{S}$ the stock is fully recovered, so the initial stock S is available again at the beginning of the second period. In this case, the second-period cost function is symmetric to that in the first period, simplifying to $\frac{q_i(q_i + q_j)}{S}$.

(a) Repeat the analysis of Section 7.3 to find appropriation levels in the separating equilibrium of the game.

(b) Repeat the analysis of Section 7.4 to find appropriation levels in the pooling equilibrium of the game.

7.4 **Separating equilibrium with market power.** Consider the study of separating equilibria in Section 7.3. Assume now that firms face a linear inverse demand function $p(x) = 1 - x$ in the first period, and

$p(Q) = 1 - Q$ in the second period. For simplicity, assume that $S_H = 10$, $S_L = 5$, $\delta = 1$, and $r = \frac{1}{4}$. Repeating the analysis in Section 7.3, answer the following questions.

(a) Identify the incentive compatibility condition for the high-stock incumbent and for the low-stock incumbent.

(b) Use the two conditions of part (a) to find the appropriation level that each type of incumbent chooses in the separating equilibrium.

(c) How do your results differ from those in Section 7.3? Interpret your results.

7.5 **Pooling equilibrium with market power.** Consider the study of pooling equilibria in Section 7.4. Assume now that firms face a linear inverse demand function $p(x) = 1 - x$ in the first period, and $p(Q) = 1 - Q$ in the second period. For simplicity, assume that $S_H = 10$, $S_L = 5$, $\delta = 1$, and $r = \frac{1}{4}$. Repeating the analysis in Section 7.4, answer the following questions:

(a) Identify the incentive compatibility condition for the high-stock incumbent and for the low-stock incumbent.

(b) Use the two conditions from part (a) to find the appropriation level that both types of incumbent select in the pooling equilibrium.

(c) How do your results differ from those in Section 7.4? Interpret your results.

7.6 **Welfare evaluation under different information contexts.** In this exercise we seek to evaluate the welfare that arises under complete information, in the separating equilibrium, and in the pooling equilibrium under a specific set of parameter values. We then rank them to understand if keeping firms exploiting the CPR under incomplete information can be welfare improving. Consider, for simplicity, the same parameter values as in previous sections of this chapter, $S_H = 10$, $S_L = 5$, $\delta = 1$, and $r = \frac{1}{4}$.

(a) Find the welfare that arises under complete information. You will need to find two numbers, one in the case that the stock is high and another when it is low.

(b) Find the welfare that emerges in the separating equilibrium of the game. In this setting, you only need to find welfare when the stock is low, as that when the stock is high coincides with that under complete information.

(c) Find the welfare that emerges in the pooling equilibrium of the game. In this context, you only need to find welfare when the stock is high, as that when the stock is low coincides with that under complete information.

(d) Compare the welfare you found in parts (a)–(c). Which of the cases 1–3 discussed in Subsection 7.5.1 emerges? Interpret your results.

APPENDIX A   Game Theory Tools

We next provide a list of basic tools on game theory that are recurrently used throughout this book. For a more detailed presentation, see Tadelis (2013) and Muñoz-Garcia and Toro-Gonzalez (2019).

A.1   BACKGROUND

Consider a setting with $N \geq 2$ players (e.g., firms exploiting a CPR), each choosing a strategy s_i from a set of available strategies S_i (known as the "strategy set"). In a CPR context, strategy s_i represents the tons of fish that fisherman i appropriates out of the range of feasible appropriation levels. For instance, if it is technologically impossible to appropriate more than 10 tons of fish, the strategy set would be the real numbers between 0 and 10, i.e., $S_i = [0, 10]$. Similarly, let s_j represent player j's strategy, where $j \neq i$, from his strategy set S_j, which may differ from player i's, S_i, if each firm has access to different technologies; otherwise, $S_i = S_j = S$. For compactness, we often use (s_i, s_{-i}) to denote a strategy profile where player i chooses s_i while his rivals select s_{-i}, defined as

$$s_{-i} \equiv (s_1, s_2, \ldots, s_{i-1}, s_{i+1}, \cdots, s_N).$$

Finally, we assume that players are rational, meaning that they seek to maximize their payoff function, and that this is common knowledge. In a two-player game, this entails that player 1 tries to maximize his payoff, that player 2 knows that player 1 seeks to maximize his payoff, that player 1 knows that player 2 knows that he seeks to maximize his payoff ...and, so on, ad infinitum. Intuitively, this will help each player put himself in his rival's shoes, anticipating the actions that his rival chooses. For compactness, we refer to this assumption as "common knowledge of rationality."

The following subsections present different solution concepts that seek to predict how players behave (e.g., which specific appropriation levels they choose) by relying on different behavioral assumptions.

A.2 STRICTLY DOMINATED STRATEGIES

In this first solution concept, rather than focusing on which specific strategies each player chooses to maximize his payoff, we seek to delete those strategies that a rational player would never select.

> **Strictly Dominated Strategy:** Player i finds strategy s_i to strictly dominate strategy s_i' if
>
> $$u_i(s_i, s_{-i}) > u_i(s_i', s_{-i})$$
>
> for every strategy profile s_{-i} of player i's rivals.

Intuitively, strategy s_i yields a higher payoff than s_i' regardless of the strategy chosen by the player's rivals. In other words, a strictly dominated strategy s_i' yields a strictly lower payoff regardless of his rivals' choice and, hence, we should expect a rational player to never choose such a strategy. We can, essentially, delete strictly dominated strategies from player i's strategy set, reducing the list of potential strategies this player considers.

Example A.1 illustrates how to find strictly dominated strategies in a two-player game.

Example A.1. Finding dominated strategies: Matrix A.1 considers a setting in which two firms simultaneously and independently choose their appropriation levels, High, Medium, or Low, denoted as H, M, or L for firm 1 (in rows), and h, m, or l for firm 2 (in columns).

		Firm 2		
		h	m	l
	H	2, 2	3, 1	5, 0
Firm 1	M	1, 3	2, 2	2.5, 2.5
	L	0, 5	2.5, 2.5	3, 3

Matrix A.1 *Strictly dominated strategies in the appropriation game.*

We can easily show that L is strictly dominated for firm 1 because it yields a strictly lower payoff than H when firm 2 chooses h in the left column (since $0 < 2$), m in the middle column (given that $2.5 < 3$), and l in the right-hand column (given that $3 < 5$). A similar argument applies to row M, because it yields a strictly lower payoff than H when firm 2 chooses h in the left column (since $1 < 2$), m in the middle column (given that $2 < 3$), and l in the right-hand column (given that $2.5 < 5$).

Therefore, strategies M and L are both strictly dominated by H. As payoffs are symmetric across firms, a similar argument applies to firm 2, which finds strategies m and l to be strictly dominated by h. $\square$

If player i finds that strategy s_i strictly dominates all his other available strategies we then say that s_i is a *strictly dominant* strategy, and we would expect him to choose that strategy, as defined below.

> **Strictly Dominant Strategy**: Player i finds strategy s_i to be strictly dominant if
>
> $$u_i(s_i, s_{-i}) > u_i(s_i', s_{-i})$$
>
> for every strategy $s_i' \in S_i$ and every strategy profile s_{-i} of player i's rivals.

Intuitively, all of his available strategies yield a strictly lower payoff than s_i regardless of the strategy profile his rivals select, and can thus be deleted, leaving him with only one surviving strategy, s_i. This strategy, then, provides player i with an unambiguously higher payoff than any of his available strategies (that is, regardless of the strategy his opponents select). In Example A.1, strategy H is strictly dominant for firm 1 as it yields a strictly higher payoff than all other strategies for this firm (i.e., a strictly higher payoff than both M and L). Similarly, strategy h is strictly dominant for firm 2.

As a remark, you may have noted the similarities between the definition of a strictly dominant strategy and that of a strictly dominated strategy. However, the former requires strategy s_i to yield a strictly higher payoff than all of the other strategies player i can choose from (i.e., every s_i' in S_i), while the latter only requires strategy s_i to impose a strictly higher payoff than another strategy s_i'.

A.3   ITERATIVE DELETION OF STRICTLY DOMINATED STRATEGIES

From rationality, we know that a player would never use strictly dominated strategies, so we can delete them from his strategy set. We can then proceed by using the definition of common knowledge of rationality, which in this context entails that every player i can put himself in his opponent's shoes, identify all strictly dominated strategies for his opponent (player j), and delete them from j's strategy set. We can, of course, proceed one more step: Player i can find which strategies survived this iterated deletion of strictly dominated strategies (IDSDS) and then remove any strategies that he finds to be strictly dominated at this point. The process continues until no player can identify any further strictly dominated strategies to delete. The remaining strategies are referred to as the strategy profile/s surviving IDSDS.

In Matrix A.1, the use of IDSDS yields a unique surviving stratcgy profile, (H, h), with associated payoff pair $(2, 2)$. In other games, however, the use of IDSDS does not necessarily provide such a precise equilibrium prediction, but rather two or more strategy profiles.

Example A.2. When IDSDS Does Not Provide a Unique Equilibrium: Consider Matrix A.2 as representing the appropriation decision of two firms. Starting IDSDS with firm 1, we find that H is strictly dominated by L, since it yields a lower payoff than L regardless of the appropriation that firm 2 chooses (i.e., independently of the column that firm 2 selects).

	Firm 2		
	h	m	l
H	2, 3	1, 4	3, 2
M	5, 3	2, 1	1, 2
L	3, 6	4, 7	5, 4

Firm 1

Matrix A.2 *When IDSDS yields more than one equilibrium – I.*

After deleting the strictly dominated strategy High from firm 1's rows in Matrix A.2, we are left with the reduced Matrix A.3, which only has two rows. We put ourselves in firm 2's shoes, to see if we can find a strictly dominated strategy for this firm. Specifically, l is strictly dominated by h, since l yields a strictly lower payoff than h regardless of the row that firm 1 selects.

	Firm 2		
	h	m	l
M	5, 3	2, 1	1, 2
L	3, 6	4, 7	5, 4

Firm 1

Matrix A.3 *When IDSDS yields more than one equilibrium – II.*

After deleting column l from firm 2's strategies, we are left with a further reduced matrix (see Matrix A.4). We can now focus our attention on firm 1 again. At this point, however, we cannot identify any more strictly dominated strategies for this firm since there is no strategy (no row in Matrix A.4) yielding a lower payoff regardless of the column firm 2 plays.[1]

[1] Indeed, firm 1 prefers M to L if firm 2 chooses h (in the left column) since $5 > 3$, but prefers L to M if firm 2 chooses m (in the right-hand column) given that $4 > 2$. A similar argument applies to firm 2, since there is no strategy (column) yielding a lower payoff regardless of the row that firm 1 selects.

Firm 2

		h	m
Firm 1	M	5,3	2,1
	L	3,6	4,7

Matrix A.4 *When IDSDS yields more than one equilibrium-III.*

Therefore, the remaining four cells in Matrix A.4 are our equilibrium prediction after applying IDSDS:

$$(M,h),(M,m),(L,h),(L,m)$$

entailing four possible outcomes. Importantly, the order of deletion does not affect the strategy profiles surviving IDSDS. As a practice, you can redo this example but starting with firm 2, trying to delete strictly dominated strategies, and then moving to firm 1. □

In some games, players may have no strictly dominated strategies that we can delete using IDSDS, which is often described as that IDSDS "does not have a bite." In this class of games, and generally in those where IDSDS provides a relatively imprecise equilibrium prediction like in Example A.2, we can apply the Nash equilibrium solution concept that we define in Section A.5, which offers the same (or more precise) equilibrium predictions than IDSDS. Before that definition, we briefly discuss weak dominance.

A.4   WEAKLY DOMINATED STRATEGIES

In some games, player i may find that his payoff from two strategies, s_i and s_i', may coincide, which yields the following weaker version of the definition of strictly dominated strategies in Section A.3.

Weakly Dominated Strategies: Player i finds strategy s_i to weakly dominate another strategy s_i' if

$$u_i(s_i, s_{-i}) \geq u_i(s_i', s_{-i})$$

for every strategy profile s_{-i} of player i's rivals, and $u_i(s_i, s_{-i}) > u_i(s_i', s_{-i})$ for at least one strategy profile s_{-i}.

Therefore, we say that player i finds that strategy s_i weakly dominates another strategy s_i' if choosing s_i provides her with a strictly higher payoff than selecting s_i' for at least one of his rivals' strategies but provides the same payoff as s_i' for the remaining strategies of his rivals.

Matrix A.5 presents a version of the appropriation game where we altered firm 1's payoffs from choosing M. Given these changes, we can claim that strategy H weakly dominates M for firm 1 because H yields the same payoff as M when firm 2 chooses h in the left column, and when it chooses m in the middle column, but H still yields a strictly higher payoff than M when firm 2 selects l in the right-hand column. If firm 1's payoffs coincide in H and M for every strategy of firm 2 (i.e., for every column), we would not be able to claim that H weakly dominates M.[2]

Firm 2

		h	m	l
	H	2,2	3,2	5,0
Firm 1	M	2,3	3,2	2.5,2.5
	L	0,5	2.5,2.5	3,3

Matrix A.5 *Equilibrium dominance in the appropriation game.*

A.5 NASH EQUILIBRIUM

In this section, we present a different solution concept that may have "more bite" than IDSDS. Fewer strategy profiles can, then, emerge as equilibria of the game. This solution concept, known as the Nash Equilibrium after Nash (1950), builds upon the notion that every player finds his best response to each of his rivals' strategies and, hence, we start with the definition of best response.

Best Response: Player i regards strategy s_i as a best response to strategy profile s_{-i}, if

$$u_i(s_i, s_{-i}) \geq u_i(s_i', s_{-i})$$

for every available strategy $s_i' \in S_i$.

Intuitively, in a two-player game, strategy s_i is a best response to player j's strategy, s_j, if, given player i's type, strategy s_i yields a weakly higher payoff than

[2] If we delete strategies that are weakly dominated for firm 1 and then move to delete those that are weakly dominated for firm 2, we may end up with a different list of surviving strategy profiles than if we start with firm 2 and then proceed with firm 1. In summary, the order of deletion matters when applying weak dominance, as opposed to IDSDS where the order of deletion does not matter. For this reason, IDSDS is more generally used than weak dominance.

any other strategy s_i' against s_j. In other words, when player j chooses s_j, player i maximizes his payoff by responding with s_i.

We next use the concept of best response to define a Nash Equilibrium.

> **Nash Equilibrium (NE)**: A strategy profile (s_i^*, s_{-i}^*) is a Nash Equilibrium if every player chooses a best response given her rivals' strategies.

In a two-player game, strategy s_i^* is player i's best response to s_j^* and, similarly, strategy s_j^* is player j's best response to s_i^*. Therefore, a strategy profile is an NE if it is a *mutual* best response: The strategy that player i chooses is a best response to that selected by player j, and vice versa. As a result, no player has unilateral incentives to deviate since doing so would lower his payoff, or keep it unchanged.[3] Example A.3 illustrates how to find an NE in the matrix we found at the end of Example A.2.

Example A.3. Finding NEs: Matrix A.6 reproduces Matrix A.4 from Example A.2 after applying IDSDS. We can first find the best responses of firm 1.

Firm 1's best responses. When firm 2 chooses h, firm 1's best response is M since $5 > 3$, which we compactly write as $BR_1(h) = M$. In contrast, when firm 2 chooses m, firm 1's best response is $BR_1(m) = L$ since $4 > 2$. These best response payoffs are underlined in Matrix A.6 (first element in every payoff pair) for easier reference.

Firm 2

		h	m
Firm 1	M	$\underline{5}, 3$	$2, 1$
	L	$3, 6$	$\underline{4}, \underline{7}$

Matrix A.6 *Finding best responses and NEs.*

Firm 2's best responses. We now focus on firm 2's best responses. When firm 1 chooses M, firm 2's best response is $BR_2(M) = m$ since $3 > 1$. However, when firm 1 chooses L, firm 2's best response is $BR_2(L) = h$ because $7 > 6$.

Therefore, the two cells with both payoffs underlined mean that firm 1 and 2 are playing best responses or, in other words, they are playing mutual best

---

[3] Another common definition of a Nash equilibrium is by focusing on every player i's beliefs about how his rivals behave. Using that approach, a Nash equilibrium is a system of beliefs (that is, a list of beliefs for each player) and a list of actions satisfying two properties: (1) every player uses a best response to his beliefs about how his rivals behave; and (2) the beliefs that players sustain are, in equilibrium, correct. For simplicity, however, we focus on the above definition.

responses to each other's strategies, which is the definition of NE. In summary, we found two NEs: (M, h) and (L, m). Comparing our results against those in Example A.2, where we found that four strategy profiles survived IDSDS, we can claim that the NE solution concept offered more precise equilibrium predictions than IDSDS did. □

A.6   SUBGAME PERFECT EQUILIBRIUM

In sequential-move games, the NE solution concept can identify equilibria that are not sequentially rational, that is, strategies that do not maximize a player's payoff given: (1) the stage of the game when he is called to move, and (2) the information he observes at that point. (For a more detailed discussion about this point, see Muñoz-Garcia, 2017, section 8.1.2). We then need a new solution concept that guarantees sequential rationality in all nodes of the game tree.

Before introducing this new solution concept, we need to define subsets of the entire game tree, where we will require players to behave optimally. Specifically, a *subgame* is a tree structure defined by a node and all its successors.[4] We are now ready to use the definition of subgame, as a part of the game tree, to characterize a new solution concept in sequential-move games.

> **Subgame Perfect Equilibrium (SPE):** A strategy profile (s_i^*, s_{-i}^*) is a Subgame Perfect Equilibrium if it specifies an NE in each subgame.

To find SPEs in a sequential-move game, we apply the notion of "backward induction," namely, we start at the terminal nodes at the end of the tree, finding optimal actions for the player/s called to move in the last subgames of the game tree. Then, we move to the second-to-last mover who, anticipating equilibrium behavior in the last subgames, chooses his optimal actions. We can repeat this process by moving one step closer to the initial node, successively finding equilibrium behavior in subgames as each player can anticipate how players behave in the subgames that unfold in subsequent stages.

Example A.4 applies this definition to a small game tree.

Example A.4. Applying Backward Induction: Consider a game between a potential entrant, choosing whether to enter the CPR where an incumbent firm operates, or staying out. If the entrant stays out, the incumbent keeps a monopoly profit of

---

[4] This means that if node a is connected to another node b with an information set (so player i does not know whether he is at node a or b), both of these nodes must be part of the same subgame. Graphically, the circle around a subgame cannot break any players' information set.

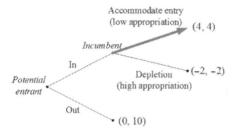

FIGURE A.1 Backward induction in the entry game.

10 while the entrant earns 0 profits. If the entrant joins the CPR, the incumbent then has the opportunity to respond, accommodating such entry by lowering its appropriation of the resource (which entails a profit of 4 to each firm) or fighting the entry through higher appropriation (which yields losses of 2 to each firm as the resource becomes depleted). Figure A.1 depicts this sequential-move game, with the potential entrant being the first mover and the incumbent the second mover. Note that, in this game, the only proper subgame is that initiated after the potential entrant joins the CPR, other than the entire game as a whole.

Applying backward induction, we first focus on the last mover, the incumbent. Comparing its payoff from accommodating entry, 4, and starting to deplete the resource, −2, we find that its best response to entry is to accommodate. We shade the branch corresponding to *Accommodate* in Figure A.1 to keep in mind the optimal response of the incumbent in this subgame.

We now move to the first mover, the entrant, who can anticipate the incumbent's subsequent choices if the entrant were to enter. As a consequence, the entrant can expect that, if it chooses to enter, the incumbent will respond with accommodation since such a strategy yields a higher payoff for the incumbent than the depletion of the CPR. Graphically, the entrant can understand that, if it enters, the game will proceed through the shaded branch of accommodation, ultimately yielding a payoff of 4 from entering. If, instead, the entrant stays out, its payoff is only 0 and, as a consequence, the optimal strategy for the entrant is to enter. We then say that the SPE after applying backward induction is

{*Enter, Accommodate*},

which indicates that the first mover (entrant) chooses to enter, and the second mover (incumbent) responds by accommodating, entailing equilibrium payoffs of (4,4). □

A.7 BAYESIAN NASH EQUILIBRIUM

In some contexts, players interact in games where at least one of them is uninformed about some relevant information, such as its rival's production costs in an oligopoly game or the available stock in a CPR. More generally, we say that, in a game of incomplete information, every player i observes its type, θ_i, where $\theta_i \in \Theta_i$, which may represent, for instance, a high or low cost of production, $\theta_i \in \{H, L\}$, but does not observe its rival's type θ_j. Players, however, know the probability distribution over types, e.g., firm i knows that its rival's type is either $\theta_j = H$ with probability q and $\theta_j = L$ with probability $1 - q$, and this information is common knowledge, where $q \in [0, 1]$. Therefore, in a simultaneous-move game, every player i's strategy must be a function of their observed type, θ_i, which we refer to as "type-dependent" and denote as $s_i(\theta_i)$.

We are now ready to adapt the definition of an NE to this incomplete information setting, by first defining a best response in this context. For compactness, let

$$\theta_{-i} = \left(\theta_1, \theta_2, \ldots, \theta_{i-1}, \theta_{i+1}, \ldots, \theta_N\right)$$

denote the profile of types by player i's rivals.

Best Response under Incomplete Information: Player i regards strategy s_i as a best response to strategy profile s_{-i}, if

$$EU_i(s_i(\theta_i), s_{-i}(\theta_{-i})) \geq EU_i(s_i'(\theta_i), s_{-i}(\theta_{-i}))$$

for every available strategy $s_i'(\theta_i) \in S_i$ and every type $\theta_i \in \Theta_i$.

Intuitively, in a two-player game, player i finds strategy $s_i(\theta_i)$ to be a best response to player j's strategy, $s_j(\theta_j)$, if, given player i's type, strategy s_i yields a weakly higher *expected* payoff than any other strategy s_i' against s_j. In other words, when player j chooses s_j, player i maximizes his payoff by responding with s_i as opposed to any other of his available strategies.

We next use the concept of best response to define a Bayesian Nash Equilibrium.

Bayesian Nash Equilibrium (BNE): A strategy profile $(s_i^*(\theta_i), s_{-i}^*(\theta_{-i}))$ is a Bayesian Nash Equilibrium if every player chooses a best response (in expectation) given his rivals' strategies.

Therefore, in a two-player game, a strategy profile is a BNE if it is a *mutual* best response, thus being analogous to the definition of an NE: the strategy that player i chooses is a best response to that selected by player j, and vice versa. As a result, no player has unilateral incentives to deviate.

For a detailed analysis of how to apply BNE in simultaneous-move games, see Muñoz-Garcia and Toro-Gonzalez (2019, chapter 7).

A.8   PERFECT BAYESIAN EQUILIBRIUM

When we consider sequential-move games under incomplete information, the application of BNE can lead to a large number of equilibria, some of them prescribing sequentially irrational behavior. Hence, it displays similar problems as when one applies the NE solution concept to solve sequential-move games of complete information.

> **Perfect Bayesian Equilibrium (PBE)**: A strategy profile $(s_i^*(\theta_i), s_{-i}^*(\theta_{-i}))$ and a system of beliefs (μ_i, μ_{-i}) over all information sets is a Perfect Bayesian Equilibrium if:
>
> (a) Every player i's strategies specify optimal actions at each information set where he is called to move, given the strategies of the other players, and given player i's beliefs μ_i.
>
> (b) Beliefs (μ_i, μ_{-i}) are consistent with Bayes' rule, whenever possible.

Intuitively, condition (a) is symmetric to the definition of BNE given that it requires every player i to choose best responses to his rivals' strategies under incomplete information, which in this case means given his beliefs about other players' types.

Condition (b), however, states that every player's beliefs must be consistent with Bayes' rule, which is only possible along the equilibrium path, that is, at information sets that are reached in equilibrium. In contrast, when player i is called to move in an information set that should not be reached in equilibrium, he cannot use Bayes' rule to update his beliefs of his rivals' types. We refer to these beliefs as "off-the-equilibrium" beliefs and, because we cannot use Bayes' rule to update them, we can specify any value to them in our search of the conditions that sustain a PBE.

In this class of games, it is common to find *separating* PBEs, where the first mover, privately informed about its type, chooses a type-dependent strategy. Formally, player i's strategy satisfies

$$s_i^*(\theta_i) \neq s_i^*(\theta_i') \text{ for any two types } \theta_i \neq \theta_i'.$$

As this player selects a different strategy for each of his types, other players can infer the first mover's type by observing his actions. Intuitively, actions are signals that convey the first mover's type to the second mover. As a result, these strategy profiles are often known as "informative" equilibria, as they lead to information transmission from the informed player (first mover) to the uninformed player (second mover).

We can also search for *pooling* PBEs where, in contrast, the first mover chooses a type-independent strategy, that is,

$$s_i^*(\theta_i) = s_i^*(\theta_i') \text{ for any two types } \theta_i \neq \theta_i'.$$

In this context, other players cannot use the first mover's actions to infer his type or, in other words, this player conceals his type from his rivals. As a consequence, these strategy profiles are also known as "uninformative" equilibria.

For more details about how to apply the PBE solution concept in sequential-move games, see Muñoz-Garcia and Toro-Gonzalez (2019, chapters 9 and 10).

APPENDIX B   Solutions to Selected End-of-Chapter Exercises

CHAPTER 2 – COMMON POOL EESOURCES IN A STATIC SETTING

Exercise 2.1 – Allowing for Different Cost Externalities

2.1 Consider the setting in Section 2.3 and, for simplicity, assume $N = 2$ firms. In addition, consider that every firm's cost function is

$$C_i(q_i, q_j) = \frac{q_i(q_i + \theta q_j)}{S},$$

where $\theta \geq 0$ denotes the severity of the cost externality. When $\theta = 0$, firm i's costs are unaffected by its rival's appropriation q_j, whereas when $\theta > 0$, firm i's costs are affected by q_j. As a remark, note that our setting in Section 2.3 can be interpreted as a special case of this more general model, where $\theta = 1$.

(a) Find every firm i's best response function, $q_i(q_j)$.

- Each firm chooses its appropriation level q_i to solve

$$\max_{q_i \geq 0} \pi_i = q_i - \frac{q_i(q_i + \theta q_j)}{S}.$$

Following Section 2.3, we normalize the price of the good to \$1. Differentiating with respect to q_i, we obtain

$$1 - \frac{2q_i + \theta q_j}{S} = 0.$$

To find the best response function, we first rearrange the equation to $S = 2q_i + \theta q_j$, and solving for q_i we find

$$q_i(q_j) = \frac{S}{2} - \frac{\theta}{2} q_j.$$

This indicates that appropriation levels are strategic substitutes, that is, an increase in firm j's appropriation induces a reduction in firm i's.

(b) How is $q_i(q_j)$ affected by an increase in parameter θ? Interpret.

- Differentiating $q_i(q_j)$ with respect to θ, we obtain that

$$\frac{\partial q_i(q_j)}{\partial \theta} = -\frac{q_j}{2}.$$

Therefore, when firm j appropriates one more unit, it affects firm i's cost more significantly as the severity of the cost externality, θ, increases. This intuition goes in line with our interpretation in part (a).

(c) Find the equilibrium appropriation q_i^*.

- In a symmetric equilibrium, appropriation levels satisfy $q_i = q_j = q_i^*$. Every firm i's best response function is

$$q_i^* = \frac{S}{2} - \frac{\theta}{2}q_i^*.$$

Rearranging yields $(1 + \theta/2)q_i^* = \frac{S}{2}$, or, multiplying both sides by 2, $(2 + \theta)q_i^* = S$. Finally, solving for q_i^*, we obtain the equilibrium appropriation

$$q_i^* = \frac{S}{2 + \theta}.$$

Therefore, as the stock becomes more abundant (higher S), equilibrium appropriation increases.

(d) How is q_i^* affected by an increase in parameter θ? Interpret.

- An increase in θ decreases the equilibrium appropriation. We can find the exact amount by which it decreases by taking a derivative:

$$\frac{\partial q_i^*}{\partial \theta} = -\frac{S}{(2 + \theta)^2} < 0.$$

A higher θ increases the negative externality from the other firm's exploitation of the resource, which increases the marginal cost for firm i. The increase in marginal cost (absent a change in the price, or marginal revenue, of the good) reduces the equilibrium appropriation from the firm.

Exercise 2.3 – Finding Socially Optimal Appropriation in a CPR with N Firms

2.3 Consider the setting in Section 2.4.1, which assumed a CPR with $N = 2$ firms. Repeat the analysis allowing for $N \geq 2$ firms.

(a) Find the socially optimal appropriation q_i^{SO}.

- In the case of $N \geq 2$ firms, the social planner solves

$$\max_{q_1,\dots,q_N} W = \sum_{i=1}^{N} \pi_i = \sum_{i=1}^{N}\left(q_i - \frac{q_i(q_i + Q_{-i})}{S}\right).$$

To find the first-order condition, it is helpful to rewrite the problem as

$$\max_{q_1,\dots,q_N \geq 0} W = \left(q_i - \frac{q_i(q_i + Q_{-i})}{S} \right)$$

$$+ \sum_{j \neq i} \left(q_j - \frac{q_j(q_j + Q_{-j})}{S} \right).$$

where $Q_{-j} \equiv \sum_{i \neq j} q_i$ denotes aggregate appropriation from all firms other than firm j. Differentiating with respect to q_i yields

$$\frac{\partial W}{\partial q_i} = 1 - \frac{2q_i + Q_{-i}}{S} - \sum_{j \neq i} \frac{q_j}{S}.$$

Note that Q_{-j} can be expressed as the sum $Q_{-j} = q_1 + q_2 + \cdots + q_{j-1} + q_{j+1} + \cdots + q_N$, thus including firm i's appropriation, q_i. Rearranging and solving for q_i, we find that

$$q_i(Q_{-i}) = \frac{S}{2} - \sum_{j \neq i} q_j$$

$$= \frac{S}{2} - Q_{-i},$$

which originates at $q_i = \frac{S}{2}$ and decreases at a rate of one for each unit of appropriation of all other firms, Q_{-i}. In a symmetric equilibrium, $q_1^{SO} = \cdots = q_N^{SO} = q_i^{SO}$ and $Q_{-i}^{SO} = \sum_{j \neq i} q_j^{SO} = (N-1)q_i^{SO}$.

Inserting this property into the above expression, we obtain that

$$q_i^{SO} = \frac{S}{2} - \underbrace{(N-1)q_i^{SO}}_{Q_{-i}^{SO}}.$$

Solving for q_i^{SO} gives the socially optimum level of appropriation

$$q_i^{SO} = \frac{S}{2N}.$$

(b) How is q_i^{SO} affected by the number of firms, N?

- To find how the socially optimal appropriation is affected by the number of firms, we take a derivative of q^{SO} with respect to N,

$$\frac{\partial q^{SO}}{\partial N} = -\frac{S}{2N^2} < 0.$$

Since this is negative, we find that the socially optimal appropriation by an individual firm decreases as the number of firms exploiting the resource increases.

Exercise 2.5 – Profit-Enhancing Appropriation Fees – I

2.5 Consider the setting in Section 2.3. Assume that a regulator sets a fee t on all firms (this is a generic fee t, rather than the socially optimal fee t^* found in Section 2.7.2).

(a) Find individual equilibrium appropriation $q^*(t)$, as a function of fee t.

- Every firm i chooses q_i to solve

$$\max_{q_i \geq 0} \; \pi_i = q_i - \frac{q_i(q_i + Q_{-i})}{S} - tq_i.$$

Differentiating with respect to q_i, yields

$$\underbrace{1}_{MR} - \underbrace{\left(\frac{2q_i + Q_{-i}}{S} + t \right)}_{MC} = 0$$

where each firm now faces the same fee t. In a symmetric equilibrium, $q_i^* = q_j^* = q^*$, which entails that $Q_{-i} = (N-1)q_i^*$. Inserting this into the first-order condition, we obtain

$$1 - \left(\frac{2q^* + (N-1)q^*}{S} + t \right) = 0.$$

Rearranging yields $1 - t = \frac{(N+1)q^*}{S}$, and then $S(1-t) = (N+1)q^*$. Solving for the individual equilibrium appropriation, we obtain

$$q^*(t) = \frac{S(1-t)}{N+1}.$$

This output is positive given that $t \in (0,1)$ by definition (note that if, instead, $t > 1$, appropriation and profits would be negative even when a single firm exploits the resource).

(b) Show that $q^*(t)$ is decreasing in fee t. How is your result affected by the number of firms, N?

- To show that $q^*(t)$ is decreasing in fee t, we can take a derivative with respect to t as follows:

$$\frac{\partial q^*(t)}{\partial t} = -\frac{S}{N+1} < 0.$$

Since S and N are both strictly positive, this derivative is negative, indicating that an increase in the fee decreases the firm's equilibrium appropriation.

- To show how $q^*(t)$ is affected by the number of firms N, we take a derivative of $q^*(t)$ with respect to N as follows:

$$\frac{\partial q^*(t)}{\partial N} = -\frac{S(1-t)}{(N+1)^2} < 0$$

since $t \in (0,1)$. This shows that the individual firm's equilibrium appropriation decreases as the number of firms increases.

(c) Show that aggregate equilibrium appropriation, $Q^*(t)$, is also decreasing in fee t. How is your result affected by the number of firms, N?

- First, the aggregate equilibrium appropriation is

$$Q^*(t) = Nq^*(t) = \frac{NS(1-t)}{N+1}.$$

Taking a derivative with respect to the fee t, we find that

$$\frac{\partial Q^*(t)}{\partial t} = -\frac{SN}{N+1} < 0.$$

So, the aggregate equilibrium appropriation is decreasing as the fee increases.

- To show how the aggregate equilibrium appropriation increases as the number of firms increases, we take the derivative of $Q^*(t)$ with respect to N as follows:

$$\frac{\partial Q^*(t)}{\partial N} = \frac{S(1-t)}{(N+1)^2} > 0$$

since $t \in (0,1)$. This means that the aggregate equilibrium appropriation increases with the number of firms in the market. Combining this with the result found in part (b), even though an individual firm's equilibrium appropriation decreases when there is an additional firm in the market, that additional firm's appropriation is greater than the decrease in all of the other firms' appropriations.

(d) Evaluate equilibrium profits $\pi^*(t)$, and find if they are increasing/decreasing in fee t. Interpret your results.

- Equilibrium profits are

$$\pi^*(t) = q^*(t) - \frac{q^*(t)(Nq^*(t))}{S} - tq^*(t)$$

$$= (1-t)q^*(t) - \frac{N}{S}(q^*(t))^2.$$

Substituting value of $q^*(t)$ yields equilibrium profit

$$\pi^*(t) = \frac{S(1-t)^2}{(N+1)^2}.$$

- Differentiating $\pi^*(t)$ with respect to fee t yields

$$\frac{\partial \pi^*(t)}{\partial t} = -\frac{2S(1-t)}{(N+1)^2} < 0$$

since $t \in (0,1)$. Intuitively, equilibrium profit decreases when the fee increases, as equilibrium appropriation declines with fee t.

Exercise 2.7 – Finding Appropriation Fees

2.7 Consider the setting in Exercise 2.2. Let us use the approach to appropriation fees we discussed in Section 2.7, as follows:

(a) Find the equilibrium appropriation $q_1(t_1)$ and $q_2(t_2)$ for each firm. (Note that each appropriation is a function of a firm-specific appropriation fee.)

- Firm 1's maximization problem is

$$\max_{q_1 \geq 0} \ \pi_1 = q_1 - \frac{q_1(q_1 + q_2)}{S} - t_1 q_1,$$

and the first-order condition is found by differentiating with respect to q_1,

$$\frac{\partial \pi_1}{\partial q_1} = 1 - \frac{2q_1 + q_2}{S} - t_1 = 0.$$

Solving for q_1, we obtain firm 1's best response function,

$$q_1(q_2) = \frac{S(1-t_1)}{2} - \frac{1}{2}q_2.$$

As in previous exercises, this best response function is increasing with the stock S and appropriation levels are strategic substitutes.

- Firm 2 has a similar maximization problem, that is,

$$\max_{q_2 \geq 0} \ \pi_2 = q_2 - \frac{\alpha q_2(q_1 + q_2)}{S} - t_2 q_2,$$

with first-order condition

$$\frac{\partial \pi_2}{\partial q_2} = 1 - \frac{\alpha(2q_2 + q_1)}{S} - t_2 = 0.$$

Solving for q_2, we find firm 2's best response function

$$q_2(q_1) = \frac{S(1-t_2)}{2\alpha} - \frac{1}{2}q_1.$$

- Next, we can solve for the equilibrium appropriation by plugging firm 2's best response function into firm 1's best response function:

$$q_1 = \frac{S(1-t_1)}{2} - \frac{1}{2}\left(\frac{S(1-t_2)}{2\alpha} - \frac{1}{2}q_1\right).$$

Solving for q_1 yields firm 1's equilibrium appropriation level

$$q_1^*(t_1) = \frac{S}{3\alpha}\left[2\alpha(1-t_1)-(1-t_2)\right].$$

- Firm 2's equilibrium appropriation level is found by plugging $q_1^*(t_1)$ into firm 2's best response function,

$$q_2 = \frac{S(1-t_2)}{2\alpha} - \frac{1}{2}\left(\frac{S}{3\alpha}\left[2\alpha(1-t_1)-(1-t_2)\right]\right).$$

Rearranging, we obtain

$$q_2^*(t_2) = \frac{S}{3\alpha}\left[2(1-t_2)-(1-t_1)\right].$$

If we set $\alpha = 1$, we find symmetric appropriations.

(b) Find the emission fee t_i that induces every firm i to appropriate q_i^{SO} units.

- First, we need to find the socially optimal appropriation by each firm, which is found by maximizing joint profits as follows:

$$\max_{q_1,q_2 \geq 0} \pi_1 + \pi_2 = \left(q_1 - \frac{q_1(q_1+q_2)}{S}\right)$$
$$+ \left(q_2 - \frac{\alpha q_2(q_1+q_2)}{S}\right).$$

Differentiating with respect to q_1 and q_2, respectively, yields

$$\frac{\partial \pi_1}{\partial q_1} = 1 - \frac{2q_1+q_2}{S} - \frac{\alpha q_2}{S} = 0$$

$$\frac{\partial \pi_2}{\partial q_2} = 1 - \frac{q_1}{S} - \frac{\alpha(2q_2+q_1)}{S} = 0.$$

Rearranging, this system of equations becomes

$$q_1 = \frac{S}{2} - \frac{1+\alpha}{2}q_2 \text{ and}$$

$$q_2 = \frac{S}{2\alpha} - \frac{1+\alpha}{2\alpha}q_1.$$

We have two cases:

- Firms are symmetric, $\alpha = 1$, and the analysis matches that of Section 2.7.2.
- Firms are asymmetric, $\alpha < 1$, and firm 2's costs are less than that of firm 1. In this second, more interesting case, only the low-cost firm 2 produces in the socially optimal equilibrium. This means that

$$q_1^{SO} = 0$$

$$q_2^{SO} = \frac{S}{2\alpha}.$$

- Now we can set the equilibrium appropriation levels $q_i^* = q_i^{SO}$ and solve the following system of equations:

$$\frac{S}{3\alpha}(2\alpha(1 - t_1) - (1 - t_2)) = 0 \text{ for firm 1 and}$$

$$\frac{S}{3\alpha}(2(1 - t_2) - (1 - t_1)) = \frac{S}{2\alpha} \text{ for firm 2.}$$

Solving for t_1 and t_2 yields

$$t_1 = \frac{3}{2(1 - 4\alpha)} + 1$$

$$t_2 = \frac{3(1 - 2\alpha)}{2(1 - 4\alpha)} - \frac{1}{2}$$

where t_1 is positive given that $\frac{3}{2(1-4\alpha)} + 1 > 0$ simplifies to $\alpha < \frac{5}{4}$, which holds given that $\alpha \in [0, 1]$ by assumption. Similarly, fee t_2 is positive since

$$\frac{3(1 - 2\alpha)}{2(1 - 4\alpha)} > \frac{1}{2}$$

simplifies to $\alpha < 1$, which is also true by definition.

(c) What happens if the regulator cannot set a firm-specific appropriation fee, (t_1, t_2), but must rather set a uniform fee t for both firms? Discuss your results.

- In the case of a uniform fee t, each firm's appropriation levels are

$$q_1^*(t) = \frac{S}{3\alpha}\left[2\alpha(1 - t) - (1 - t)\right]$$

$$= \frac{S(1 - t)(2\alpha - 1)}{3\alpha}.$$

$$q_2^*(t) = \frac{S}{3\alpha}\left[2(1 - t) - (1 - t)\right]$$

$$= \frac{S(1 - t)}{3\alpha}.$$

The regulator cannot find a unique fee that induces each firm to appropriate exactly the socially optimal level. However, it can set a uniform fee t that induces the aggregate socially optimal appropriation, as follows:

$$\frac{S(1 - t)(2\alpha - 1)}{3\alpha} + \frac{S(1 - t)}{3\alpha} = 0 + \frac{S}{2\alpha},$$

which simplifies to

$$S\left(4t - 4 + \frac{3}{\alpha}\right) = 0.$$

Solving for t, we get the uniform fee

$$t^U = 1 - \frac{3}{4\alpha},$$

which is positive if $\alpha > \frac{3}{4}$. Otherwise, the fee becomes a per-unit subsidy.

- It is easy to show that this fee does not lead firm 1 to produce the socially optimal output $q_1^{SO} = 0$, since

$$q_1^*(t^U) = \frac{S(1 - t^U)(2\alpha - 1)}{3\alpha}$$

$$= \frac{S(2\alpha - 1)}{4\alpha^2}.$$

Similarly, the uniform fee does not lead firm 2 to produce the socially optimal output $q_2^{SO} = \frac{S}{2\alpha}$, given that

$$q_2^*(t^U) = \frac{S(1 - t^U)}{3\alpha}$$

$$= \frac{S}{4\alpha^2}.$$

Therefore, while aggregate appropriation is socially optimal, its distribution between firm 1 and 2 is not efficient, namely, firm 1 appropriates a socially excessive amount while firm 2 appropriates a socially insufficient amount.

Exercise 2.9 – Equity Shares; Based on Ellis (2001) and Heintzelman et al. (2009)

2.9 Consider our discussion of equilibrium appropriation levels in Section 2.3. Assume now that, before choosing its appropriation level q_i, every firm i selects an equity share $\alpha_i \in [0, 1/2]$ into firm j's profit to solve

$$\max_{\alpha_i \geq 0} \ (1 - \alpha_j)\pi_i + \alpha_i \pi_j.$$

In words, when $\alpha_j = \alpha_i = 0$, firm i's objective function reduces to its own profits, $(1 - 0)\pi_i + 0\pi_j = \pi_i$; if $\alpha_j = 0$ but $\alpha_i > 0$, firm i's objective function is $(1 - 0)\pi_i + \alpha_i\pi_j = \pi_i + \alpha_i\pi_j$, that is, its own profits plus a share of firm j's; and if both equity shares are positive, $\alpha_j, \alpha_i > 0$, firm i maximizes a weighted average of its own and firm j's profits.

For simplicity, we next consider equity shares α_i and α_j as given (exogenous) and study how appropriation levels are affected by these shares.

(a) For a given pair of equity shares α_i and α_j, find firm i's best response function $q_i(q_j)$. This function should depend on equity shares α_i and α_j.

How is it affected by a marginal increase in α_i? And how is it affected by a marginal increase in α_j? Interpret.

- Firm i's maximization problem is

$$\max_{q_1 \geq 0} \underbrace{(1 - \alpha_j)\left(q_i - \frac{q_i(q_i + q_j)}{S}\right)}_{\pi_i} + \underbrace{\alpha_i\left(q_j - \frac{q_j(q_i + q_j)}{S}\right)}_{\pi_j}.$$

Differentiating with respect to q_i, we get firm i's first-order condition

$$(1 - \alpha_j)\left(1 - \frac{2q_i + q_j}{S}\right) - \alpha_i\frac{q_j}{S} = 0.$$

Solving for q_i, we find firm i's best response function

$$q_i(q_j) = \frac{S}{2} - \frac{1}{2}q_j - \underbrace{\frac{\alpha_i}{1 - \alpha_j}\frac{q_j}{2S}}_{\text{New term}}.$$

From the new term, it is clear how the addition of the equity shares affects firm i's best response function. This term indicates that firm i reduces its appropriation for a given increase in q_j, relative to the setting where firms hold no equity in each other's profits, $\alpha_i = \alpha_j = 0$.

- Differentiating the best response function with respect to α_i yields

$$\frac{\partial q_i(q_j)}{\partial \alpha_i} = -\frac{1}{1 - \alpha_j}\frac{q_j}{2S} < 0,$$

which is negative. Therefore, as firm i's equity share in firm j's profits increases, firm i decreases its appropriation level. Intuitively, firm i's appropriation increases firm j's costs and decreases its profit, which firm i has a greater equity in as α_i increases. In other words, firm i's equity share helps this firm internalize part of the cost externality that its appropriation causes firm j.

- Differentiating the best response function with respect to α_j yields

$$\frac{\partial q_i(q_j)}{\partial \alpha_j} = -\frac{\alpha_i}{(1 - \alpha_j)^2}\frac{q_j}{2S} < 0.$$

An increase in firm j's equity of firm i's profits reduces the share of firm i's total profits that come from firm i's production, and increases the share of total profits that come from firm j's production. This means that firm i decreases its appropriation level in order to increase the profit from its equity in firm j.

(b) Find the equilibrium appropriation levels, q_i^* and q_j^*, and evaluate second-period profits, π_i^*. How are they affected by a marginal increase in each firm's equity shares?

- In a symmetric equilibrium, such that $q_i^* = q_j^*$, firm i's best response function is

$$q_i^* = \frac{S}{2} - \frac{1}{2}q_i^* - \frac{\alpha_i}{1 - \alpha_j}\frac{q_i^*}{2S}.$$

Solving for q^*, we get each firm's appropriation level

$$q_i^* = \frac{(1 - \alpha_j)S^2}{\alpha_i + 3(1 - \alpha_j)S}.$$

- Taking a derivative with respect to α_i yields

$$\frac{\partial q_i^*}{\partial \alpha_i} = -\frac{(1 - \alpha_j)S^2}{(\alpha_i + 3(1 - \alpha_j)S)^2} < 0.$$

So, the firm's appropriation decreases as its equity share in the other firm increases.

- Taking a derivative with respect to α_j yields

$$\frac{\partial q_i^*}{\partial \alpha_j} = -\frac{\alpha_i S^2}{\alpha_i + 3(1 - \alpha_j)S^2} < 0.$$

Then, the firm's appropriation decreases as its rival's equity share in its own profits increases.

(c) Is the "tragedy of the commons" ameliorated by the presence of equity shares? Interpret.

- Without equity shares, each firm's appropriation level is $q^* = \frac{S}{3}$. If $q^* > q_i^*$, then the tragedy of the commons is ameliorated in this context:

$$\frac{S}{3} > \frac{(1 - \alpha_j)S^2}{\alpha_i + 3(1 - \alpha_j)S}$$

or, after rearranging,

$$\alpha_i + 3(1 - \alpha_j)S > 3(1 - \alpha_j)S.$$

which further simplifies to $\alpha_i > 0$. In other words, equity shares induce both firms to reduce their appropriation, which helps ameliorate the tragedy of the commons.

CHAPTER 3 – COMMON POOL RESOURCES
IN A DYNAMIC SETTING

Exercise 3.1 – Firms Facing Downward Sloping Demand Curve

3.1 Consider our analysis of equilibrium behavior in Section 3.3, where we assume that firms take market price as given (and have normalized it to $p = \$1$). Assume now that the incumbent faces a linear inverse demand curve $p(x) = 1 - bx$ in the first period, where x denotes the incumbent's first-period appropriation and, similarly, firms face linear inverse demand curve $p(Q) = 1 - bQ$ in the second period where Q represents second-period aggregate appropriation. In both periods, assume that parameter $b \geq 0$. (Note that when $b = 0$, the inverse demand collapses to $p = \$1$ in both periods, yielding the same results as in Section 3.3, whereas when $b > 0$ market price decreases as firms increase their appropriation.)

(a) *Second period.* Find every firm i's best response function, $q_i(q_j)$. How is $q_i(q_j)$ affected by an increase in parameter b? Interpret.

- We operate by backward induction, taking first-period appropriation x as given. In the second period, every firm i chooses q_i to solve

$$\max_{q_i \geq 0} \ \pi_i^{2nd} = \left[1 - b(q_i + q_j)\right] q_i - \frac{q_i(q_i + q_j)}{S - (1 - r)x}.$$

Differentiating with respect to q_i yields

$$\frac{\partial \pi_i^{2nd}}{\partial q_i} = 1 - 2bq_i - bq_j - \frac{2q_i + q_j}{S - (1 - r)x} = 0.$$

Rearranging first gives

$$2\left(b + \frac{1}{S - (1 - r)x}\right) q_i = 1 - \left(b + \frac{1}{S - (1 - r)x}\right) q_j,$$

and then we can solve for firm i's best response function

$$q_i(q_j) = \frac{1}{2}\left(\frac{S - (1 - r)x}{b(S - (1 - r)x) + 1}\right) - \frac{1}{2} q_j.$$

Note that when firms face an inverse demand curve, instead of a normalized price, the only change to the best response function is on its intercept. In particular,

$$\frac{\partial q_i(q_j)}{\partial b} = -\frac{1}{2}\frac{(S - (1 - r)x)^2}{(b(S - (1 - r)x) + 1)^2} < 0.$$

Therefore, as b increases, the inverse demand curve becomes steeper and each additional unit appropriated decreases the price, leading every firm to reduce its appropriation.

(b) Find every firm's second-period equilibrium appropriation $q_i^*(x)$, as a function of the incumbent's first-period appropriation x. How is $q_i^*(x)$ affected by an increase in parameter b? Interpret.

- In a symmetric equilibrium, $q_i = q_j = q_i^*$, which simplifies the best response function to

$$q_i^* = \frac{1}{2}\left(\frac{S - (1 - r)x}{b(S - (1 - r)x) + 1}\right) - \frac{1}{2}q_i^*.$$

Solving for the second-period appropriation as a function of first-period appropriation, we have that

$$q_i^* = \frac{1}{3}\left(\frac{S - (1 - r)x}{b(S - (1 - r)x) + 1}\right),$$

which is positive as long as first-period appropriation, x, satisfies $x < \frac{S}{1-r}$.

- To see how second-period appropriation is impacted by b, we take the derivative

$$\frac{\partial q_i^*}{\partial b} = -\frac{1}{3}\frac{(S - (1 - r)x)^2}{(b(S - (1 - r)x) + 1)^2} < 0.$$

The intuition follows that of part (a), where any appropriation decreases the marginal revenue to each firm, and the firm responds by decreasing its appropriation. A higher b only amplifies the decrease in marginal revenue, thus, firms further reduce their appropriation as b increases.

(c) *First period.* Find the incumbent's first-period equilibrium appropriation, x^*. For simplicity, assume no discounting, and parameter values $S = 2$ and $r = \frac{1}{2}$. Then, evaluate your results at $b = \frac{1}{2}$ and at $b = 1$. How is x^* affected by an increase in parameter b? Interpret.

- We first need to find firm i's second-period profits π_i^{2nd},

$$\pi_i^{2nd} = \left[1 - b(q_i^* + q_i^*)\right]q_i^* - \frac{q_i^*(q_i^* + q_i^*)}{S - (1 - r)x}$$

$$= q_i^* - 2b(q_i^*)^2 - \frac{2(q_i^*)^2}{S - (1 - r)x}$$

$$= \frac{S - (1 - r)x}{9\left[b(S - (1 - r)x) + 1\right]}.$$

Inserting parameter values $S = 2$ and $r = \frac{1}{2}$, we obtain

$$\pi_i^{2nd} = \frac{2 - \frac{1}{2}x}{9\left[b\left(2 - \frac{1}{2}x\right) + 1\right]}$$

$$= \frac{4 - x}{9[2 + b(4 - x)]}.$$

- In the first period, the incumbent solves

$$\max_{x \geq 0} \ \pi^{1st} + \pi_i^{2nd} = \left[(1 - bx)x - \frac{x^2}{2}\right] + \underbrace{\left[\frac{4 - x}{9[2 + b(4 - x)]}\right]}_{\pi_i^{2nd}}$$

since the exercise assumes no discounting of second-period payoffs and $S = 2$. Differentiating with respect to x, we find

$$1 - (1 + 2b)x - \frac{2}{9\left[2 + b(4 - x)\right]^2} = 0.$$

Solving for x in this first-order condition yields a highly nonlinear expression with several roots. For simplicity, we now evaluate this first-order condition at $b = \frac{1}{2}$, as described in the question, to obtain

$$1 - 2x - \frac{8}{9(8 - x)^2} = 0,$$

which yields three roots: two of them imaginary numbers and $x = 0.49$. Operating similarly, we can evaluate the first-order condition now at $b = 1$, to obtain

$$1 - 3x - \frac{2}{9(6 - x)^2} = 0,$$

which yields three roots: two of them imaginary numbers and $x = 0.33$. Therefore, the incumbent decreases its first-period appropriation as the price becomes more sensitive to appropriation levels (higher b).

Exercise 3.3 – Alternative Second-Period Cost Function

3.3 In this chapter, we considered a second-period cost function that produces tractable mathematical results about first- and second-period equilibrium appropriation. However, another well-known second-period cost function in the literature is

$$C_i(q_i, q_j) = \frac{q_i(q_i + q_j)}{S(1 + g) - x},$$

where $g \geq 0$ denotes the growth rate of the initial stock, S, and x represents the incumbent's first-period appropriation. Intuitively, when $g = 0$, the stock does not regenerate and the net stock available at the beginning of the second period is $S - x$; as captured by the denominator of the cost function. In contrast, when $g = \frac{x}{S}$, the stock is fully recovered, so the initial stock S is available again at the beginning of the second period. In this case, the second-period cost function is symmetric to that in the first period, simplifying to $\frac{q_i(q_i+q_j)}{S}$.

(a) *Second period.* Find every firm i's best response function, $q_i(q_j)$. How is $q_i(q_j)$ affected by an increase in the growth rate g? Interpret.

- Taking first-period appropriation x as given, in the second period every firm i solves

$$\max_{q_i \geq 0} \; \pi_i^{2nd} = q_i - \frac{q_i(q_i + q_j)}{S(1+g) - x}.$$

Differentiating with respect to q_i yields

$$\frac{\partial \pi_i^{2nd}}{\partial q_i} = 1 - \frac{2q_i + q_j}{S(1+g) - x} = 0.$$

Solving for firm i's best response function, we find

$$q_i(q_j) = \frac{S(1+g) - x}{2} - \frac{1}{2}q_j.$$

- Differentiating with respect to g, we can find how every firm i's best response function is affected by an increase in the growth rate,

$$\frac{\partial q_i(q_j)}{\partial g} = \frac{1}{2}S > 0.$$

That is, an increase in the growth rate increases each firm's best response in the second period. A bigger growth rate means that more of the stock is available in the second period, and a bigger stock decreases the marginal cost of appropriation, hence increasing each firm's appropriation.

(b) Find every firm's second-period equilibrium appropriation $q_i^*(x)$, as a function of the incumbent's first-period appropriation x. How is $q_i^*(x)$ affected by an increase in the growth rate g? Interpret.

- In a symmetric equilibrium, every firm i appropriates $q_i = q_j = q_i^*$, which simplifies the best response function to

$$q_i^* = \frac{S(1+g) - x}{2} - \frac{1}{2}q_i^*.$$

Solving for q_i^*, we get every firm i's second-period appropriation as a function of the incumbent's first-period appropriation x,

$$q_i^*(x) = \frac{S(1+g) - x}{3}.$$

- Differentiating the second-period appropriation with respect to g, we find that

$$\frac{\partial q_i^*(x)}{\partial g} = \frac{1}{3}S > 0.$$

This derivative is unambiguously positive, meaning that the second-period appropriation is increasing in the growth rate. Intuitively, as the stock in the second period becomes more abundant due to a greater growth rate, the firm's marginal cost decreases (while marginal revenue is constant), thus, inducing every firm to increase its appropriation.

(c) *First period.* Find the incumbent's first-period equilibrium appropriation, x^*. How is x^* affected by an increase in the growth rate g? Interpret.

- The incumbent's second-period profit is

$$\pi_i^{2nd} = q_i^* - \frac{q_i^*(q_i^* + q_i^*)}{S(1+g) - x} = q_i^* - \frac{2(q_i^*)^2}{S(1+g) - x},$$

which simplifies to

$$\pi_i^{2nd} = \frac{S(1+g) - x}{9}.$$

Using this information, the incumbent's first-period problem is

$$\max_{x \geq 0} \ \pi^{1st} + \pi_i^{2nd} = \left[x - \frac{x^2}{S} \right] + \delta \left[\frac{S(1+g) - x}{9} \right].$$

Differentiating with respect to x yields

$$1 - \frac{2x}{S} - \delta\frac{1}{9} = 0.$$

Solving for x, we find the incumbent's first-period equilibrium appropriation

$$x^* = \frac{S}{2}\left(1 - \delta\frac{1}{9}\right).$$

- Differentiating the first-period appropriation with respect to g yields

$$\frac{\partial x^*}{\partial g} = 0.$$

This means that the growth rate of the stock has no impact on first-period appropriation. Intuitively, the growth rate increases the total initial stock from the first period and is not dependent upon first-period appropriation.

Exercise 3.5 – Finding Socially Optimal Appropriation When N Firms Compete in the Second Period

3.5 Consider the setting in Exercise 3.4.

(a) *Second period.* Find the socially optimal appropriation level in the second period, $q_i^{SO}(x)$. How is it affected by an increase in the number of firms N?

- In the second period, the social planner solves

$$\max_{q_1,\ldots,q_N \geq 0} \sum_{i=1}^{N} \pi_i^{2nd} = \sum_{i=1}^{N} \left(q_i - \frac{q_i(q_i + Q_{-i})}{S - (1 - r)x} \right).$$

Since $Q_{-i} \equiv \sum_{j\neq i} q_j$ and $Q_{-j} \equiv \sum_{i\neq j} q_i$, it is helpful to rewrite this problem as

$$\max_{q_1,\ldots,q_N \geq 0} \left(q_i - \frac{q_i(q_i + Q_{-i})}{S - (1 - r)x} \right) + \sum_{j\neq i} \left(q_j - \frac{q_j(q_j + Q_{-j})}{S - (1 - r)x} \right).$$

Differentiating with respect to q_i yields

$$1 - \frac{2q_i + Q_{-i}}{S - (1 - r)x} - \sum_{j\neq i} \frac{q_j}{S - (1 - r)x} = 0.$$

Solving for q_i, we find

$$q_i = \frac{S - (1 - r)x}{2} - Q_{-i}.$$

In a symmetric equilibrium, we have that $q_1^{SO} = \ldots = q_N^{SO} = q_i^{SO}$ and $Q_{-i} = (N - 1)q_i^{SO}$. Inserting these properties into the above expression, we obtain

$$q_i^{SO} = \frac{S - (1 - r)x}{2} - (N - 1)q_i^{SO}.$$

Solving for the socially optimal level of appropriation, we find

$$q_i^{SO}(x) = \frac{S - (1 - r)x}{2N}.$$

- Differentiating second-period appropriation with respect to N, we find

$$\frac{\partial q_i^{SO}(x)}{\partial N} = -\frac{S - (1 - r)x}{2N^2} < 0.$$

Therefore, as the number of firms increases, the individual firm appropriation decreases.

(b) *First period.* Find the socially optimal appropriation level in the first period, x^{SO}. How is it affected by an increase in the number of firms N?

- First, we need to find second-period welfare:

$$W^{2nd} = N\left[q_i^{SO} - \frac{q_i^{SO}(Nq_i^{SO})}{S - (1-r)x}\right]$$

$$= \frac{S - (1-r)x}{4}.$$

The social planner anticipates the second-period welfare, and how it depends on first-period appropriation, solving

$$\max_{x \geq 0} \ \pi^{1st} + \delta W^{2nd} = \left[x - \frac{x^2}{S}\right] + \delta\left[\frac{S - (1-r)x}{4}\right].$$

Differentiating with respect to x, we obtain

$$1 - \frac{2x}{S} - \frac{\delta(1-r)}{4} = 0.$$

Solving for x, we obtain the socially optimal first-period appropriation

$$x^{SO} = \frac{S}{2} - \frac{S\delta(1-r)}{8}.$$

- As the number of firms N does not appear in the equilibrium first-period appropriation, N does not impact x^{SO}.

(c) *Evaluating inefficiencies.* Use your results from Exercises b and 3.4 to find the static inefficiency, $SI = q^*(x) - q^{SO}(x)$, and the dynamic inefficiency, $DI = x^* - x^{SO}$. How are they affected by the number of firms operating in the second period, N? Show that both of these inefficiencies collapse to zero when $N = 1$.

- *Static inefficiency.* Second-stage private appropriation is

$$q_i^*(x) = \frac{S - (1-r)x}{1+N},$$

and the socially optimal appropriation is

$$q_i^{SO}(x) = \frac{S - (1-r)x}{2N}.$$

The static inefficiency is

$$SI = q^*(x) - q^{SO}(x)$$

$$= \frac{S - (1-r)x}{1+N} - \frac{S - (1-r)x}{2N}$$

$$= \frac{(N-1)\left[S - (1-r)x\right]}{2N(N+1)}.$$

If we take a derivative with respect to N, we find that

$$\frac{\partial SI}{\partial N} = \left(\frac{1}{2N^2(N+1)^2} - \frac{N-2}{2N(N+1)^2}\right)\left[S - (1-r)x\right].$$

We can determine the sign of the derivative by evaluating the first term in parentheses, which is positive if

$$\frac{1}{2N^2(N+1)^2} > \frac{N-2}{2N(N+1)^2},$$

which simplifies to $N < \frac{1}{\sqrt{2}-1} \simeq 2.41$. This means that when N increases from 1 to 2 firms, the static inefficiency increases, and for $N > 2$ firms the static inefficiency decreases. When $N = 1$, we can see that the static inefficiency collapses to zero:

$$SI = \frac{(1-1)(S - (1-r)x)}{2(1)(1+1)} = 0.$$

However, when $r = 1$ and/or $\delta = 0$, the value of SI is not zero.

- *Dynamic inefficiency.* First-stage private appropriation is

$$x^* = \frac{S}{2} - \frac{\delta S(1-r)}{2(N+1)^2},$$

and the socially optimal appropriation is

$$x^{SO} = \frac{S}{2} - \frac{\delta S(1-r)}{8}.$$

Therefore, the dynamic inefficiency is

$$DI = x^* - x^{SO}$$

$$= \left(\frac{S}{2} - \frac{\delta S(1-r)}{2(N+1)^2}\right) - \left(\frac{S}{2} - \frac{\delta S(1-r)}{8}\right)$$

$$= \frac{\delta S(N-1)(N+3)(1-r)}{8(N+1)^2}.$$

If we take a derivative with respect to N, we find that

$$\frac{\partial DI}{\partial N} = \frac{\delta S(1-r)}{(N+1)^3} > 0.$$

Intuitively, the dynamic inefficiency increases as the number of firms in the second stage increases. When $N = 1$, we can easily see that $DI = 0$, but as N increases, the private appropriation increases in the first stage as the incumbent appropriates more in the period when there is less competition. In addition, when $\delta = 0$ or $r = 1$, we observe that the dynamic inefficiency collapses to zero as well.

This happens because, essentially, first-period actions have no payoff effects in future periods. This is either because future players do not assign a positive value to future payoffs ($\delta = 0$) or because the stock is fully regenerated ($r = 1$), thus making the stock completely available again at the beginning of the second period.

Exercise 3.7 – Two Firms Competing in Both Periods

3.7 Consider our analysis of equilibrium behavior in Sections 3.3 and 3.4, with only one incumbent in the first period and two firms in the second period. Let us now assume that two incumbent firms, 1 and 2, operate in the first period and the *same two firms* keep operating in the second period.

(a) Repeat the equilibrium analysis of Section 3.3. How are first- and second-period equilibrium appropriation levels affected as a result of having one more firm operating in the first period?

- The second-stage appropriation remains the same, where aggregate first-stage appropriation is now $X = x_i + x_j$, and every firm i in the first stage solves

$$\max_{x_i \geq 0} \ \pi_i^{1st} + \delta \pi_i^{2nd}$$

$$= \left[x_i - \frac{x_i(x_i + x_j)}{S} \right] + \delta \left[\frac{S - (1 - r)(x_i + x_j)}{9} \right].$$

Differentiating with respect to x_i yields

$$1 - \frac{2x_i}{S} - \frac{x_j}{S} - \delta \frac{(1 - r)}{9} = 0.$$

This first-order condition differs from that in Section 3.3 by the inclusion of the $-\frac{x_j}{S}$ term, as firm i in the first stage takes into account firm j's first-period appropriation on first-period costs. Solving for x_i, we get firm i's best response function

$$x_i(x_j) = \frac{S[9 - \delta(1 - r)]}{18} - \frac{1}{2}x_j.$$

If $x_j = 0$, and firm i is a monopoly, we obtain the equilibrium appropriation found in Section 3.3. The inclusion of a second firm in the first stage implies that firm i now takes into account the impact of its rival's appropriation on its marginal cost. In a symmetric equilibrium, $x_i^* = x_j^*$, implying that the above equation becomes

$$x_i^* = \frac{S[9 - \delta(1 - r)]}{18} - \frac{1}{2}x_i^*.$$

Solving for x_i^*, we get every firm i's first-period appropriation,

$$x_i^* = \underbrace{\frac{2}{3}\frac{S[9 - \delta(1 - r)]}{18}}_{x^*} = \frac{S[9 - \delta(1 - r)]}{27}.$$

Compared to the situation where only one firm operates in the first stage, where this firm chooses a first-period appropriation

$$x^* = \frac{S}{2} - \frac{\delta S(1 - r)}{18}$$
$$= \frac{S[9 - \delta(1 - r)]}{18},$$

we can see that when two firms operate, each firm produces exactly $\frac{2}{3}$ of that as the incumbent since the ratio of first-period appropriations $\frac{x_i^*}{x^*}$ simplifies to

$$\frac{x_i^*}{x^*} = \frac{\frac{S[9-\delta(1-r)]}{27}}{\frac{S[9-\delta(1-r)]}{18}} = \frac{2}{3}.$$

(b) Repeat the socially optimal analysis of Section 3.4. How do first- and second-period socially optimal appropriation levels change as a result of having one more firm operating in the first period?

• Again, the results we found in the second stage in Section 3.4 hold here too. In the firststage, the regulator solves

$$\max_{x_i, x_j \geq 0} \left[x_i - \frac{x_i(x_i + x_j)}{S} + x_j - \frac{x_j(x_i + x_j)}{S} \right]$$
$$+ \delta \left[\frac{2[S - (1 - r)(x_i + x_j)]}{9} \right].$$

Taking a derivative with respect to x_i yields

$$1 - \frac{2x_i}{S} - \frac{2x_j}{S} - \delta\frac{2(1 - r)}{9} = 0.$$

In a symmetric equilibrium, $x_i^{SO} = x_j^{SO}$, and the first-order condition becomes

$$1 - \frac{2x_i^{SO}}{S} - \frac{2x_i^{SO}}{S} - \delta\frac{2(1 - r)}{9} = 0.$$

Solving for x_i^{SO}, we obtain

$$x_i^{SO} = \frac{1}{2}\underbrace{\frac{S[9 - 2\delta(1-r)]}{18}}_{x^{SO}} = \frac{S[9 - 2\delta(1-r)]}{36}.$$

Hence, when two firms operate in the first stage, their individual socially optimal appropriation is exactly half that of the case where only one firm operates in the first stage. In other words, aggregate socially optimal appropriation is unaffected by the number of firms, but the individual socially optimal appropriation per firm decreases with the number of firms exploiting the resource.

(c) Use your results from parts (a) and (b) to find the static inefficiency, $SI = q^*(x) - q^{SO}(x)$, and the dynamic inefficiency, $DI = x^* - x^{SO}$, where x^* now denotes the first-period appropriation every firm i selects and x^{SO} represents the individual first-period appropriation selected by the social planner. How do each of these inefficiencies compare to those identified in Section 3.5? Are they larger or smaller? Interpret.

- *Static inefficiency.* The static inefficiency does not change from that presented in Section 3.5 as the private and socially optimal appropriations are the same in both cases.
- *Dynamic inefficiency.* The dynamic inefficiency in the case where two firms operate in the first stage is

$$\begin{aligned}
DI_2 &= x^* - x^{SO} \\
&= \frac{S[9 - \delta(1-r)]}{27} - \frac{S[9 - 2\delta(1-r)]}{36} \\
&= \frac{S[9 + 2\delta(1-r)]}{108}.
\end{aligned}$$

In this case, we see that even if $\delta = 0$, a dynamic inefficiency still exists. That is, the firms do not take into account the impact of their appropriation on their rivals' profit in the first stage.

When we directly compare this dynamic inefficiency, DI_2, to that in the case of only one firm operating in the first stage, where $DI = \frac{5[S\delta(1-r)]}{57}$ from Section 3.5, we obtain

$$\begin{aligned}
DI_2 - DI &= \frac{S[9 + 2\delta(1-r)]}{108} - \frac{5[S\delta(1-r)]}{57} \\
&= \frac{S[171 - 7\delta(1-r)]}{513},
\end{aligned}$$

which is positive since $\delta, r \in [0,1]$. (That is, even if $\delta = r = 1$, the numerator in the above expression is positive.)

This means that the dynamic inefficiency is larger in the case where two firms operate in the first stage than when only one firm operates. Intuitively, when two firms operate in the first stage, neither takes into account the impact of their appropriation on their rival's profits in either the first or second stage, thus amplifying the inefficiency from when there is only one firm.

Exercise 3.9 – Asymmetric Discount Factors

3.9 Consider our analysis of socially optimal appropriation in Section 3.4. Repeat the analysis assuming now that the incumbent firm's discount factor is δ_I while the regulator's is δ_R. How are the results in that section affected?

- First, we need to find the private and socially optimal appropriations if the regulator and incumbent firm have different discount factors:

$$x^* = \frac{S[9 - \delta_I(1 - r)]}{18}$$

$$x^{SO} = \frac{S[4 - \delta_R(1 - r)]}{8}.$$

The difference of these two terms is, then,

$$x^* - x^{SO} = \frac{4S[9 - \delta_I(1 - r)]}{72} - \frac{9S[4 - \delta_R(1 - r)]}{72}$$

$$= \frac{S(1 - r)}{72}(9\delta_R - 4\delta_I).$$

When the discount factors coincide, $\delta_R = \delta_I$, we get the same answer as Section 3.4. If the regulator cares more about future welfare than the incumbent, that is, $\delta_R > \delta_I$, then the difference between the private and social appropriations grows. If the opposite is true and the incumbent cares more about future profits than the regulator, that is, $\delta_R < \delta_I$, then the difference between the socially optimal appropriation and the private appropriation shrinks.

CHAPTER 4 – ENTRY DETERRENCE IN THE COMMONS

Exercise 4.1 – Firms Facing a Downward-Sloping Demand Curve

4.1 Consider the setting in this chapter, where we assumed that firms took the market price as given. Consider now that firms face a downward-sloping demand function $p(x) = 1 - bx$ in the first period, and $p(Q) = 1 - bQ$ in the second period, where parameter $b \geq 0$. In the case that $b = 0$, the price collapses to $p = \$1$ in both periods, yielding the same results as in this chapter, but otherwise firms should face fewer incentives to appropriate. Repeat the analysis of Section 4.2. For simplicity, examine first-period appropriation assuming no discounting, and parameter values $S = 10$, $r = b = \frac{1}{2}$, and $F = \frac{1}{100}$.

- **Second-period appropriation.**

  - *No entry.* If there is no entry, the incumbent is the only firm exploiting the resource in the second period. The incumbent chooses its second-period appropriation, q, to solve

$$\max_{q \geq 0} \pi^{2nd} = (1 - bq)q - \frac{q^2}{S - (1 - r)x}.$$

  Differentiating with respect to q yields

$$1 - 2bq - \frac{2q}{S - (1 - r)x} = 0.$$

  Solving for q, we obtain the incumbent's second-period appropriation under no entry, as follows:

$$q^{NE}(x) = \frac{S - (1 - r)x}{2b[S - (1 - r)x] + 2}.$$

  Inserting $q^{NE}(x)$ into the objective function gives the incumbent's second-period profit without entry:

$$\Pi_{NE}^{2nd} = (1 - bq^{NE}(x))q^{NE}(x) - \frac{q^{NE}(x)^2}{S - (1 - r)x}$$

$$= \frac{S - (1 - r)x}{4b[S - (1 - r)x] + 4}.$$

  - *Entry.* When a new firm enters, every firm i simultaneously and independently chooses its second-period appropriation, q_i, to solve

$$\max_{q_i \geq 0} \pi_i^{2nd} = (1 - bq_i - bq_j)q_i - \frac{q_i(q_i + q_j)}{S - (1 - r)x}.$$

  Differentiating with respect to q_i yields

$$1 - 2bq_i - bq_j - \frac{2q_i + q_j}{S - (1 - r)x} = 0.$$

  Solving for q_i, we find firm i's best response function

$$q_i(q_j) = \frac{S - (1 - r)x}{2b[S - (1 - r)x] + 2} - \frac{q_j}{2}.$$

In a symmetric equilibrium, $q_i^* = q_j^* = q^*$. Inserting this property in the above best response function, we obtain

$$q^* = \frac{S - (1 - r)x}{2b[S - (1 - r)x] + 2} - \frac{q^*}{2}.$$

Solving for q^* gives second-period equilibrium appropriation with entry

$$q^E(x) = \frac{S - (1 - r)x}{3b[S - (1 - r)x] + 3}.$$

Inserting $q^E(x)$ into firm i's objective function, we find that second-period profit under entry is

$$\Pi_E^{2nd} = (1 - bQ^E(x))q^E(x) - \frac{q^E(x)(q^E(x) + q^E(x))}{S - (1 - r)x}$$

$$= \frac{S - (1 - r)x}{9b[S - (1 - r)x] + 9}.$$

- *Enter or not?* The entrant enters if its second-period profit offsets its fixed entry cost, $F \geq 0$, that is, $\Pi_E^{2nd} - F \geq 0$, or more explicitly,

$$\frac{S - (1 - r)x}{9b[S - (1 - r)x] + 9} \geq F,$$

which, solving for x, yields

$$x \leq \frac{S - 9F(1 + bS)}{(1 - r)(1 - 9bF)} \equiv x_{ED}.$$

That is, the incumbent's first-period appropriation is sufficiently low.

- **First-period appropriation:**

  - *Allowing entry.* When the incumbent chooses a first-period appropriation smaller than x_{ED}, it allows entry, thus making profit Π_E^{2nd} in the second period. The incumbent then solves

$$\max_{x < x_{ED}} \pi^{1st} + \delta\Pi_E^{2nd} = \left[x - \frac{x^2}{S} \right] + \delta\underbrace{\left[\frac{S - (1 - r)x}{9b[S - (1 - r)x] + 9} \right]}_{\Pi_E^{2nd}}.$$

Differentiating with respect to x yields

$$1 - \frac{2x}{S} - \delta\frac{(1 - r)}{9\left[1 + b(S - (1 - r)x) \right]^2} = 0.$$

This first-order condition is highly nonlinear, not allowing for an explicit solution for x. Evaluating it at no discounting, $S = 10$, $r = \frac{1}{2}$, and $b = \frac{1}{2}$, the first-order condition becomes

$$1 - \frac{x}{5} - \frac{8}{9(24 - x)^2} = 0.$$

Solving for x, we obtain a first-period appropriation $x_E - 4.98$. Therefore, the incumbent's overall profit when allowing entry is

$$\Pi^{AE} = \left[x_E - \frac{x_E^2}{S} \right] + \delta \left[\frac{S - (1 - r)x_E}{9b[S - (1 - r)x_E] + 9} \right]$$

$$= 2.67.$$

- *Entry deterrence.* When the incumbent chooses a first-period appropriation larger than x_{ED}, it deters entry, thus making profit Π_{NE}^{2nd} in the second period. The incumbent then solves

$$\max_{x \geq x_{ED}} \quad \pi^{1st} + \delta\Pi_{NE}^{2nd} = \left[x - \frac{x^2}{S} \right] + \delta \underbrace{\left[\frac{S - (1 - r)x}{4b[S - (1 - r)x] + 4} \right]}_{\Pi_{NE}^{2nd}}.$$

Differentiating with respect to x yields

$$1 - \frac{2x}{S} - \delta \frac{(1 - r)}{4\left[1 + b(S - (1 - r)x) \right]^2} < 0.$$

Therefore, the incumbent's discounted sum of profits is monotonically decreasing in its first-period appropriation, x, which implies that when this firm seeks to deter entry, it chooses the minimal first-period appropriation that achieves this objective, x_{ED}. Inserting $x = x_{ED}$ into the discounted sum of profits, we obtain

$$\Pi^{ED} = \left[x_{ED} - \frac{x_{ED}^2}{S} \right] + \delta \left[\frac{S - (1 - r)x_{ED}}{4b[S - (1 - r)x_{ED}] + 4} \right]$$

$$= \delta \frac{9F}{4} - \frac{[9F - rS(1 - 9bF)(9F(1 + bS) - S)]}{(1 - r)^2(1 - 9bF)^2}.$$

which, evaluated at the same parameter values as when the firm allows entry and $F = \frac{1}{100}$, yields a negative profit of $\Pi^{ED} = -19.41$.

- *Deterring entry?* In the above parameter values, the incumbent allows entry since $\Pi^{AE} = 2.67 \geq -19.41 = \Pi^{ED}$.

Exercise 4.3 – Using a Different Welfare Function to Measure Inefficiencies

4.3 Assume that the social planner considers a welfare function $W = CS + PS$, where $CS = \frac{x^2}{2}$ in the first period and, similarly, $CS = \frac{Q^2}{2}$ in the second period, where $Q = q_1 + q_2$ denotes aggregate appropriation. Our analysis of Section 4.2 should be unaffected, since they only examine firms' equilibrium behavior. However, our measurement of the dynamic inefficiency in Section 4.3 is affected given that x^{SO} is now different.

Is the dynamic inefficiency $DI = x_{ED} - x^{SO}$ greater than when the social planner considers welfare function $W = PS$? Interpret. For simplicity, your analysis of first-period appropriation can assume no discounting and parameter values $S = 10$, $r = \frac{1}{10}$, and $F = \frac{1}{100}$.

- **Finding socially optimal appropriation.**

  - *Second period.* To find socially optimal appropriation in the second period, we have to maximize social welfare $W^{2nd} = CS^{2nd} + PS^{2nd}$, where $CS^{2nd} = \frac{Q^2}{2}$ while $PS^{2nd} = \pi_i^{2nd} + \pi_j^{2nd}$. Therefore, the social planner chooses q_i and q_j to solve

$$
\max_{q_i, q_j \geq 0} W^{2nd} = \underbrace{\frac{(q_i + q_j)^2}{2}}_{CS^{2nd}}
$$

$$
+ \underbrace{\left(q_i - \frac{q_i(q_i + q_j)}{S - (1-r)x} \right) + \left(q_j - \frac{q_j(q_i + q_j)}{S - (1-r)x} \right)}_{PS^{2nd}}.
$$

Differentiating with respect to q_i yields

$$
(q_i + q_j) + \left(1 - \frac{2q_i + q_j}{S - (1-r)x} \right) + \frac{q_j}{S - (1-r)x} = 0.
$$

Rearranging, and solving for q_i, we obtain

$$
q_i = \frac{2}{2 - [S - (1-r)x]} - 1 - q_j.
$$

Similarly, when we differentiate with respect to q_j, we find that

$$
(q_i + q_j) - \frac{q_i}{S - (1-r)x} + \left(1 - \frac{2q_j + q_i}{S - (1-r)x} \right) = 0.
$$

Rearranging, and solving for q_j, we obtain

$$
q_j = \frac{2}{2 - [S - (1-r)x]} - 1 - q_i.
$$

In a symmetric socially optimal appropriation, $q_i^{SO} = q_j^{SO} = q^{SO}$. Inserting this property in either of the above first-order conditions, we find that

$$
q^{SO} = \frac{2}{2 - [S - (1-r)x]} - 1 - q^{SO}.
$$

Solving for q^{SO} yields a second-period socially optimal appropriation of

$$
q^{SO} = \frac{S - (1-r)x}{2[2 - S - (1-r)x]}.
$$

Inserting q^{SO} in the second-period welfare, we obtain

$$W^{2nd} = \frac{S - (1-r)x}{2\left[2 - S - (1-r)x\right]}.$$

- *First period.* In the first period, the social planner anticipates the second-period welfare found above, W^{2nd}, and considers first-period welfare $W^{1st} = CS^{1st} + PS^{1st}$, where $CS^{1st} = \frac{x^2}{2}$ and $PS^{1st} = \pi^{1st}$. Therefore, the social planner chooses x to solve

$$\max_{x \geq 0} \underbrace{\frac{x^2}{2}}_{CS^{1st}} + \underbrace{\left(x - \frac{x^2}{S}\right)}_{PS^{1st}} + \delta \underbrace{\left(\frac{S - (1-r)x}{2\left[S - (1-r)x - 2\right]}\right)}_{W^{2nd}}.$$

Differentiating with respect to x yields

$$x + 1 - \frac{2x}{S} - \frac{\delta(1-r)}{\left[S - (1-r)x - 2\right]^2} = 0.$$

This first-order condition is highly nonlinear, which does not allow for an explicit expression of the first-period socially optimal appropriation, x^{SO}. We can, nonetheless, evaluate the first-order condition at specific parameter values, such as no discounting, $S = 10$ and $r = \frac{1}{10}$, to obtain

$$1 + \frac{4x}{5} - \frac{1}{(8-x)^2} = 0.$$

which, solving for x, yields $x^{SO} = 8.51$.

- *Dynamic inefficiency.* We can now use x^{SO} to measure the dynamic inefficiency, $DI = x_{ED} - x^{SO}$. The entry-deterring appropriation level x_{ED}, evaluated at the above parameter values and an entry cost of $F = \frac{1}{100}$, becomes

$$\frac{S - 9F}{1 - r} = \frac{10 - 9\frac{1}{100}}{1 - \frac{1}{10}} = 11.01.$$

Then, the dynamic inefficiency in this context is

$$DI = x_{ED} - x^{SO}$$
$$= 11.01 - 8.51$$
$$= 2.50.$$

In contrast, the dynamic inefficiency in Section 4.3 (where the regulator only considers PS in the welfare function), evaluated at the above parameter values, becomes

$$DI = x_{ED} - x^{SO}$$

$$= \frac{S - 9F}{1 - r} - \frac{S[9 - 2\delta(1 - r)]}{18}$$

$$= \frac{10 - 9\frac{1}{100}}{1 - \frac{1}{10}} - \frac{10[9 - 2 \times 0.9]}{18}$$

$$= 10.05.$$

Comparing the dynamic inefficiencies in both settings, we see that they are greater when the regulator only considers PS in the welfare function (10.05) than when he considers both CS and PS (2.50). Intuitively, the equilibrium first-period appropriation x_{ED} coincides in both contexts, but the first-period socially optimal appropriation x_{SO} is larger when the regulator considers CS and PS, thus shrinking the extent of the dynamic inefficiency.

Exercise 4.5 – Two Incumbent Firms Seeking to Deter Entry

4.5 Consider again our analysis in Section 4.2, but assume now that two (rather than one) incumbent firms exploit the CPR during the first stage. Both incumbents are symmetric. Find for which values of S the incumbent practices entry deterrence, and compare your results with those in Section 4.2. [*Hint*: See Espinola-Arredondo and Muñoz-Garcia (2013a), which characterizes equilibrium behavior in the commons with N incumbents facing potential entry. Lemma 1 and Proposition 1 should be particularly helpful.]

- **Second-period appropriation:**

  - *No entry.* If there is no entry, the incumbents are the only firms exploiting the resource in the second period. Therefore, every firm i chooses its second-period appropriation q_i to solve

    $$\max_{q_i \geq 0} \pi_i^{2nd} = q_i - \frac{q_i(q_i + q_j)}{S - (1 - r)X},$$

    where $X \equiv x_1 + x_2$ denotes aggregate first-period appropriation. Differentiating with respect to q_i yields

    $$1 - \frac{2q_i + q_j}{S - (1 - r)X} = 0$$

    and, solving for q_i, we obtain firm i's best response function in the second period, as follows:

    $$q_i(q_j) = \frac{S - (1 - r)X}{2} - \frac{q_j}{2}.$$

In a symmetric equilibrium, $q_i = q_j = q$. Inserting this property in the above best response function yields

$$q = \frac{S - (1-r)X}{2} - \frac{q}{2}.$$

Solving for q, we find the equilibrium second-period appropriation under no entry:

$$q^{NE}(X) = \frac{S - (1-r)X}{3}.$$

Therefore, second-period aggregate appropriation is

$$Q^{NE}(X) = 2q^{NE}(X) = \frac{2(S - (1-r)X)}{3}.$$

Inserting $q^{NE}(x)$ in firm i's objective function gives the incumbent's second-period profit without entry.

$$\Pi_{NE}^{2nd} = q^{NE}(X) - \frac{q^{NE}(X)(q^{NE}(X) + q^{NE}(X))}{S - (1-r)X}$$

$$= \frac{S - (1-r)X}{9}.$$

- *Entry.* If there is entry, the two incumbents and the entrant simultaneously and independently choose their second-period appropriation q_i. That is, every firm $i = \{1,2,3\}$ chooses q_i to solve

$$\max_{q_i \geq 0} \; \pi_i^{2nd} = q_i - \frac{q_i(q_i + q_j + q_k)}{S - (1-r)X}$$

where $i \neq j \neq k$ and $X \equiv x_1 + x_2$ denotes aggregate first-period appropriation by the two incumbent firms. Differentiating with respect to q_i yields

$$1 - \frac{2q_i + q_j + q_k}{S - (1-r)X} = 0.$$

Solving for q_i gives firm i's best response function

$$q_i(q_j, q_k) = \frac{S - (1-r)X}{2} - \frac{q_j}{2} - \frac{q_k}{2}.$$

In a symmetric equilibrium, $q_i = q_j = q_k = q^*$, so the above best response function becomes

$$q^* = \frac{S - (1-r)X}{2} - \frac{q^*}{2} - \frac{q^*}{2}.$$

Solving for q^*, we find the equilibrium second-period appropriation with entry for every firm i

$$q^E(X) = \frac{S - (1-r)X}{4}.$$

Therefore, aggregate second-period appropriation under entry is

$$Q^E(X) = 3q^E(X)$$
$$= \frac{3(S - (1 - r)X)}{4}.$$

Inserting $q^E(X)$ in firm i's objective function, we find second-period profit when entry occurs to be

$$\Pi_E^{2nd} = q^E(X) - \frac{q^E(X)(q^E(X) + q^E(X) + q^E(X))}{S - (1 - r)X}$$
$$= \frac{S - (1 - r)X}{16}.$$

Since, $\Pi_{NE}^{2nd} = \frac{S - (1-r)X}{9} > \frac{S - (1-r)X}{16} = \Pi_E^{2nd}$, the incumbent's second-period profit is higher without entry than with the entry of a new firm.

– *Enter or not?* In the second period, the entrant enters if and only if $\Pi_E^{2nd} - F \geq 0$, or

$$\frac{S - (1 - r)X}{16} \geq F.$$

Solving for X yields

$$X \leq \frac{S - 16F}{1 - r} \equiv X_{ED}.$$

Then, the firm enters in the second period if the incumbent's aggregate first-period appropriation is less than X_{ED}, $X < X_{ED}$. Otherwise, the incumbent deters entry.

- **First-period appropriation.**

  – *Allowing entry.* When the incumbents allow entry, then every incumbent chooses its first-period appropriation x_i such that $X < X_{ED}$, that solves

  $$\max_{x_i, \, x_i + x_j < X_{ED}} \pi^{1st} + \delta\Pi_E^{2nd}$$
  $$= \left[x_i - \frac{x_i(x_i + x_j)}{S} \right] + \delta \left[\frac{S - (1 - r)X}{16} \right].$$

  Differentiating with respect to x_i yields

  $$1 - \frac{2x_i + x_j}{S} - \frac{\delta(1 - r)}{16} = 0.$$

  Solving for x_i, gives incumbent i's best response function when incumbents (as a whole) allow entry:

  $$x_i(x_j) = \frac{S\left[16 - \delta(1 - r)\right]}{32} - \frac{x_j}{2}.$$

In a symmetric equilibrium, $x_i = x_j = x$, which simplifies the above best response function to

$$x = \frac{S[16 - \delta(1-r)]}{32} - \frac{x}{2}.$$

Solving for x, we find first-period equilibrium appropriation when incumbents as a whole allow entry:

$$x_i^E = \frac{S[16 - \delta(1-r)]}{48}.$$

Inserting x_i^E in $\pi^{1st} + \delta \Pi_E^{2nd}$, we obtain the incumbent's profit from allowing entry:

$$\Pi^{AE} = \left[x_i^E - \frac{x_i^E(x_i^E + x_j^E)}{S}\right] + \delta\left[\frac{S - (1-r)(x_i^E + x_j^E)}{16}\right]$$

$$= \frac{S[64 + \delta(16 + \delta + r(20 + (r-2)\delta))]}{576}.$$

- *Entry deterrence.* To deter entry, the incumbent chooses a first-period appropriation x_i, and aggregate first-period appropriation must exceed X_{ED}. Formally, every incumbent i solves

$$\max_{x_i,\; x_i + x_j \geq X_{ED}} \pi^{1st} + \delta \Pi_{NE}^{2nd}$$

$$= \left[x_i - \frac{x_i(x_i + x_j)}{S}\right] + \delta\left[\frac{S - (1-r)X}{9}\right].$$

Differentiating with respect to x_i yields

$$1 - \frac{2x_i + x_j}{S} - \frac{\delta(1-r)}{9}.$$

In a symmetric equilibrium, $x_i = x_j = x$, which simplifies the above first-order condition to

$$1 - \frac{3x}{S} - \frac{\delta(1-r)}{9} < 0.$$

This first-order condition is unambiguously negative, implying that incumbent i's profit from deterring entry decreases in x_i. Therefore, this incumbent chooses minimal first-period appropriation that deters entry, $x_i = x_j = \frac{X_{ED}}{2}$. Inserting this result into the above objective function, we find that incumbent i's profits from deterring entry are

$$\Pi^{ED} = \frac{(16F - S)(Sr - 16F)}{2(1-r)^2 S} + \frac{16F\delta}{9}.$$

- *Deterring entry?* Every incumbent i deters entry if $\Pi^{ED} \geq \Pi^{AE}$. For simplicity, consider the same parameter values as in Section 4.2, that is, no discounting $(\delta = 1)$, and parameter values $r = \frac{1}{4}$ and $F = \frac{1}{100}$. In this context, the above profit condition $\Pi^{ED} \geq \Pi^{AE}$ simplifies to

$$\frac{2\left(550 - \frac{64}{S} - 625S\right)}{5625} \geq \frac{1369}{9216}S.$$

Solving for S, we find that $0.173 < S < 0.354$. It implies that incumbents deter entry if $S < 0.354$. Intuitively, the resource is relatively scarce and, then, the incumbent makes it sufficiently unattractive for the potential entrant to join the CPR. In contrast, when the stock is relatively abundant, $S > 0.354$, it is unprofitable for the incumbent to deplete the CPR enough to prevent entry, leading the incumbent to allow entry.

- *Comparison with Section 4.2.* In the setting where a single incumbent operates in the CPR, we found that under the same parameter conditions, the incumbent practices entry deterrence only if $S < 0.19$. Therefore, the presence of more incumbent firms expands the range of S for which entry deterrence can be sustained in equilibrium.

    Intuitively, the cost of practicing entry deterrence (depleting the available resource in future periods) is fully internalized when one incumbent operates in the first period, but this cost is not internalized when two or more incumbent firms operate, making this practice more likely to be supported.

CHAPTER 5 – REPEATED INTERACTION IN THE COMMONS

Exercise 5.1 – Asymmetric Payoffs

5.1 Consider the CPR game of Matrix 5.1, but assume that firm 1's payoffs are different from firm 2's. In particular, assume that every firm i's payoffs are a_i, b_i, c_i, and d_i, where $b_i > a_i > d_i > c_i$.

(a) What is the minimal discount factor sustaining cooperation if $b_1 - a_1 > b_2 - a_2$ and $b_1 - d_1 = b_2 - d_2$? Interpret.

- For easier reference, we include here the modified Matrix 5.1.

Firm 2

		High approp.	Low approp.
Firm 1	High approp.	d_1, d_2	b_1, c_2
	Low approp.	c_1, b_2	a_1, a_2

Matrix B.1 *CPR game with asymmetric payoffs.*

- If no previous cheating occurs, the GTS dictates that every player cooperates in the next period, earning a payoff of a_i, yielding a stream of discounted payoffs

$$a_i + \delta a_i + \delta^2 a_i + \cdots = a_i \frac{1}{1-\delta}.$$

If, instead, the player cheats in the current period (playing High appropriation while its opponent chooses Low appropriation), its defection is detected by the other firm, yielding a payoff of d_i thereafter. As a result, its stream of discounted payoffs from cheating becomes

$$b_i + \delta d_i + \delta^2 d_i + \cdots = b_i + d_i \frac{\delta}{1-\delta}.$$

Therefore, after a history of cooperation, every firm keeps cooperating, if

$$a_i \frac{1}{1-\delta} \geq b_i + d_i \frac{\delta}{1-\delta}.$$

Solving for δ, we obtain

$$\delta \geq \frac{b_i - a_i}{b_i - d_i} \equiv \bar{\delta}_i.$$

Therefore, firm 1 will keep cooperating if $\delta \geq \bar{\delta}_1$ while firm 2 will keep cooperating if $\delta \geq \bar{\delta}_2$. Since $b_1 - a_1 > b_2 - a_2$ and $b_1 - d_1 = b_2 - d_2$ by assumption, we obtain that cutoffs $\bar{\delta}_1$ and $\bar{\delta}_2$ satisfy $\bar{\delta}_1 > \bar{\delta}_2$ or, more explicitly,

$$\frac{b_1 - a_1}{b_1 - d_1} > \frac{b_2 - a_2}{b_2 - d_2}$$

so condition $\delta \geq \bar{\delta}_1$ is more demanding than $\delta \geq \bar{\delta}_2$. Therefore, cooperating is sustained as long as the common discount factor δ satisfies $\delta \geq \bar{\delta}_1$.
- Intuitively, recall that, for any firm i, term $b_i - a_i$ measures the instantaneous gain from cheating, while term $b_i - d_i$ captures the loss that this firm suffers thereafter because of its deviation. Therefore, assumption $b_1 - a_1 > b_2 - a_2$ and $b_1 - d_1 = b_2 - d_2$ in this exercise can be interpreted, informally, as indicating that firm 1 has more incentives to cheat than firm 2, while both firms symmetrically suffer from the punishment of permanently reverting to High appropriation after cheating is detected. As a consequence, firm 2 is willing to cooperate under less restrictive values of δ.

(b) What is the minimal discount factor sustaining cooperation if $b_1 - a_1 = b_2 - a_2$ and $b_1 - d_1 < b_2 - d_2$? Interpret.

- Since $b_1 - a_1 = b_2 - a_2$ and $b_1 - d_1 < b_2 - d_2$ in this setting, we obtain that cutoffs $\bar{\delta}_1$ and $\bar{\delta}_2$ satisfy $\bar{\delta}_1 > \bar{\delta}_2$ or, more explicitly,

$$\frac{b_1 - a_1}{b_1 - d_1} \geq \frac{b_2 - a_2}{b_2 - d_2}.$$

We, then, find that cooperation can be sustained under the same parameter conditions as in part (a), that is, when the common discount factor δ satisfies $\delta \geq \bar{\delta}_1$.

- We can provide an intuitive explanation as in part (a). In this setting, assumption $b_1 - a_1 = b_2 - a_2$ and $b_1 - d_1 < b_2 - d_2$ indicates that both firms have the same instantaneous gain from cheating, but firm 2 suffers more from the punishment that cheating triggers than firm 1 does. As a result, firm 2 is willing to cooperate under less restrictive values of δ.

Exercise 5.3 – Altering Players' Payoffs – II

5.3 Consider the infinitely repeated CPR game of Section 5.4. Assume that a regulator sets a lump-sum tax t that firms pay when choosing High appropriation implying that Matrix 5.1 becomes:

		Firm 2	
		High approp.	Low approp.
Firm 1	High approp.	$d-t, d-t$	$b-t, c$
	Low approp.	$c, b-t$	a, a

(a) Find the NE of the game, and explain how it is affected by tax t.

- If $t < d - c$ and $t < b - a$, the NE is (High, High).

  - If firm 2 chooses High appropriation, firm 1's best response is High since $d - t > c$; if firm 2 chooses Low appropriation, firm 1's best response is still High since $b - t > a$.
  - Similarly, if firm 1 chooses High appropriation, firm 2's best response is High since $d - t > c$; if firm 1 chooses Low appropriation, firm 2's best response is High since $b - t > a$.
  - Therefore, the NE is (High, High).

- If $t < d - c$ and $t > b - a$, the Nash equilibria are (High, High) and (Low, Low).

- If firm 2 chooses High appropriation, firm 1's best response is High since $d - t > c$; if firm 2 chooses Low appropriation, firm 1's best response is Low since $b - t < a$.
- Similarly, if firm 1 chooses High appropriation, firm 2's best response is High since $d - t > c$; if firm 1 chooses Low appropriation, firm 2's best response is High since $b - t < a$.
- Therefore, the Nash equilibria are (High, High) and (Low, Low).

• If $t > d - c$ and $t < b - a$, the Nash equilibria are (High, Low) and (Low, High).

- If firm 2 chooses High appropriation, firm 1's best response is Low since $d - t < c$; if firm 2 chooses Low appropriation, firm 1's best response is High since $b - t > a$.
- Similarly, if firm 1 chooses High appropriation, firm 2's best response is Low since $d - t < c$; if firm 1 chooses Low appropriation, firm 2's best response is High since $b - t > a$.
- Therefore, the Nash equilibria are (High, Low) and (Low, High).

• If $t > d - c$ and $t > b - a$, the NE is (Low, Low).

- If firm 2 chooses High appropriation, firm 1's best response is Low since $d - t < c$; if firm 2 chooses Low appropriation, firm 1's best response is Low since $b - t < a$.
- Similarly, if firm 1 chooses High appropriation, firm 2's best response is Low since $d - t < c$; if firm 1 chooses Low appropriation, firm 2's best response is Low since $b - t < a$.
- Therefore, the NE is (Low, Low).

(b) If the game is finitely repeated two periods, can the cooperative outcome (Low, Low) be sustained as an SPE of the game? How are your results affected by t? Interpret.

- Depending on the value of tax t, we can identify different SPEs (for presentation purposes, we list the different values of t in the same order as in part (a)).
- If tax t satisfies $t < d - c$ and $t < b - a$, the unique NE of the unrepeated game is (High, High). In order to sustain the cooperative outcome (Low, Low) in the first period, we can consider the following strategy profile, where every player chooses Low in the first period and, in the second

period, if both players chose Low in the previous period, every player chooses High. Operating by backward induction, we start with the second period.

- In the second period, High is a best response to High, as shown in part (a), so (High, High) is the equilibrium outcome in the second period, yielding an equilibrium payoff of $d - t$ for each firm.

- In the first period, if firm j chooses Low (as prescribed in this strategy profile) and firm i responds with Low, its payoff is a, yielding a payoff stream of $a + (d - t)$.

  If, instead, firm i unilaterally deviates to High, its first-period payoff is $b - t$, which is higher than its payoff from choosing Low, a, if $b - t > a$ or $b - a > t$, which holds in this case. (This indicates that every firm i improves its first-period payoff by unilaterally deviating from Low to High.) Therefore, firm i's payoff stream from deviating is $a + (b - t)$.

- We can then conclude that every firm i has incentives to select Low in the first period if its payoff stream satisfies

$$a + (d - t) > a + (b - t),$$

which simplifies to $d > b$, which does not hold by definition. Therefore, we cannot sustain the cooperative outcome (Low, Low) as an SPE when t satisfies $t < d - c$ and $t < b - a$.

• If tax t satisfies $t < d - c$ and $t > b - a$, as shown in part (a), there are two NEs in the unrepeated game, (Low, Low) and (High, High). Then, the cooperative outcome (Low, Low) can be sustained at every period of the twice-repeated game.

• If tax t satisfies $t > d - c$ and $t < b - a$, as shown in part (a), there are two NEs in the unrepeated game, (Low, Low) and (High, High). As in the previous case, the cooperative outcome (Low, Low) can also be sustained at every period of the twice-repeated game.

• If tax t satisfies $t > d - c$ and $t > b - a$, as shown in part (a), the unique NE of the unrepeated game is (Low, Low). Therefore, the cooperative outcome (Low, Low) can be sustained at every period of the twice-repeated game.

(c) If the game is infinitely repeated, which is the minimal discount factor sustaining the cooperative outcome (Low, Low) as an SPE of the game? How are your results affected by t? Interpret.

- We start at any given period. If no previous cheating occurs, the GTS dictates that every player cooperates in the next period, earning a payoff of a, yielding a stream of discounted payoffs

$$a + \delta a + \delta^2 a + \cdots = a\frac{1}{1-\delta}.$$

If instead, the player cheats in the current period (playing High appropriation while its opponent chooses Low appropriation), it earns $b - t$ in this period. However, its defection is detected by the other firm, yielding a payoff of $d - t$ thereafter. As a result, its stream of discounted payoffs from cheating becomes

$$(b - t) + \delta(d - t) + \delta^2(d - t) + \cdots = (b - t) + (d - t)\frac{\delta}{1-\delta}.$$

Therefore, after a history of cooperation, every firm keeps cooperating, if

$$a\frac{1}{1-\delta} \geq (b - t) + (d - t)\frac{\delta}{1-\delta}.$$

Solving for δ, we obtain

$$\delta \geq \frac{b - a - t}{b - d} \equiv \bar{\delta}(t),$$

where the minimal discount factor $\bar{\delta}(t)$ is decreasing in t, expanding the range of discount factors that sustain cooperation. Intuitively, a higher lump-sum tax t makes deviations to High appropriation less attractive, facilitating players' cooperation.

Exercise 5.5 – *N Firms Exploiting the Commons*

5.5 Consider the CPR game of Matrix 5.1. Let us now extend it to N firms. For simplicity, assume that if all firms choose Low appropriation, every firm earns a; if all firms choose High appropriation, they all earn d; and if one or more firms choose High appropriation while at least one of its rivals chooses Low appropriation, the firm/s selecting High appropriation earn b while the firm/s choosing Low appropriation earn c.

(a) What is the minimal discount factor supporting cooperation?

- The analysis considers any firm i and its $N - 1$ rivals, so it yields the same results as the setting with two firms, as we show at the end of part (a) below.
- *Cooperation.* If no previous cheating occurs, the GTS dictates that every player cooperates in the next period, earning a payoff of a, yielding a stream of discounted payoffs

$$a + \delta a + \delta^2 a + \cdots = a\frac{1}{1 - \delta}.$$

- *Deviation.* If instead, the player cheats in the current period (playing High appropriation while all its opponents ($N - 1$ firms) choose Low appropriation), it earns b in that period. Its defection is, however, detected by the other firms, yielding a payoff of d thereafter. As a result, its stream of discounted payoffs from cheating becomes

$$b + \delta d + \delta^2 d + \cdots = b + d\frac{\delta}{1 - \delta}.$$

- *Comparison.* Therefore, after a history of cooperation, every firm keeps cooperating, if

$$a\frac{1}{1 - \delta} \geq b + d\frac{\delta}{1 - \delta}.$$

Solving for δ, we obtain a minimal discount factor of

$$\delta \geq \frac{b - a}{b - d} \equiv \bar{\delta}.$$

(b) How is the minimal discount factor you found in part (a) affected by the number of firms, N? Interpret.

- The minimal discount factor $\bar{\delta}$ does not depend on the number of firms exploiting the CPR, N.

(c) Show that when only $N = 2$ firms exploit the commons, you obtain the same results as in Section 5.4.

- When $N = 2$, the minimal discount factor is still $\bar{\delta} = \frac{b-a}{b-d}$ which, as expected, coincides with that in Section 5.4.

Exercise 5.7 – Temporary Punishments

5.7 Consider the CPR game of Matrix 5.1. We now study a GTS where firms, upon observing a firm defecting to High appropriation, respond by defecting to High appropriation during $T \geq 1$ periods (rather than thereafter, as assumed in this chapter).

Under which parameter conditions can cooperation be sustained? [*Hint*: At the end of your analysis, solve for the minimal number of punishment periods that sustains cooperation, rather than solving for the minimal discount factor].

- *Cooperation.* If no previous cheating occurs, the GTS dictates that every player cooperates in the next period, earning a payoff of a, yielding a stream of discounted payoffs

$$a + \delta a + \delta^2 a + \cdots + \delta^T a + \delta^{T+1} a + \cdots$$

- *Deviation.* If instead, the player cheats in the current period (playing High appropriation while its opponent chooses Low appropriation), it earns b in this period. Its defection is, however, detected by the other firm, yielding a payoff of d during N periods. As a result, its stream of discounted payoffs from cheating becomes

$$b + \delta d + \delta^2 d + \cdots + \delta^T d + \delta^{T+1} a + \cdots$$

- *Comparison.* Therefore, after a history of cooperation, every firm keeps cooperating, if

$$a + \delta a + \delta^2 a + \cdots + \delta^T a + \delta^{T+1} a + \cdots$$
$$\geq b + \delta d + \delta^2 d + \cdots + \delta^T d + \delta^{T+1} a + \cdots$$

Rearranging yields

$$a\left(\frac{\delta^{T+1} - 1}{\delta - 1}\right) \geq b + d\left(\frac{\delta^{T+1} - \delta}{\delta - 1}\right),$$

which simplifies to

$$\delta^{T+1} \leq \frac{(a - b) - (b - d)\delta}{a - d}.$$

This expression is highly nonlinear in δ, and does not allow for an explicit function of the minimal discount factor, $\bar{\delta}$. We can, nonetheless, gain some intuition of our results by solving for T, which represents the length of the punishment phase, as follows:

$$T + 1 \geq \ln \frac{(a - b) - (b - d)\delta}{a - d}.$$

Rearranging yields

$$T \geq \frac{\ln \frac{(a-b)-(b-d)\delta}{a-d}}{\ln \delta} - 1 \equiv \hat{T}.$$

Intuitively, the number of punishment periods, T, must be longer than cutoff $\hat{T}$, for firms to be discouraged from deviating, so cooperation can be sustained.

CHAPTER 6 – COMMONS UNDER INCOMPLETE INFORMATION

Exercise 6.1 – Socially Optimal Appropriation

6.1 Consider the setting in Section 6.2.

(a) Assuming that the social planner has a welfare function $W = PS$, find the socially optimal appropriation for each firm, x^{SO}, and evaluate the static inefficiency, $x_i^* - x^{SO}$. Is this inefficiency greater than that under complete information?

- In this setting, the social planner considers the sum of the expected profits of firms i and j, and chooses appropriation levels x_i and x_j, as follows:

$$\max_{x_i, x_j \geq 0} \ p \underbrace{\left(x_i - \frac{x_i \left(x_i + X_{-i} \right)}{S_H} \right)}_{\pi_i \text{ if the stock is high}} + (1 - p) \underbrace{\left(x_i - \frac{x_i \left(x_i + X_{-i} \right)}{S_L} \right)}_{\pi_i \text{ if the stock is low}}$$

$$+ p \underbrace{\left(x_j - \frac{x_j \left(x_j + X_{-j} \right)}{S_H} \right)}_{\pi_j \text{ if the stock is high}} + (1 - p) \underbrace{\left(x_j - \frac{x_j \left(x_j + X_{-j} \right)}{S_L} \right)}_{\pi_j \text{ if the stock is low}}.$$

Differentiating with respect to x_i yields

$$p \left(1 - \frac{2x_i + X_{-i}}{S_H} \right) + (1 - p) \left(1 - \frac{2x_i + X_{-i}}{S_L} \right)$$
$$- p \left(\frac{x_j}{S_H} \right) - (1 - p) \left(\frac{x_j}{S_L} \right) = 0.$$

Solving for x_i, we obtain

$$x_i(x_j, X_{-i}) = \frac{S_H S_L}{2[pS_L + (1 - p)S_H]} - \frac{1}{2}(x_j + X_{-i}).$$

In a symmetric appropriation profile $x_i^{SO} = x_j^{SO} = x^{SO}$, which implies that $X_{-i}^{SO} = (N - 1)x^{SO}$ or $x_j^{SO} + X_{-i}^{SO} = Nx^{SO}$. Therefore, the above expression simplifies to

$$x^{SO} = \frac{S_H S_L}{2[pS_L + (1 - p)S_H]} - \frac{N}{2}x^{SO}.$$

Solving for x^{SO} yields the socially optimal appropriation

$$x^{SO} = \frac{S_H S_L}{(N + 2)[pS_L + (1 - p)S_H]}.$$

- *Static inefficiency.* To evaluate static inefficiency under incomplete information, recall from Section 6.2 that equilibrium appropriation is $x^* = \frac{S_H S_L}{(N+1)[pS_L + (1-p)S_H]}$. Hence, the static inefficiency is

$$SI = x^* - x^{SO}$$

$$= \frac{S_H S_L}{(N+1)[pS_L + (1-p)S_H]} - \frac{S_H S_L}{(N+2)[pS_L + (1-p)S_H]}$$

$$= \frac{S_H S_L}{(N+2)(N+1)[pS_L + (1-p)S_H]}.$$

Comparing this result against the static inefficiency under complete information (i.e., $SI_L = \frac{S_L}{(N+2)(N+1)}$ when the stock is low and $SI_H = \frac{S_H}{(N+2)(N+1)}$ when the stock is high), we find that

$$SI_H - SI$$

$$= \frac{S_H}{(N+2)(N+1)} - \frac{S_H S_L}{(N+2)(N+1)[pS_L + (1-p)S_H]}$$

$$= \frac{pS_H(S_L - S_H)}{(N+2)(N+1)[pS_L + (1-p)S_H]}.$$

which is unambiguously negative since $S_L < S_H$, implying that $SI_H < SI$.

Similarly,

$$SI_L - SI$$

$$= \frac{S_L}{(N+2)(N+1)} - \frac{S_H S_L}{(N+2)(N+1)[pS_L + (1-p)S_H]}$$

$$= \frac{pS_L(S_L - S_H)}{(N+2)(N+1)[pS_L + (1-p)S_H]}.$$

which is also negative since $S_H > S_L$. Therefore, we can conclude that $SI_L < SI$. Intuitively, incomplete information gives rise to additional inefficiencies as opposed to when when firms are informed about the stock level (either high or low).

(b) Assuming that the social planner has a welfare function $W = CS + PS$, find the socially optimal appropriation for each firm, x^{SO}, and evaluate the static inefficiency, $x_i^* - x^{SO}$. Is this inefficiency greater than that under complete information?

- In this setting, the social planner considers consumer surplus, $\frac{(x_i+x_j)^2}{2}$, plus the expected profits of both firm i and j, and solves

$$\max_{x_i, x_j \geq 0} \frac{(x_i + x_j)^2}{2} + \underbrace{p \left(x_i - \frac{x_i (x_i + X_{-i})}{S_H} \right)}_{\pi_i \text{ if the stock is high}}$$

$$+ \underbrace{(1-p) \left(x_i - \frac{x_i (x_i + X_{-i})}{S_L} \right)}_{\pi_i \text{ if the stock is low}}$$

$$+ \underbrace{p \left(x_j - \frac{x_j (x_j + X_{-j})}{S_H} \right)}_{\pi_j \text{ if the stock is high}} + \underbrace{(1-p) \left(x_j - \frac{x_j (x_j + X_{-j})}{S_L} \right)}_{\pi_j \text{ if the stock is low}}.$$

Differentiating with respect to x_i yields

$$x_i + x_j + p \left(1 - \frac{2x_i + X_{-i}}{S_H} \right) + (1-p) \left(1 - \frac{2x_i + X_{-i}}{S_L} \right)$$

$$- p \left(\frac{x_j}{S_H} \right) - (1-p) \left(\frac{x_j}{S_L} \right) = 0.$$

Solving for x_i, we obtain

$$x_i(x_j, X_{-i}) = \frac{S_H S_L}{2(pS_L + (1-p)S_H) - S_H S_L}$$

$$- \frac{(pS_L + (1-p)S_H)(X_{-i} - x_j) - S_H S_L x_j}{2(pS_L + (1-p)S_H) - S_H S_L}.$$

In a symmetric appropriation profile $x_i^{SO} = x_j^{SO} = x^{SO}$, which implies that $X_{-i}^{SO} = (N-1)x^{SO}$. Therefore, the above expression simplifies to

$$x^{SO} = \frac{S_H S_L}{2(pS_L + (1-p)S_H) - S_H S_L}$$

$$- \frac{(N-2)[pS_L + (1-p)S_H] - S_H S_L}{2(pS_L + (1-p)S_H) - S_H S_L} x^{SO}.$$

Solving for x^{SO} yields the socially optimal appropriation

$$x^{SO} = \frac{S_H S_L}{(N+2)[pS_L + (1-p)S_H] - 2S_H S_L}.$$

- *Static inefficiency.* To evaluate static inefficiency under incomplete information, recall from Section 6.2 that equilibrium first-period appropriation is $x^* = \frac{S_H S_L}{(N+1)[pS_L+(1-p)S_H]}$. Hence, the static inefficiency is

$$SI = x^* - x^{SO}$$

$$= \frac{S_H S_L}{(N+1)[pS_L + (1-p)S_H]}$$

$$- \frac{S_H S_L}{(N+2)[pS_L + (1-p)S_H] - 2S_H S_L}$$

$$= \frac{S_H S_L}{(N+1)[pS_L + (1-p)S_H]}$$

$$+ \frac{S_L}{2S_L - (N+2)\left[(1-p) + pS_L\right]}.$$

Comparing this result against the static inefficiency under complete information (i.e., $SI_L = \frac{2S_L[S_H + S_H S_L]}{(N+2)N[2S_H S_L - S_H]}$ when the stock is low and $SI_H = \frac{2S_H[S_L + S_H S_L]}{(N+2)N[2S_H S_L - S_L]}$ when the stock is high), we find that the difference $SI_H - SI$ is

$$\frac{2S_H[S_L + S_H S_L]}{(N+2)N[2S_H S_L - S_L]} - \left(\frac{S_H S_L}{(N+1)[pS_L + (1-p)S_H]} \right.$$

$$\left. + \frac{S_L}{2S_L - (N+2)\left[(1-p) + pS_L\right]} \right).$$

which is negative if the number of firms, N, is sufficiently low. Solving for N in the above equation produces a large expression that is difficult to interpret. For illustration purposes, we evaluate the above equation at $S_H = 10$ and $S_L = 5$, yielding

$$\frac{220}{19N(N+2)} - \frac{10(18+p)}{(N+1)(2-p)[2(8+p) - N(2-p)]}.$$

Evaluating this expression at $p = 0$, we obtain

$$\frac{220}{19N(N+2)} - \frac{45}{(N+1)(8-N)}.$$

which is negative for all the admissible number of firms, i.e., $N \geq 2$. Therefore, static inefficiencies satisfy $SI_H < SI$, implying that the static inefficiency is greater under incomplete information, SI, than complete information, SI_H, as in part (a). A similar argument holds for all values of p, yielding that $SI_H < SI$ given that $N \geq 2$.

- Similarly, the difference $SI_L - SI$ is

$$\frac{2S_L[S_H + S_H S_L]}{(N+2)N[2S_H S_L - S_H]} - \left(\frac{S_H S_L}{(N+1)[pS_L + (1-p)S_H]} \right.$$

$$\left. + \frac{S_L}{2S_L - (N+2)\left[(1-p) + pS_L\right]} \right).$$

which is negative if the number of firms, N, is sufficiently low. Solving for N in the above equation produces a large expression that is difficult to interpret. For illustration purposes, we evaluate the above equation at the same parameter values as above, $S_H = 10$ and $S_L = 5$, yielding

$$\frac{20}{3N(N+2)} - \frac{10(18+p)}{(N+1)(2-p)[2(8+p)-N(2-p)]}.$$

Evaluating this expression at $p = 0$, we obtain

$$\frac{20}{3N(N+2)} - \frac{45}{8+7N-N^2}.$$

which is negative for all the admissible number of firms, i.e., $N \geq 2$. Therefore, static inefficiencies satisfy $SI_L < SI$, implying that the static inefficiency is greater under incomplete information, SI, than complete information, SI_L, as in part (a). A similar argument holds for all values of p, yielding that $SI_L < SI$ given that $N \geq 2$.

Exercise 6.3 – Two-Period Interaction, but only One of Them Facing Uncertainty

6.3 Consider the setting in Section 6.2, but extended to a two-period game. Consider a regeneration rate r and assume that firms are uninformed about the stock only during the first period, but are informed before the second period starts. To facilitate your calculations, you may assume parameter values $S_H = 10$ and $S_L = 5$.

- Operating by backward induction, we start analyzing second-period appropriation, which resembles a complete-information game as firms observe the available stock at the beginning of the second period. We then examine the incumbent's first-period appropriation decision.
- *Second period.* Every firm i chooses q_i that solves

$$\max_{q_i \geq 0} \quad q_i - \frac{q_i(q_i + q_j)}{S_k - (1-r)x},$$

where $k = \{H, L\}$ denotes the stock level, which both firms observe at the beginning of the second period.

Differentiating with respect to q_i, we find

$$q_i - \frac{2q_i + q_j}{S_k - (1-r)x} = 0,$$

and, solving for q_i, we obtain

$$q_i(q_j) = \frac{S_k - (1-r)x}{2} - \frac{1}{2}q_j,$$

which is increasing in the stock, S_k and in the regeneration rate, r.

In a symmetric equilibrium, $q_i = q_j$ for every firm $j \neq i$. Inserting this property in the above best response function yields

$$q_i = \frac{S_k - (1-r)x}{2} - \frac{1}{2}q_i.$$

Solving for q_i, we find the equilibrium second-period appropriation

$$q_k = \frac{S_k - (1-r)x}{3}.$$

Inserting appropriation level q_k into firm i's profit function, we obtain its second-period profit, that is,

$$\Pi_k^{2nd} = q_k - \frac{q_k (q_k + q_k)}{S_k - (1-r)x}$$

$$= \frac{S_k - (1-r)x}{9}.$$

- *First period.* To solve for the first-period equilibrium appropriation, we express firm i's expected second-period profits, as follows:

$$\mathbb{E}(\Pi_i^{2nd}) = p \underbrace{\left(\frac{S_H - (1-r)x}{9}\right)}_{\text{Profit if the stock is high}} + (1-p) \underbrace{\left(\frac{S_L - (1-r)x}{9}\right)}_{\text{Profit if the stock is low}}$$

$$= \frac{p(S_H - (1-r)x) + (1-p)(S_L - (1-r)x)}{9}.$$

where, intuitively, the numerator represents the expected available stock in the second period.

In the first period, the incumbent is the only firm operating, and chooses its appropriation level x to maximize the sum of its expected first- and second-period profits, as follows:

$$\max_{x \geq 0} \quad \underbrace{p\left(x - \frac{x^2}{S_H}\right) + (1-p)\left(x - \frac{x^2}{S_L}\right)}_{\mathbb{E}(\pi_i^{1st})}$$

$$+ \delta \underbrace{\left(\frac{p(S_H - (1-r)x) + (1-p)(S_L - (1-r)x)}{9}\right)}_{\mathbb{E}(\Pi_i^{2nd})}.$$

Differentiating with respect to x yields

$$1 - \frac{2[(1-p)S_H + pS_L]x}{S_H S_L} - \delta\frac{(1-r)}{9} = 0.$$

Solving for x, we obtain the first-period equilibrium

$$x^* = \frac{S_H S_L[9 - \delta(1-r)]}{18[pS_L + (1-p)S_H]}.$$

For illustration purposes, we evaluate our results assuming no discounting, $\delta = 1$, a regeneration rate of $r = \frac{1}{2}$, and stock levels of $S_H = 10$ and $S_L = 5$, which yields

$$(x^*, q_H, q_L) = \left(\frac{85}{18(2-p)}, \frac{20-x}{6}, \frac{10-x}{6} \right),$$

where first-period appropriation, x^*, increases in the probability that the stock is high, p, and second-period appropriation (when both firms observe that the stock is high and low) is decreasing in first-period appropriation, x. As expected, second-period appropriation is greater when the stock is high than when it is low since $\frac{20-x}{6} > \frac{10-x}{6}$.

Exercise 6.5 – Allowing for Market Power – Asymmetrically Informed Players

6.5 Consider the setting in Section 6.3, but allow for players to face a linear inverse demand function $p(X) = 1 - X$, where X denotes aggregate appropriation. Repeat our analysis and compare your results.

How are the equilibrium appropriation decisions for the privately informed firm and for the uninformed firm affected by market power? To facilitate your calculations, you may assume no discounting, and $S_H = 10$ and $S_L = 5$.

- We begin by finding the best response of the privately informed firm, when observing a high and low stock. We then find the best response function of the uninformed firm. Finally, we combine all best responses to solve for equilibrium appropriation.
- *Privately informed firm – high stock*: The privately informed firm i chooses x_H to solve

$$\max_{x_H \geq 0} \left[1 - (x_H + x_U) \right] x_H - \frac{x_H (x_H + x_U)}{S_H}.$$

Differentiating with respect to x_H yields

$$1 - 2x_H - x_U - \frac{2x_H + x_U}{S_H} = 0.$$

Solving for x_H, we find the best response function of the privately informed firm observing a high stock,

$$x_H(x_U) = \frac{S_H}{2(S_H + 1)} - \frac{1}{2}x_U,$$

which is increasing in the stock, S_H, but decreasing in the appropriation decision of the uniformed firm, x_U.

Comparing this best response function with that in Section 6.3, where prices are given, where we found that $x_H(x_U) = \frac{S_H}{2} - \frac{1}{2}x_U$, we can conclude that, for a given appropriation of the uninformed firm, x_U, the informed firm appropriates less when prices decrease in appropriation than otherwise. Graphically, the best response function we found in this exercise is a parallel downward shift in that of Section 6.3.

- *Privately informed firm – low stock*: When observing a low stock, the privately informed firm i chooses x_L to solve

$$\max_{x_L \geq 0} \left[1 - (x_L + x_U)\right]x_L - \frac{x_L\left(x_L + x_U\right)}{S_L},$$

which is analogous to the above problem, but evaluated at a low stock S_L. Differentiating with respect to x_L yields

$$1 - 2x_L - x_U - \frac{2x_L + x_U}{S_L} = 0.$$

Solving for x_L, we find the following best response function:

$$x_L(x_U) = \frac{S_L}{2(S_L + 1)} - \frac{1}{2}x_U$$

which, as expected, is increasing in the stock, S_L but decreasing in the appropriation decision of the uniformed firm, x_U.

- *Uniformed firm*: The firm that does not observe the stock level (firm j) solves an expected profit maximization problem:

$$\max_{x_j \geq 0} p \underbrace{\left[(1 - (x_U + x_H))x_U - \frac{x_U\left(x_U + x_H\right)}{S_H}\right]}_{\text{Profit if the stock is high}}$$

$$+ (1 - p)\underbrace{\left[(1 - (x_U + x_L))x_U - \frac{x_U\left(x_U + x_L\right)}{S_L}\right]}_{\text{Profit if the stock is low}}.$$

Differentiating with respect to x_U yields

$$p\left[1 - 2x_U - x_H - \frac{2x_U + x_H}{S_H}\right]$$
$$+ (1 - p)\left[1 - 2x_U - x_L - \frac{2x_U + x_L}{S_L}\right] = 0.$$

Solving for x_U, we find the best response function of the uninformed firm,

$$x_U(x_H, x_L) = \frac{S_L S_H - (1 - p)S_H\left(S_L + 1\right)x_L - pS_L\left(S_H + 1\right)x_H}{2[pS_L + (1 - p)S_H + S_L S_H]},$$

which is decreasing in both x_L and x_H.

- *Equilibrium appropriation:* We can now insert best responses $x_L(x_U)$ and $x_H(x_U)$ into $x_U(x_H, x_L)$, which yields

$$x_U = \frac{S_L S_H - (1-p)S_H (S_L+1) \overbrace{\left(\frac{S_L}{2(S_L+1)} - \frac{1}{2}x_U\right)}^{x_L(x_U)} - pS_L (S_H+1) \overbrace{\left(\frac{S_H}{2(S_H+1)} - \frac{1}{2}x_U\right)}^{x_H(x_U)}}{2[pS_L + (1-p)S_H + S_L S_H]}.$$

which, rearranging, simplifies to

$$x_U = \frac{S_L S_H}{4[pS_L + (1-p)S_H + S_L S_H]}$$
$$+ \frac{S_H(S_L+1) - p(S_H - S_L)}{4[pS_L + (1-p)S_H + S_L S_H]}x_U.$$

Solving for x_U, we obtain the equilibrium appropriation for the uninformed firm

$$x_U^* = \frac{S_L S_H}{3[pS_L + (1-p)S_H + S_L S_H]}.$$

Therefore, substituting x_U^* into the best responses of the privately informed firm, we find

$$x_L^* = \frac{S_L}{2(S_L+1)} - \frac{1}{2}\overbrace{\left(\frac{S_L S_H}{3[pS_L + (1-p)S_H + S_L S_H]}\right)}^{x_U^*}$$
$$= \frac{S_L}{2}\left(\frac{1}{S_L+1} - \frac{S_H}{3[pS_L + (1-p)S_H + S_L S_H]}\right)$$

and

$$x_H^* = \frac{S_H}{2(S_H+1)} - \frac{1}{2}\overbrace{\left(\frac{S_L S_H}{3[pS_L + (1-p)S_H + S_L S_H]}\right)}^{x_U^*}$$
$$= \frac{S_H}{2}\left(\frac{1}{S_H+1} - \frac{S_L}{3[pS_L + (1-p)S_H + S_L S_H]}\right).$$

In summary, the BNE of this game is (x_H^*, x_L^*, x_U^*). For illustration purposes, we evaluate the above BNE assuming no discounting and $S_H = 10$ and $S_L = 5$, which yields

$$(x_H^*, x_L^*, x_U^*) = \left(\frac{5}{11} - \frac{5}{3(12-p)}, \frac{5}{12} - \frac{5}{3(12-p)}, \frac{10}{3(12-p)}\right).$$

These results show that, by allowing for market power, the equilibrium appropriation is lower than when firms take prices as given – which holds for each of the above three appropriation levels. Intuitively, allowing for market power, firms have incentives to reduce their individual appropriation level both when they are informed and uninformed about the available stock.

- *Equilibrium comparison.* We compare equilibrium appropriation in different information contexts.

  - *Uninformed firm:* We begin by comparing the equilibrium appropriation that the firm chooses under complete information, $x_H = \frac{S_H}{1+S_H}$,[1] and in the above incomplete information setting where one of the firms is uninformed, x_U^*. Hence, we obtain

$$
\begin{aligned}
x_H - x_U^* &= \frac{S_H}{1+S_H} - \frac{S_L S_H}{3[pS_L + (1-p)S_H + S_L S_H]} \\
&= \frac{S_H}{1+S_H}\left(1 - \frac{S_L(1+S_H)}{3[pS_L + (1-p)S_H + S_L S_H]}\right).
\end{aligned}
$$

which is positive when S_H satisfies

$$
S_H > \frac{S_L(1-3p)}{3(1-p) + 2S_L} \equiv \overline{S}_H.
$$

Therefore, if $S_H > \overline{S}_H$, we have that $x_H > x_U^*$.[2] Intuitively, allowing for market power leads the uninformed the firm to exploit the resource less intensively than when it knows with certainty that the stock is abundant.

Similarly, when the stock is low, we find that

$$
\begin{aligned}
x_L - x_U^* &= \frac{S_L}{1+S_L} - \frac{S_L S_H}{3[pS_L + (1-p)S_H + S_L S_H]} \\
&= \frac{S_L}{1+S_L}\left(1 - \frac{3p(S_H - S_L) + 2S_H(1+S_L)}{3[pS_L + (1-p)S_H + S_L S_H]}\right).
\end{aligned}
$$

which is negative. Therefore, we conclude that $x_L < x_U^*$, implying that the uninformed firm appropriates the resource less intensively than when it observes a scarce resource.

  - *Privately informed firm – high stock:* Similarly, we can compare the equilibrium appropriation that the firm chooses under complete

---

[1] Note that when $p = 1$, the equilibrium appropriation under incomplete information collapses to $x_H = \frac{S_H}{1+S_H}$, coinciding with that under a complete information setting where firms observe a high stock. Similarly, when $p = 0$, equilibrium appropriation under incomplete information simplifies to $x_L = \frac{S_L}{1+S_L}$, as in a complete information setting where firms observe a low stock.

[2] As an example, when $S_L = 5$ and $p = \frac{1}{2}$, this cutoff becomes $\overline{S}_H = -0.21$, implying that condition $S_H > \overline{S}_H$ holds for all positive values of S_H. A similar argument applies to all other probabilities $p \in [0,1]$, which originates at $\overline{S}_H = 0.38$ when $p = 0$, and decreases in p, reaching $\overline{S}_H = -1$ when $p = 1$.

information, $x_H = \frac{S_H}{1+S_H}$, and in the above incomplete information setting where the firm is privately informed about the stock being abundant, x_H^*. Hence, we obtain

$$x_H - x_H^*$$

$$= \frac{S_H}{1+S_H} - \frac{S_H}{2}\left(\frac{1}{S_H+1} - \frac{S_L}{3[pS_L + (1-p)S_H + S_LS_H]}\right)$$

$$= \frac{S_H}{1+S_H}\left(\frac{1}{2} + \frac{S_L(1+S_H)}{3[pS_L + (1-p)S_H + S_LS_H]}\right),$$

which is positive. Hence, we find that $x_H > x_H^*$. Intuitively, allowing for market power, the privately informed firm exploits the resource less intensively when it is the only firm observing that the stock is abundant than when all firms observe the stock.

- *Privately informed firm – low stock*: Following a similar comparison when the stock is low, we find that

$$x_L - x_L^*$$

$$= \frac{S_L}{1+S_L} - \frac{S_L}{2}\left(\frac{1}{1+S_L} - \frac{S_H}{3[pS_L + (1-p)S_H + S_LS_H]}\right)$$

$$= \frac{S_L}{1+S_L}\left(\frac{1}{2} + \frac{S_H(1+S_L)}{6[pS_L + (1-p)S_H + S_LS_H]}\right),$$

which is positive. Therefore, we conclude that $x_L > x_L^*$, exhibiting a similar intuition as in our analysis where the stock was high.

CHAPTER 7 – SIGNALING IN THE COMMONS

Exercise 7.1 – Separating Equilibrium When the Potential Entrant Enjoys a Cost Advantage

7.1 Consider the separating equilibrium we found in Section 7.3. Assume now that the potential entrant enjoys a cost advantage relative to the incumbent, so its cost function is $C_E(q_I, q_E) = \alpha \frac{q_E(q_I+q_E)}{S-(1-r)x}$, where $\alpha \in [1/2, 1]$ measures this firm's cost advantage. Intuitively, if $\alpha = 1$ the potential entrant does not benefit from a cost advantage, but otherwise it does.

Repeating the analysis in Section 7.3, identify the incentive compatibility condition for the high-stock incumbent and for the low-stock incumbent. Then use these two conditions to find the appropriation level that each type of incumbent chooses in the separating equilibrium. For simplicity, you can consider the same parameter values as in the chapter, namely, no discounting, $S_H = 10$, and $S_L = 5$.

(a) How are your equilibrium results affected by parameter α? Interpret your results.

- **High-stock incumbent:**

  - *Allowing entry.* The incumbent chooses the same first-period appropriation as in a complete information setting with subsequent entry. If entry occurs, in the second period, the incumbent solves

$$\max_{q_I \geq 0} \; \pi_I^{2nd} = q_I - \frac{q_I(q_I + q_E)}{S - (1 - r)x}.$$

Differentiating with respect to q_I and solving for q_I, we obtain the incumbent's best response function

$$q_I(q_E) = \frac{S - (1 - r)x}{2} - \frac{q_E}{2}.$$

In the second period, the entrant solves

$$\max_{q_E \geq 0} \; \pi_E^{2nd} = q_E - \frac{\alpha q_E(q_E + q_I)}{S - (1 - r)x}.$$

Differentiating with respect to q_E and solving for q_E, we obtain the entrant's best response function

$$q_E(q_I) = \frac{S - (1 - r)x}{2\alpha} - \frac{q_I}{2}.$$

Simultaneously solving for q_E and q_I in best response functions $q_I(q_E)$ and $q_E(q_I)$ yields equilibrium appropriation levels

$$q_I = \frac{2\alpha - 1}{3\alpha}[S - (1 - r)x] \text{ and}$$

$$q_E = \frac{2 - \alpha}{3\alpha}[S - (1 - r)x].$$

Plugging appropriation levels q_E and q_I into π_E^{2nd} and π_I^{2nd} yields second-period profits

$$\pi_I^{2nd} = \frac{(2\alpha - 1)^2}{9\alpha^2}[S - (1 - r)x] \text{ and}$$

$$\pi_E^{2nd} = \frac{(2 - \alpha)^2}{9\alpha^2}[S - (1 - r)x].$$

Therefore, in the first period the incumbent anticipates second-period profits π_I^{2nd}, and chooses the first-period appropriation x that solves

$$\max_{x \geq 0} \left[x - \frac{x^2}{S_H} \right] + \delta \underbrace{\left[\frac{(2\alpha^2 - 1)^2}{9\alpha^2} [S_H - (1 - r)x] \right]}_{\pi_I^{2nd}}.$$

Differentiating with respect to x yields

$$1 - \frac{2x}{S_H} - \delta \frac{(2\alpha^2 - 1)^2(1 - r)}{9\alpha^2} = 0.$$

Solving for x, we obtain

$$x_{H,E} = \frac{[9\alpha^2 - \delta(2\alpha - 1)^2(1 - r)]S_H}{18\alpha^2}.$$

As in the chapter, we label this first-period appropriation x_H rather than $x_{H,E}$. Inserting x_H into the incumbent's objective function in the first period yields an overall profit from allowing entry,

$$\Pi_H^{AE} = \left[x_H - \frac{x_H^2}{S_H} \right] + \delta \left[\frac{(2\alpha^2 - 1)^2}{9\alpha^2} [S_H - (1 - r)x_H] \right].$$

By choosing first-period appropriation level x_H the incumbent maximizes its discounted stream of profits but does not deter entry.

− *Deterring entry.* To prevent entry, the incumbent could deviate toward the low-stock incumbent's appropriation level, x_L, inducing the entrant to believe that the stock is low. Under complete information, in the second period under no entry, the incumbent chooses its second-period appropriation q that solves

$$\max_{q \geq 0} \pi^{2nd} = q - \frac{q^2}{S - (1 - r)x}.$$

Differentiating with respect to q yields

$$1 - \frac{2q}{S - (1 - r)x} = 0.$$

Solving for q, we find the incumbent's second-period appropriation under no entry

$$q^{NE}(x) = \frac{S - (1 - r)x}{2}.$$

Therefore, the incumbent's second-period profit when entry does not occur, evaluated at $q^{NE}(x)$, is

$$\Pi_{NE}^{2nd} = q^{NE}(x) - \frac{(q^{NE}(x))^2}{S - (1 - r)x}$$

$$= \frac{S - (1 - r)x}{4}.$$

Choosing x_L in the first period yields an overall profit

$$\Pi_H^{ED} = \left[x_L - \frac{x_L^2}{S_H} \right] + \delta \left[\frac{S_H - (1-r)x_L}{4} \right].$$

- *Allowing or deterring entry?* For the high-stock incumbent to choose x_H in the separating equilibrium, rather than mimicking the low-stock incumbent, the overall profits from allowing entry must exceed those from deterring entry, that is, $\Pi_H^{AE} \geq \Pi_H^{ED}$. This incentive compatibility condition of the high-stock incumbent, IC_H, is, formally,

$$\left[x_H - \frac{x_H^2}{S_H} \right] - \left[x_L - \frac{x_L^2}{S_H} \right]$$

$$\geq \delta \left[\frac{S_H - (1-r)x_L}{4} - \frac{(2\alpha^2 - 1)^2}{9\alpha^2} [S_H - (1-r)x_H] \right].$$

- **Low-stock incumbent:**

  - *Deterring entry.* If the low-stock incumbent chooses the first-period appropriation that this separating equilibrium prescribes, x_L, it deters entry, yielding overall profit

$$\Pi_L^{ED} = \left[x_L - \frac{x_L^2}{S_L} \right] + \delta \left[\frac{S_L - (1-r)x_L}{4} \right].$$

  - *Allowing entry.* If, instead, the incumbent deviates toward the appropriation level of the high-stock incumbent, x_H, it attracts entry. Conditional on entry, however, x_H does not yield the highest profit for the low-stock incumbent. The first-period appropriation that, conditional on entry, maximizes the low-stock incumbent's overall profits, solves

$$\max_{x \geq 0} \left[x - \frac{x^2}{S_L} \right] + \delta \underbrace{\left[\frac{(2\alpha^2 - 1)^2}{9\alpha^2} [S_L - (1-r)x] \right]}_{\pi_I^{2nd}}.$$

Differentiating with respect to x yields

$$\bullet 1 - \frac{2x}{S_L} - \delta \frac{(2\alpha^2 - 1)^2(1-r)}{9\alpha^2} = 0.$$

Solving for x, we obtain a first-period appropriation level

$$x_{L,E} = \frac{[9\alpha^2 - \delta(2\alpha - 1)^2(1-r)]S_L}{18\alpha^2}.$$

Inserting $x_{L,E}$ into the low-stock incumbent's objective function, this firm attracts entry and earns overall profits of

$$\Pi_L^{AE} = \left[x_{L,E} - \frac{x_{L,E}^2}{S_L} \right] + \delta \left[\frac{(2\alpha^2 - 1)^2}{9\alpha^2} [S_L - (1 - r)x_{L,E}] \right].$$

  – *Allowing or deterring entry?* Therefore, the low-stock incumbent chooses first-period appropriation x_L, deterring entry, rather than $x_{L,E}$, attracting entry, as required in this separating equilibrium, if and only if $\Pi_L^{ED} \geq \Pi_L^{AE}$. This incentive compatibility condition of the low-stock incumbent, IC_L, is, formally,

$$\left[x_{L,E} - \frac{x_{L,E}^2}{S_L} \right] - \left[x_L - \frac{x_L^2}{S_L} \right]$$

$$\leq \delta \left[\frac{S_L - (1 - r)x_L}{4} - \frac{(2\alpha^2 - 1)^2}{9\alpha^2} [S_L - (1 - r)x_{L,E}] \right].$$

- **Solving for x_L.** To find x_L, we need to simultaneously solve for it in the above incentive compatibility conditions IC_L and IC_H. For illustration purposes, we assume the same parameter values as in the chapter, $S_H = 10$, $S_L = 5$, and $\delta = 1$. Solving this context for x_L in IC_H, we obtain that the first-period appropriation x_L must lie in the interval

$$x_L \in \left[\frac{5[\alpha^2(r + 3) - A]}{8\alpha^2}, \frac{5[\alpha^2(r + 3) - A]}{4\alpha^2} \right]$$

where, for compactness,

$$A \equiv \frac{4}{3} \left[\frac{32\alpha^5(1 - r)^2}{9} - \frac{8\alpha^6(4r^2 + r + 13)}{9} \right.$$

$$+ \frac{\alpha^4(721r^2 + 358r + 2521)}{144} + \frac{2\alpha^2(4r^2 - 11r + 1)}{3}$$

$$\left. - \frac{64\alpha^3(1 - r)^2}{9} - \frac{(1 - r)^2}{9} \right]^{\frac{1}{2}}.$$

Since all appropriation levels in this range convey the low stock to the potential entrant, deterring entry, this type of incumbent chooses the highest of them (the upper bound), as follows:

$$x_L = \frac{5[\alpha^2(3 + r) - A]}{4\alpha^2}.$$

- **Separating effort.** To find how much the low-stock incumbent's behavior in the separating equilibrium differs from its appropriation under complete information, we first find its equilibrium appropriation

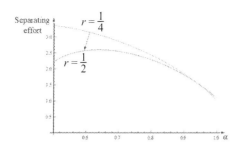

$r = \dfrac{1}{4}$

$r = \dfrac{1}{2}$

FIGURE B.I Separating effort evaluated at $r = \frac{1}{2}$ and at $r = \frac{1}{4}$.

in a complete information context. In this setting, the entrant observes the low stock and, thus, does not enter. From the previous calculation, we know that, conditional on no entry, the low-stock incumbent's second period profit is

$$\Pi_{NE}^{2nd} = \frac{S_L - (1 - r)x}{4}.$$

Therefore, the incumbent's optimal first-period appropriation under complete information solves

$$\max_{x \geq 0} \left[x - \frac{x^2}{S_L} \right] + \delta \left[\frac{S_L - (1 - r)x}{4} \right].$$

Differentiating with respect to x yields

$$1 - \frac{2x}{S_L} - \frac{\delta(1 - r)}{4} = 0.$$

Solving for x, we obtain

$$x_{L,NE} = \frac{S_L[4 - \delta(1 - r)]}{8}.$$

Evaluating $x_{L,NE}$ at $S_L = 5$, $\delta = 1$, this appropriation level simplifies to $x_{L,NE} = \frac{5(3+r)}{8}$. Therefore, the separating effort is

$$\text{Separating effort} = x_{L,NE} - x_L$$

$$= \frac{5(3 + r)}{8} - \frac{5[\alpha^2(r + 3) - A]}{4\alpha^2}$$

$$= \frac{10A - 5\alpha^2(3 + r)}{8\alpha^2}.$$

For illustration purposes, Figure B.1 evaluates this separating effort at $r = \frac{1}{2}$ and at $r = \frac{1}{4}$, and plots it against α in the horizontal axis. When $r = \frac{1}{4}$, a given increase in α (shrinking the entrant's cost advantage relative to the incumbent) reduces the incumbent's incentives to deter entry as the entrant becomes less threatening (higher post-entry profits). As a consequence, the incumbent's separating effort decreases in α.

When the regeneration rate increases to $r = \frac{1}{2}$, the available stock in the second period is more abundant, for a given first-period exploitation, reducing the incumbent's incentives to overexploit the CPR in the first period to deter entry. Graphically, the separating effort shifts downward as r increases.

(b) Show that when $\alpha = 1$ your results coincide with those in Section 7.3.

- If $\alpha = 1$, the separating effort simplifies to $\frac{A-5(3+r)}{8}$ where term A evaluated at $\alpha = 1$ is now

$$A \equiv \frac{4}{3}\left[\frac{32(1-r)^2}{9} - \frac{8(4r^2+r+13)}{9} + \frac{(721r^2+358r+2521)}{144}\right.$$

$$\left. + \frac{2(4r^2-11r+1)}{3} - \frac{64(1-r)^2}{9} - \frac{(1-r)^2}{9}\right]^{\frac{1}{2}},$$

which further simplifies to

$$A \equiv 4\sqrt{\frac{65r^2}{1296} + \frac{115r}{648} + \frac{425}{1296}}$$

$$= \frac{1}{9}\sqrt{65r^2 + 230r + 425}.$$

Therefore, the range of x_L is now

$$x_L \in \left[\frac{5[27+9r-\sqrt{5(85+r(46+13r))}]}{72}, \frac{5[27+9r-\sqrt{5(85+r(46+13r))}]}{36}\right],$$

which coincides with the separating effort found in Section 7.4.

Exercise 7.3 – Considering a Different Second-Period Cost Function

7.3. Chapters 3, 4, and 7 considered a second-period cost function that yields tractable first- and second-period equilibrium appropriation. Another second-period cost function used in the literature is

$$C_i(q_i, q_j) = \frac{q_i(q_i+q_j)}{S(1+g)-x},$$

where $g \geq 0$ denotes the growth rate of the initial stock, S, and x represents the incumbent's first-period appropriation. Intuitively, when $g = 0$, the stock does not regenerate and the net stock available at the beginning of the second period is $S - x$, as captured by the denominator of the cost function. In contrast, when $g = \frac{x}{S}$, the stock is fully recovered, so the initial stock S is available again at the beginning of the second period. In this case, the second-period cost function is symmetric to that in the first period, simplifying to $\frac{q_i(q_i+q_j)}{S}$.

(a) Repeat the analysis of Section 7.3 to find appropriation levels in the separating equilibrium of the game.

- **Complete information:**

  - *No entry.* If entry does not occur, the incumbent chooses the second-period appropriation q that solves

  $$\max_{q \geq 0} \pi^{2nd} = q - \frac{q^2}{S(1+g) - x}.$$

  Differentiating with respect to q yields

  $$1 - \frac{2q}{S(1+g) - x} = 0.$$

  Solving for q, we find the incumbent's second-period appropriation under no entry

  $$q^{NE}(x) = \frac{S(1+g) - x}{2}.$$

  Therefore, the incumbent's second-period profit when entry does not occur, evaluated at $q^{NE}(x)$, is

  $$\Pi^{2nd}_{NE} = q^{NE}(x) - \frac{q^{NE}(x)^2}{S(1+g) - x}$$
  $$= \frac{S(1+g) - x}{4}.$$

  Conditional on no entry, the incumbent chooses its first-period appropriation x to maximize

  $$\max_{x \geq 0} \pi^{1st} + \delta\Pi^{2nd}_{NE} = \left[x - \frac{x^2}{S}\right] + \delta\underbrace{\left[\frac{S(1+g) - x}{4}\right]}_{\Pi^{2nd}_{NE}}.$$

  Differentiating with respect to x yields

  $$1 - \frac{2x}{S} - \frac{\delta}{4} = 0.$$

  Solving for x, we obtain

  $$x_{NE} = \frac{S(4 - \delta)}{8}.$$

Inserting x_{NE} in the incumbent's objective function, we find that its overall profits when entry does not ensue are

$$\Pi^{ED} = \frac{S[\delta^2 + 8\delta(1 + 2g) + 16]}{64}.$$

– *Entry.* If entry occurs, every firm $i = \{1,2\}$ chooses its second-period appropriation q_i to solve

$$\max_{q_i \geq 0} \ \pi_i^{2nd} = q_i - \frac{q_i(q_i + q_j)}{S(1 + g) - x}.$$

Differentiating with respect to q_i yields

$$1 - \frac{2q_i + q_j}{S(1 + g) - x} = 0.$$

Solving for q_i, we obtain firm i's best response function

$$q_i(q_j) = \frac{S(1 + g) - x}{2} - \frac{q_j}{2}.$$

In a symmetric equilibrium, all firms choose the same second-period appropriation, $q_i = q_j = q^*$, which reduces the best response function to

$$q^* = \frac{S(1 + g) - x}{2} - \frac{q^*}{2}.$$

Rearranging and solving for q^*, we obtain the second-period appropriation under entry

$$q^E(x) = \frac{S(1 + g) - x}{3}.$$

Therefore, firm i's second-period profits under entry are

$$\Pi_E^{2nd} = q^E(x) - \frac{q^E(x)[q^E(x) + q^E(x)]}{S(1 + g) - x}$$
$$= \frac{S(1 + g) - x}{9}.$$

Anticipating this profit under entry, the incumbent chooses its first-period appropriation to solve

$$\max_{x \geq 0} \ \pi^{1st} + \delta\Pi_E^{2nd} = \left[x - \frac{x^2}{S}\right] + \delta\underbrace{\left[\frac{S(1 + g) - x}{9}\right]}_{\Pi_E^{2nd}}.$$

Differentiating with respect to x yields

$$1 - \frac{2x}{S} - \frac{\delta}{9} = 0.$$

Solving for x, we obtain a first-period appropriation

$$x_E = \frac{S(9 - \delta)}{18}.$$

Inserting x_E in the incumbent's objective function, we find that its overall profits when allowing entry are

$$\Pi^{AE} = \frac{S[\delta^2 + 18\delta(1 + 2g) + 81]}{324}.$$

- **High-stock incumbent:**

  – *Allowing entry.* The incumbent chooses the same first-period appropriation as in a complete information setting with subsequent entry, denoted by $x_E = \frac{S(9-\delta)}{18}$ as in the complete information case. To clarify that we deal with the high-stock incumbent, we relabel x_E as x_H, which yields an overall profit

$$\Pi_H^{AE} = \left[x_H - \frac{x_H^2}{S_H} \right] + \delta \left[\frac{S_H(1 + g) - x_H}{9} \right].$$

  – *Deterring entry.* To prevent entry, the incumbent could deviate toward the low-stock incumbent's appropriation level, x_L, inducing the entrant to believe that the stock is low. Choosing x_L yields an overall profit

$$\Pi_H^{ED} = \left[x_L - \frac{x_L^2}{S_H} \right] + \delta \left[\frac{S_H(1 + g) - x_L}{4} \right]$$

where both profit expressions are a function of the incumbent's true stock, S_H.

  – *Allow or deter entry?* Therefore, for the high-stock incumbent to choose x_H in the separating equilibrium, rather than mimicking the low-stock incumbent, the overall profits from allowing entry must exceed those from deterring entry, that is, $\Pi_H^{AE} \geq \Pi_H^{ED}$. This incentive compatibility condition of the high-stock incumbent, IC_H, is, formally,

$$\left[x_H - \frac{x_H^2}{S_H} \right] - \left[x_L - \frac{x_L^2}{S_H} \right]$$

$$\geq \delta \left[\frac{S_H(1 + g) - x_L}{4} - \frac{S_H(1 + g) - x_H}{9} \right].$$

Plugging $x_H = \frac{S_H(9-\delta)}{18}$ into IC_H yields

$$\frac{324 x_L^2}{S_H} - 82 x_L(4 - \delta) + S_H \left[81 - 9(7 + 5g)\delta + \delta^2 \right] = 0.$$

Solving for x_L, we obtain

$$x_L \leq -\frac{36S_H - 9S_H\delta + \sqrt{5}\sqrt{\delta\left(72 + 144gS^2 + 13S^2\delta\right)}}{72}$$

or

$$x_L \geq \frac{36S_H - 9S_H\delta - \sqrt{5}\sqrt{\delta\left(72 + 144gS^2 + 13S^2\delta\right)}}{72}.$$

• **Low-stock incumbent:**

  – *Deterring entry.* If the low-stock incumbent chooses the first-period appropriation that this separating equilibrium prescribes, x_L, it deters entry, yielding overall profit

  $$\Pi_L^{ED} = \left[x_L - \frac{x_L^2}{S_L}\right] + \delta\left[\frac{S_L(1+g) - x_L}{4}\right].$$

  – *Allowing entry.* The first-period appropriation that, conditional on entry, maximizes the low-stock incumbent's overall profits solves

  $$\max_{x \geq 0} \left[x - \frac{x^2}{S_L}\right] + \delta\left[\frac{S_L(1+g) - x}{9}\right].$$

  Differentiating with respect to x yields

  $$1 - \frac{2x}{S_L} - \frac{\delta}{9} = 0.$$

  Solving for x, we obtain a first-period appropriation $x_{L,E} = \frac{S_L(9-\delta)}{18}$. Inserting $x_{L,E}$ in the low-stock incumbent's objective function, this firm allows entry and earns a profit of

  $$\Pi_L^{AE} = \left[x_{L,E} - \frac{x_{L,E}^2}{S_L}\right] + \delta\left[\frac{S_L(1+g) - x_{L,E}}{9}\right].$$

  – *Allow or deter entry?* The low-stock incumbent chooses first-period appropriation x_L, deterring entry, rather than $x_{L,E}$, attracting entry, if and only if $\Pi_L^{ED} \geq \Pi_L^{AE}$. This incentive compatibility condition of the low-stock incumbent, IC_L, is, formally

  $$\left[x_{L,E} - \frac{x_{L,E}^2}{S_L}\right] - \left[x_L - \frac{x_L^2}{S_L}\right]$$
  $$\leq \delta\left[\frac{S_L(1+g) - x_L}{4} - \frac{S_L(1+g) - x_{L,E}}{9}\right].$$

Plugging $x_{L,E} = \frac{S_L(9-\delta)}{18}$ into IC_L yields

$$\frac{324x_L^2}{S_L} - 81x_L(4 - \delta) + S_L\left[81 - 9(7 + 5g)\delta + \delta^2\right] = 0.$$

Solving for x_L, we obtain

$$\frac{9S_L(4 - \delta) - \sqrt{5}\sqrt{S_L^2\delta(72 + 144g + 13\delta)}}{72} \leq x_L$$

and

$$x_L \leq \frac{9S_L(4 - \delta) + \sqrt{5}\sqrt{S_L^2\delta(72 + 144g + 13\delta)}}{72}.$$

Since all appropriation levels in this range convey the low stock to the potential entrant, deterring entry, this type of incumbent chooses the highest of them:

$$x_L = \frac{9S_L(4 - \delta) + \sqrt{5}\sqrt{S_L^2\delta(72 + 144g + 13\delta)}}{72}.$$

(b) Repeat the analysis of Section 7.4 to find appropriation levels in the pooling equilibrium of the game.

- **Low-stock incumbent:** By selecting the same appropriation level as under complete information, $x_{L,NE} = \frac{S_L(4-\delta)}{8}$, this type of incumbent deters entry. This appropriation level maximizes the incumbent's overall profit, thus becoming a rather attractive option. This type of incumbent does not have incentives to deviate from appropriation level $x_{L,NE}$.

- **High-stock incumbent:**

  - *Deter entry.* By selecting appropriation level $x_{L,NE}$, this type of incumbent also deters entry, earning overall profit

    $$\Pi_H^{ED} = \left[x_{L,NE} - \frac{x_{L,NE}^2}{S_H}\right] + \delta\left[\frac{S_H(1 + g) - x_{L,NE}}{4}\right].$$

  - *Allow entry.* If, instead, the high-stock incumbent deviates to any other appropriation level, $x \neq x_{L,NE}$, entry occurs. In that setting, the incumbent chooses its first-period appropriation, x, to solve

    $$\max_{x \geq 0}\left[x - \frac{x^2}{S_H}\right] + \delta\left[\frac{S_H(1 + g) - x}{9}\right].$$

    Differentiating with respect to x yields

    $$1 - \frac{2x}{S_H} - \frac{\delta}{9} = 0.$$

Solving for x, we find a first-period appropriation $x_{H,E} = \frac{S_H(9-\delta)}{18}$. Inserting $x_{H,E}$ in the high-stock incumbent's objective function, this firm attracts entry and earns a profit of

$$\Pi_H^{AE} = \left[x_{H,E} - \frac{x_{H,E}^2}{S_H} \right] + \delta \left[\frac{S_H(1+g) - x_{H,E}}{9} \right].$$

- *Allow or deter entry?* Therefore, the high-stock incumbent chooses appropriation level $x_{L,NE}$, deterring entry, rather than $x_{H,E}$, which attracts entry, if and only if $\Pi_H^{ED} \geq \Pi_H^{AE}$ yields the incentive compatibility condition

$$\left[x_{L,NE} - \frac{x_{L,NE}^2}{S_H} \right] - \left[x_{H,E} - \frac{x_{H,E}^2}{S_H} \right]$$

$$\geq \delta \left[\frac{S_H(1+g) - x_{H,E}}{9} - \frac{S_H(1+g) - x_{L,NE}}{4} \right].$$

Plugging $x_{L,NE} = \frac{S_L(4-\delta)}{8}$ and $x_{H,E} = \frac{S_H(9-\delta)}{18}$ into the incentive compatibility condition yields

$$\frac{81 S_L^2 (4-\delta)^2}{S_H} + 16 S_H \left[81 - 9(7 + 5g)\delta + \delta^2 \right] \geq 162 S_L (4-\delta)^2.$$

This inequality holds under relatively general parameter values. For instance, under no discounting, the inequality simplifies to

$$\frac{729 S_L^2}{S_H} + S_H(304 - 720g) \geq 1,458 S_L,$$

which, solving for g, yields $g < \frac{19}{45} + \frac{81 S_L (S_L - 2S_H)}{80 S_H^2}$. Intuitively, the high-stock incumbent mimics the appropriation level of the low-stock incumbent if the resource does not grow quickly enough across periods. Otherwise, the high-stock incumbent behaves as under complete information, choosing $x_{H,E}$, which attracts entry in the second period.[3]

---

[3] For the standard parameter values considered in previous exercises (i.e., no discounting, $S_H = 10$ and $S_L = 5$), the incentive compatibility condition of the high-stock incumbent further simplifies to $971 + 2,880g \geq 0$, which is unambiguously positive for all values of growth rate g.

- Therefore, the pooling effort is

$$\text{Pooling effort} = x_{H.E} - x_{L.NE}$$
$$= \frac{S_H(9-\delta)}{18} - \frac{S_L(4-\delta)}{8}$$
$$= \frac{4S_H(9-\delta) - 9S_L(4-\delta)}{72},$$

which is unaffected by g.

Exercise 7.5 – Pooling Equilibrium with Market Power

7.5 Consider the study of pooling equilibria in Section 7.4. Assume now that firms face a linear inverse demand function $p(x) = 1 - x$ in the first period, and $p(Q) = 1 - Q$ in the second period. For simplicity, assume that $S_H = 10$, $S_L = 5$, $\delta = 1$, and $r = \frac{1}{4}$. Repeating the analysis in Section 7.4, answer the following questions.

(a) Identify the incentive compatibility condition for the high-stock incumbent and for the low-stock incumbent.

- **Complete information.** First, we find equilibrium appropriation when information is complete.

  - *Second period, no entry.* If entry does not occur, the incumbent chooses its first-period appropriation, q, to solve

  $$\max_{q \geq 0} \ \pi^{2nd} = (1-q)q - \frac{q^2}{S - (1-r)x}.$$

  Differentiating with respect to q yields

  $$1 - 2q - \frac{2q}{S - (1-r)x} = 0.$$

  Solving for q, we find second-period appropriation level

  $$q^{NE}(x) = \frac{1}{2}\left[\frac{S - (1-r)x}{S - (1-r)x + 1}\right].$$

  Plugging $q^{NE}(x)$ into π^{2nd} yields the second-period profit for the incumbent under no entry

  $$\pi_{NE}^{2nd} = \frac{1}{4}\left[\frac{S - (1-r)x}{S - (1-r)x + 1}\right].$$

  - *Second period, entry.* After entry, every firm i chooses its second-period appropriation q to solve

  $$\max_{q_i \geq 0} \ \pi_i^{2nd} = (1 - q_i - q_j)q_i - \frac{q_i(q_i + q_j)}{S - (1-r)x}.$$

Differentiating with respect to q_i yields

$$1 - 2q_i - q_j - \frac{q_j + 2q_i}{S - (1 - r)x} = 0.$$

Solving for q_i, we obtain firm i's best response function

$$q_i(q_j) = \frac{1}{2}\left[\frac{S - (1 - r)x}{S - (1 - r)x + 1}\right] - \frac{1}{2}q_j.$$

In a symmetric equilibrium, both firms appropriate the same amount, $q^* = q_i = q_j$. Inserting this property in the above best response function yields

$$q = \frac{1}{2}\left[\frac{S - (1 - r)x}{S - (1 - r)x + 1}\right] - \frac{1}{2}q,$$

and solving for q, we find the equilibrium second-period appropriation with entry

$$q^* = \frac{1}{3}\left[\frac{S - (1 - r)x}{S - (1 - r)x + 1}\right].$$

Plugging q^* into π_i^{2nd}, we obtain second-period profits under entry

$$\pi_E^{2nd} = \frac{1}{9}\left[\frac{S - (1 - r)x}{S - (1 - r)x + 1}\right].$$

- *First period followed by no entry.* If no entry occurs in the second period, the incumbent chooses its first-period appropriation to solve

$$\max_{x \geq 0}\left[(1 - x)x - \frac{x^2}{S}\right] + \delta \underbrace{\frac{1}{4}\left[\frac{S - (1 - r)x}{S - (1 - r)x + 1}\right]}_{\pi_{NE}^{2nd}}.$$

Differentiating with respect to x yields

$$1 - \frac{2x(S + 1)}{S} - \delta \frac{1 - r}{4\left[S - (1 - r)x + 1\right]^2} = 0.$$

The equation is highly nonlinear and does not allow for an explicit function of x_{NE}. We can, nonetheless, find first-period appropriation for specific parameter values. For instance, under no discounting, $S = 5$ and $r = \frac{1}{4}$, this first-order condition simplifies to

$$1 - \frac{12x}{5} - \frac{1}{3(8 - x)^2} = 0,$$

which yields $x_{NE} = 0.415$ (the other two roots are not real numbers). Therefore, this firm earns a profit

$$\Pi^{NE} = \left[(1 - x_{NE})x_{NE} - \frac{x_{NE}^2}{S}\right] + \delta \frac{1}{4}\left[\frac{S - (1 - r)x_{NE}}{S - (1 - r)x_{NE} + 1}\right].$$

- *First period followed by entry.* If entry ensues in the second period, the incumbent chooses its first-period appropriation to solve

$$\max_{x \geq 0} \left[(1-x)x - \frac{x^2}{S} \right] + \delta \underbrace{\frac{1}{9} \left[\frac{S - (1-r)x}{S - (1-r)x + 1} \right]}_{\pi_E^{2nd}}.$$

Differentiating with respect to x yields

$$1 - \frac{2x(S+1)}{S} - \delta \frac{1-r}{9 \left[S - (1-r)x + 1 \right]^2} = 0.$$

The equation is highly nonlinear and does not allow for an explicit function of x_E. As in the case of no entry, we can still find first-period appropriation for specific parameter values. For instance, under no discounting, $S = 5$ and $r = \frac{1}{4}$, this first-order condition simplifies to

$$1 - \frac{12x}{5} - \frac{4}{27(8-x)^2} = 0,$$

which yields $x_E = 0.416$ (the other two roots are not real numbers).

Inserting x_E in the incumbent's objective function, we find that this firm earns a profit

$$\Pi^E = \left[(1 - x_E)x_E - \frac{x_E^2}{S} \right] + \delta \frac{1}{9} \left[\frac{S - (1-r)x_E}{S - (1-r)x_E + 1} \right].$$

- **Low-stock incumbent:** Conditional on no entry, the low-stock incumbent's optimal first-period appropriation $x_{L,NE}$, under complete information, maximizes its overall profits. By selecting the same appropriation level as under complete information, $x_{L,NE}$, this type of incumbent deters entry and maximizes the incumbent's overall profit, implying that this firm does not have incentives to deviate from appropriation $x_{L,NE}$.

- **High-stock incumbent:**

  - *Deterring entry.* By selecting appropriation level $x_{L,NE}$, this type of incumbent deters entry, earning an overall profit

$$\Pi_H^{ED} = \left[(1 - x_{L,NE})x_{L,NE} - \frac{x_{L,NE}^2}{S_H} \right] + \delta \frac{1}{4} \left[\frac{S_H - (1-r)x_{L,NE}}{S_H - (1-r)x_{L,NE} + 1} \right].$$

– *Allowing entry.* If, instead, the high-stock incumbent deviates to any other appropriation level, $x \neq x_{L,NE}$, it attracts entry. The incumbent chooses x to solve

$$\max_{x \geq 0} \left[(1-x)x - \frac{x^2}{S_H} \right] + \delta \frac{1}{9} \left[\frac{S_H - (1-r)x}{S_H - (1-r)x + 1} \right],$$

which yields $x_{H,E}$. The equation is highly nonlinear and does not allow for an explicit function of $x_{H,E}$. Inserting $x_{H,E}$ into this incumbent's objective function yields

$$\Pi_H^{AE} = \left[(1 - x_{H,E})x_{H,E} - \frac{x_{H,E}^2}{S_H} \right]$$

$$+ \delta \frac{1}{9} \left[\frac{S_H - (1-r)x_{H,E}}{S_H - (1-r)x_{H,E} + 1} \right].$$

– *Allow or deter entry?* Therefore, the high-stock incumbent chooses appropriation $x_{L,NE}$, deterring entry, rather than $x_{H,E}$, which attracts entry, if and only if $\Pi_H^{ED} \geq \Pi_H^{AE}$. The incentive compatibility condition is

$$\left[(1 - x_{L,NE})x_{L,NE} - \frac{x_{L,NE}^2}{S_H} \right] - \left[(1 - x_{H,E})x_{H,E} - \frac{x_{H,E}^2}{S_H} \right]$$

$$\geq \frac{\delta}{9} \left[\frac{S_H - (1-r)x_{H,E}}{S_H - (1-r)x_{H,E} + 1} \right] - \frac{\delta}{4} \left[\frac{S_H - (1-r)x_{L,NE}}{S_H - (1-r)x_{L,NE} + 1} \right].$$

(b) Use the two conditions from part (a) to find the appropriation level that both types of incumbent select in the pooling equilibrium.

• Evaluating profit Π_L^{NE} at $S_L = 5$, $\delta = 1$, and $r = \frac{1}{4}$ yields

$$\Pi_L^{NE} = \left[(1 - x_{L,NE})x_{L,NE} - \frac{x_{L,NE}^2}{5} \right] + \frac{\delta}{4} \left[\frac{5 - \frac{3}{4}x_{L,NE}}{6 - \frac{3}{4}x_{L,NE}} \right].$$

Differentiating with respect to $x_{L,NE}$ yields

$$\frac{36x_{L,NE}^3 - 591x_{L,NE}^2 + 2544x_{L,NE} - 955}{15(x_{L,NE} - 8)^2} = 0.$$

Solving for $x_{L,NE}$, we obtain

$$x_{L,NE} = 0.4143.$$

Therefore, the profits from deterring entry are

$$\Pi_H^{ED} = \left[(1 - x_{L,NE})x_{L,NE} - \frac{x_{L,NE}^2}{10}\right] + \frac{1}{4}\left[\frac{10 - \frac{3}{4}x_{L,NE}}{11 - \frac{3}{4}x_{L,NE}}\right]$$

$$= \left[0.4143 - 0.4143^2 - \frac{0.4143^2}{10}\right] + \frac{1}{4}\left[\frac{10 - \frac{3}{4} \times 0.4143}{11 - \frac{3}{4} \times 0.4143}\right]$$

$$= 0.4521.$$

Similarly, evaluating profit Π_H^{AE} at $S_H = 10$, $\delta = 1$, and $r = \frac{1}{4}$ yields

$$\Pi_H^{AE} = (1 - x_{H,E})x_{H,E} - \frac{x_{H,E}^2}{10} + \frac{1}{9}\left[\frac{10 - \frac{3}{4}x_{H,E}}{11 - \frac{3}{4}x_{H,E}}\right].$$

Differentiating with respect to $x_{H,E}$ yields

$$1 - \frac{11}{5}x_{H,E} - \frac{1}{12\left(11 - \frac{3}{4}x_{H,E}\right)^2} = 0.$$

Solving for $x_{H,E}$, we obtain

$$x_{H,E} = 0.45.$$

Therefore, the profits from allowing entry are

$$\Pi_H^{AE} = \left[(1 - x_E)x_E - \frac{x_E^2}{10}\right] + \frac{1}{9}\left[\frac{10 - \frac{3}{4}x_E}{11 - \frac{3}{4}x_E}\right]$$

$$= \left[0.45 - 0.45^2 - \frac{0.45^2}{10}\right] + \frac{1}{9}\left[\frac{10 - \frac{3}{4} \times 0.45}{11 - \frac{3}{4} \times 0.45}\right]$$

$$= 0.3279.$$

Since $\Pi_H^{ED} = 0.4521 > \Pi_H^{AE} = 0.3279$, the high-stock incumbent chooses $x_{L,NE} = 0.4143$ to deter entry.

(c) How do your results differ from those in Section 7.4? Interpret your results.

- If we assume $r = \frac{1}{4}$ in Section 7.4, we obtain

$$x_{H,E} = \frac{S_H[9 - \delta(1 - r)]}{18}$$

$$= \frac{10\left[9 - \frac{3}{4}\right]}{18}$$

$$= 4.583 > 0.4521$$

and

$$x_{L,NE} = \frac{S_L[4 - \delta(1 - r)]}{8}$$

$$= \frac{5\left[4 - \frac{3}{4}\right]}{8}$$

$$= 2.03 > 0.4143.$$

Intuitively, when firms face a downward-sloping demand curve, they appropriate fewer units of the resource than when they take prices as given, but still have incentives to deter entry.

Bibliography

Angner, E. (2016) *A Course in Behavioral Economics*, 2nd ed., Red Globe Press.

Apesteguia, J. (2006) "Does information matter in the commons? Experimental evidence," *Journal of Economic Behavior and Organization*, 60, pp. 55–69.

Araral, E. (2014) "Ostrom, Hardin and the commons. A critical appreciation and revisionist view," *Environmental Science and Policy*, 36, pp. 1–92.

Belleflamme, P. and M. Peitz (2015) *Industrial Organization: Markets and Strategies*, 2nd ed., Cambridge University Press.

Budescu, D. V., A. Rapoport, and R. Suleiman (1995) "Common pool resource dilemmas under uncertainty: Qualitative tests of equilibrium solutions," *Games and Economic Behavior*, 10, pp. 171–201.

Camerer, C. F. (2003) *Behavioral Game Theory: Experiments in Strategic Interaction* (Roundtable Series in Behavioral Economics), Princeton University Press.

Carpenter, J. P. (2000) "Negotiation in the commons: Incorporating field and experimental evidence into a theory of local collective action," *Journal of Institutional and Theoretical Economics*, 156, pp. 661–83.

Casari, M. and C. H. Plott (2003) "Decentralized management of common property resources: Experiments with a centuries-old institution," *Journal of Economic Behavior and Organization*, 51, pp. 217–47.

Cho, I. and D. Kreps (1987) "Signaling games and stable equilibria," *Quarterly Journal of Economics*, 102, pp. 179–221.

Chu, C. (2009) "Thirty years later: The global growth of ITQs and their influence on stock status in marine fisheries," *Fish and Fisheries*, 10, pp. 217–30.

Conrad, J. M. (2010) *Resource Economics*, 2nd ed., Cambridge University Press.

Conrad, J. M. and C. W. Clark (1987) *Natural Resource Economics: Notes and Problems*, Cambridge University Press.

Cornes, R., C. Mason, and T. Sandler (1986) "The commons and the optimal number of firms," Quarterly Journal of Economics, 11, pp. 641–6.

Costello, C., S. D. Gaines, and J. Lynham (2008) "Can catch shares prevent fisheries collapse?" *Science*, 321, pp. 1678–81.

Dal Bó, P. and G. R. Fréchette (2011) "The evolution of cooperation in infinitely repeated games: Experimental evidence," *American Economic Review*, 101, pp. 411–29.

Dasgupta, P. S. and G. M. Heal (1979) *Economic Theory and Exhaustible Resources,* Cambridge University Press.

Dockner, E., S. Jorgensen, N. Van Long, and G. Sorger (2000) *Differential Games in Economics and Management Science,* Cambridge University Press.

Duffy, J. and J. Ochs (2009) "Cooperative behavior and the frequency of social interaction," *Games and Economic Behavior,* 66, pp. 785–812.

Dutta, P. K. and R. K. Sundaram (1993) "The tragedy of the commons?," *Economic Theory,* 3, 413–26.

Ellis, C. J. (2001) "Common pool equities: An arbitrage based non-cooperative solution to the common pool resource problem," *Journal of Environmental Economics and Management,* 42, 140–55.

Esteban E. and J. Albiac (2011) "Groundwater and ecosystems damages: Questioning the Gisser–Sanchez effect," *Ecological Economics,* 70, pp. 2062–9.

Espinola-Arredondo, A. and F. Muñoz-Garcia (2011) "Can incomplete information lead to under-exploitation in the commons?," *Journal of Environmental Economics and Management,* 62, pp. 402–13.

Espinola-Arredondo, A. and F. Muñoz-Garcia (2013a) "Don't forget to protect abundant resources," *Strategic Behavior and the Environment,* 3, pp. 251–78.

Espinola-Arredondo, A. and F. Muñoz-Garcia (2013b) "Asymmetric information may protect the commons: The welfare benefits of uninformed regulators," *Economics Letters,* 121, pp. 463–467.

Faysee, N. (2005) "Coping with the tragedy of the commons: Game structure and design of rules," *Journal of Economic Surveys,* 19, pp. 239–61.

Food and Agriculture Organization (2005) "Review of the state of the world marine fisheries resources," FAO Fisheries Technical Paper, no. 457, Rome.

Gardner, R., M. R. Moore, and J. M. Walker (1997) "Governing a groundwater commons: A strategic and laboratory analysis of western water law," *Economic Inquiry,* 2, pp. 218–34.

Gilbert, R. and X. Vives (1986) "Entry deterrence and the free-rider problem," *Review of Economic Studies,* 53, pp. 71–86.

Gordon, H. S. (1954) "The economic theory of a common-property resource: The fishery," *The Journal of Political Economy,* 62, pp. 124–42.

Hackett, S., E. Schlager, and J. Walker (1994) "The role of communication in resolving commons dilemmas: Experimental evidence with heterogeneous appropriators," *Journal of Environmental Economics and Management,* 27, pp. 99–126.

Hardin, G. (1968) "The tragedy of the commons," *Science,* 162, pp. 1243–8.

Haughton, M. (2002) "Fisheries subsidy and the role of regional fisheries management organizations: The Caribbean experience," paper presented at the UNEP workshop on fisheries subsidies and sustainable fisheries management, April 26–27, 2001, UNEP, Geneva.

Heintzelman, M. D., S. W. Salant, and S. Schott (2009) "Putting free-riding to work: A partnership solution to the common-property problem," *Journal of Environmental Economics and Management*, 57, pp. 309–20.

Herr, A., R. Gardner, and J. M. Walker (1997) "An experimental study of time-independent and time-dependent externalities in the commons," *Games and Economic Behavior*, 18, pp. 79–96.

Johnson, R. and G. Libecap (1980) "Agency costs and the assignment of property rights: The case of Southwestern Indian reservations," *Southern Economic Journal*, 47, pp. 332–47.

Keser, C. and R. Gardner (1999) "Strategic behavior of experimental subjects in a common pool resource game," *International Journal of Game Theory*, 28, pp 241–52.

Kotchen, M. J. and S. W. Salant (2011) "A free lunch in the commons," *Journal of Environmental Economics and Management*, 61, pp. 245–53.

Lambertini, L. (2015) *Oligopoly, the Environment and Natural Resources* (Routledge Explorations in Environmental Economics), Routledge.

Libecap, G. (2009) "The tragedy of the commons: Property rights and markets as solutions to resource and environmental problems," *The Australian Journal of Agricultural and Resource Economics*, 53, pp. 129–44.

Mason, C., R. Cornes, and T. Sandler (1988) "Expectations, the commons, and optimal group size," *Journal of Environmental Economics and Management*, 15, pp. 99–110.

Mason, C. and S. Polasky (1994) "Entry deterrence in the commons," *International Economic Review*, 35, pp. 507–25.

Mason, C. and S. Polasky (1997) "The optimal number of firms in the commons: A dynamic approach," *Canadian Journal of Economics*, 30, pp. 1143–60.

Mason, C. and S. Polasky (2002) "Strategic preemption in a common-property resource: A continuous time approach," Environmental and Resource Economics, 23, pp. 255–78.

McLean, J. (1849) *Notes of a Twenty-Five Year's Service in the Hudson's Bay Territory*, R. Bentley.

Milgrom, P. and J. Roberts (1982) "Entry deterrence and limit pricing under incomplete information," *Econometrica*, 50, pp. 443–66.

Montero, J.-P. (2008) "A simple auction mechanism for the optimal allocation of the commons," *American Economic Review*, 98, pp. 496–518.

Muñoz-Garcia, F. (2017) *Advanced Microeconomic Theory: An Intuitive Approach with Examples*, The MIT Press.

Muñoz-Garcia, F. and D. Toro-Gonzalez (2019) *Strategy and Game Theory: Practice Exercises with Answers*, 2nd ed., Springer-Verlag.

Nash, J. F. Jr. (1950) "Equilibrium points in n-person games," *PNAS*, 36, pp. 48–9.

Ostrom, E. (1990) *Governing the Commons: The Evolution of Institutions for Collective Actions*, Cambridge University Press.

Ostrom, E. (1994) *Rules, Games, and Common-Pool Resources*, The University of Michigan Press.

Ostrom, E. (2000) "Collective action and the evolution of social norms," *Journal of Economic Perspectives*, 14, pp. 137–58.

Pereau, J.-C., L. Mouyseet, and L. Doyen (2018) "Groundwater management in a food security context," *Environmental and Resource Economics*, 71, pp. 319–36.

Polasky, S. and O. Bin (2001) "Entry deterrence and signaling in a nonrenewable resource model," *Journal of Environmental Economics and Management*, 42, pp. 235–56.

Polasky, S., N. Tauri, G. Ellis, and C. F. Mason (2006) "Cooperation in the commons," *Economic Theory*, 29, pp. 71–88.

Suleiman, R. and A. Rapoport (1988) "Environmental and social uncertainty in single-trial resource dilemmas," *Acta Psychologica*, 68, pp. 99–112.

Suleiman, R., A. Rapoport, and D. Budescu (1996) "Fixed position and property rights in sequential resource dilemmas under uncertainty," *Acta Psychologica*, 93, pp. 229–45.

Tadelis, S. (2013) *Game Theory: An Introduction*, Princeton University Press.

Walker, J. M. and R. Gardner (1992) "Probabilistic destruction of common-pool resources: Experimental evidence," *Economic Journal*, 102, pp. 1149–61.

Walker, J. M., R. Gardner, A. Herr, and E. Ostrom (2000) "Collective choice in the commons: Experimental results on proposed allocation rules and votes," *Economic Journal*, 110, pp. 212–34.

Wiggins, S. and S. Libecap (1985) "Oil field utilization: Contractual failure in the presence of imperfect information," *American Economic Review*, 75, 368–85.

Index

Printed in the United States
by Baker & Taylor Publisher Services